Star Wars:
The Essential Guide to
Droids

Star Wars:
The Essential Guide to Droids

By Daniel Wallace

Original illustrations by Bill Hughes
Schematics by Troy Vigil

BOXTREE

First published 1999 by The Ballantine Publishing Group, a division of Random House Inc., New York and simultaneously in Canada by
Random House of Canada Limited, Toronto

First published in Great Britain 1999 by Boxtree
an imprint of Macmillan Publishers Ltd
25 Eccleston Place London SW1W 9NF
Basingstoke and Oxford

Associated companies throughout the world

ISBN 0 7522 2413 1

Text by Daniel Wallace
Original illustrations by Bill Hughes
Schematics by Troy Vigil

1 3 5 7 9 8 6 4 2

A CIP catalogue record for this book is available from
the British Library.

Printed by Butler and Tanner Ltd., Frome and London

Author's Dedication
To Daniel David Zoch, my friend.

Artists' Dedication

To Heidi, Beth, Brian, Chris, and Yoda.
Thanks for your patience, support and wisdom.
—Bill Hughes

My work is dedicated to the Jedi Masters of my life: Dad; my partner Stacey;
and my best friend Armando.
—Troy Vigil

Table of Contents

Author's Acknowledgments

The droids featured between these covers are the brainchildren of literally hundreds of individuals, beginning with George Lucas and including conceptual artists, prop builders, fiction novelists, computer programmers— far too many to list here. This book would have been impossible without their creative minds.

Expert editors Sue Rostoni at Lucasfilm and Steve Saffel at Ballantine did all the hard work and took none of the credit. My heartfelt thanks to both of you.

As always, the ever-helpful folks at Lucasfilm deserve much praise, particularly Lucy Autrey Wilson, Allan Kausch, and Cara Evangelista.

I'm in awe of Bill Hughes and Troy Vigil, artists who can summon up two-ton metal behemoths with a simple gesture from a pen or computer mouse. It was a pleasure to work among such talent.

A few special reference sources were invaluable in the writing and research of this project. My fervent gratitude goes out to the following heroes: Eric Trautmann, Drew Campbell, David West Reynolds, Steve Sansweet, Tom Veitch, and Pablo Hidalgo. Thanks also to Aaron Allston, Kevin J. Anderson, Joe Bongiorno, Jack Camden, Craig Robert Carey, Erin Endom, Steve Guilfoyle, Rich Handley, Michael Kogge, Rebecca Moesta, Alex Newborn, Timothy O'Brien, Curtis Saxton, Mike Stackpole, and John Whitman.

My family and friends make everything possible with their love, advice, and support.

And finally, a very special thanks to George Lucas, creator of a cosmos.

Artists' Acknowledgments

A special thank you to the Jedi Knights of Lucasfilm Licensing: Sue Rostoni, Lucy Autrey Wilson, and Cara Evangelista, for their guidance, generosity and professionalism.
—Troy Vigil

As a young man growing up in Houston during the sixties, space travel was the stock and trade of many of my neighbors. In real life we were going to the moon. On television and in the movies we were exploring the galaxy in huge starships, battling fantastic robots and, occasionally, even getting lost out there. But somehow its appeal seemed to fade. Maybe I was growing up. Maybe the stars had lost some of their luster.

In 1977 George Lucas made the stars glow again for me with his exciting adventure, *Star Wars*. He had created a world filled with images that I'd never seen before and populated it with characters I could call friends. I'd like to thank George Lucas for fanning the flame and giving me more room to dream.

I'd also like to thank the creative people I've worked with: Nick Polydoros, James Brown, and Dan Dunn for their love of ink on paper; Larry Byrd for the stories we've told together; Ryder Windham for my career; and Chris Nelson for the many hours we've spent discussing whether or not 3PO is powered by a fusion cell or a sync-pulse singularity generator.

Lastly, I'd like to give a special thanks to Dan, Troy, and Sue Rostoni at Lucasfilm for making this project a true joy for me.
—Bill Hughes

Introduction

"Did you hear that? They've shut down the main reactor. We'll be destroyed for sure. This is madness!"—C-3PO to R2-D2

When *Star Wars: A New Hope* unspooled across theater screens over two decades ago, the audience's first glimpse of the strange denizens inhabiting this "galaxy far far away" wasn't of a hot-tempered princess or a black-garbed Dark Lord. It wasn't of a self-assured smuggler or a wide-eyed farmboy. It wasn't even of a Jawa, Ewok, or Wookiee. The individuals George Lucas chose to inaugurate his epic space saga looked like a stiff golden statuette and a squat, warbling fireplug. They were droids, and as See-Threepio and Artoo-Detoo, the peculiar pair would become one of the most beloved movie duos of all time.

The word "robot," derived from a Czech term meaning "forced labor," was coined in 1920. It wasn't long before the silver screen took notice. In 1926, Fritz Lang's silent classic *Metropolis* introduced the first—a statuesque stunner named Maria whose graceful art-deco lines would later help inspire the conceptual design of C-3PO. A number of memorable movie mechanicals followed, including the mute brute Gort from *The Day the Earth Stood Still*, the delightfully deadpan Robby the Robot in *Forbidden Planet*, HAL 9000, the coldly calculating computer from *2001*, and Yul Brynner's turn as a haywire theme-park attraction in *Westworld*. All were unforgettable characters, but their advanced silicon brains couldn't hide the fact that they were hardware without heart and software without soul. Lacking personalities audiences could identify with, movie robots fell into two neat categories: subservient drones and emotionless menaces.

Star Wars broke that mold. Artoo and Threepio were bickering buddies more akin to Laurel and Hardy than clockwork and cogwheels. Thanks largely to the men inside the metal, actors Kenny Baker and Anthony Daniels, the droids were just as *human* as anyone else in the cast—and they got all the best lines, too. Threepio might be a sophisticated translation machine fluent in over six million forms of communication, but it is his exasperated response to a door slamming shut in his face ("how *typical!*") that elicits a sympathetic laugh. And despite the fact that Artoo could speak only in whistles, sound engineer Ben Burtt created a warmly expressive nonverbal language by mixing synthesized electronic tones with the sound of his own voice.

See-Threepio and Artoo-Detoo may have greeted us at the door, but more droids—*many* more—waited for us in the dusty corners of Mos Eisley and the cavernous hallways of the Death Star. The movie trilogy's "lived-in" design scheme meant that most of these whirring gadgets had rust spots and flaking paint jobs, but their appearances were always funny, intriguing, and bizarre, from the gleefully sadistic torturer in Jabba the Hutt's boiler room to the marching carton aboard the Jawa sandcrawler that unaccountably blurted out "gonk, gonk."

The sheer variety of sizes, forms, and appearances hammered home one obvious fact—when folks in the *Star Wars* universe have a problem, they build a droid. Specialized robots fill every conceivable niche from trash collection to surgery, and it has taken twenty years of novels, comics, computer games, television cartoons, and newspaper strips to showcase their full product range.

The Essential Guide to Droids is proud to present one hundred of these universal gizmos. We like to think we covered all the cool ones.

Daniel Wallace
Detroit, Michigan

A Guide to Major Manufacturers

Droids are intelligent mechanical contraptions that are vital to the smooth operation of galactic society. Every day, millions of subservient automatons negotiate treaties, repair hyperdrives, cure plagues, incinerate garbage, nurse children, haul cargo, deliver messages, cook meals, and kill enemies. At the same time, droids are often ignored and unappreciated, treated as chattel by many owners and looked at with outright hostility by others. Though antidroid prejudice is a reality among the unenlightened, the few owners who have spent long stretches of time with their droids have discovered that they can be trusted companions and loyal friends.

Unlike machines, all droids possess intelligence to some degree. Unlike computers, most droids are designed for mobility on limbs, wheels, or antigravity fields. The manufacture and sale of droids is a lucrative business dominated by the "Big Two"—Cybot Galactica and Industrial Automaton. Other major droid players include Arakyd Industries, Genetech Corporation, MerenData, and Veril Line Systems.

Of the millions of droid manufacturing plants in the galaxy, the two largest are Mechis III and Telti, which together produce a sizable percentage of all new automatons. Both locations are entire worlds covered with sprawling construction facilities and fully automated assembly lines; any human interaction in the fabrication process other than the most minimal supervision is unnecessary and counterproductive. The major droid companies pay these two worlds a negotiated fee for the use of their assembly plants, a cost that is acceptable given the speed and accuracy with which they can churn out large orders. Arakyd Industries, Genetech Corporation, SoroSuub Corporation, and Veril Line Systems are some of the companies that employ Mechis III for a major share of their production. Industrial Automaton and Cybot Galactica rely heavily on Telti. The novice Jedi Knight Brakiss recently served as manager of the Telti plants, while Mechis III is currently operated by the Thul family of Alderaan.

In addition to the more common droids produced by major manufacturers, there are many mechanicals that are difficult to classify for a number of reasons. Some droids are so ancient that verifiable information on their manufacture has been lost in the fog of history. Some are unique creations concocted by ingenious, oddball inventors, yet others are products of restricted alien governments.

Manufacturers

Accutronics

Accutronics, a former subsidiary of Industrial Automaton, was an early forerunner in the marketing of droids to families with young children. Their remarkable success in persuading the public to view metallic machines as loving caregivers has allowed the company to move out from IA's shadow and become the leader in their niche. Accutronics' corporate headquarters is located on Eriadu and its satellite offices are found throughout the Outer Rim.
- Model E
- TDL Nanny Droid

Arakyd Industries

The rise of the militaristic Empire was very good for Arakyd Industries. Through political maneuvering and competitive infighting the company set itself up as the only logical choice to receive the first Imperial droid contracts; they shrewdly exploited this early windfall by working hard to become the galaxy's leading military supplier. Recent consumer-market models from Arakyd have been moderately successful, but only account for a small fraction of their total yearly output. Despite the company's past history, the New Republic has worked closely with Arakyd since the collapse of Imperial rule.
- Death Star Droid
- G-2RD Guard
- Mark X Executioner
- Seeker Messenger Droid
- Moon Moth
- Tracker Droid
- Probot Series

Balmorran Arms

Balmorra, home to Balmorran Arms, is an ancient factory world at the edge of the Core. The Empire used the planet's huge assembly plants to churn out the majority of its AT-ST scout walkers, but Balmorra's master weapon-smiths also designed several unique tools, including the SD-9 and SD-10 robotic infantry soldiers, for Emperor Palpatine. During the rampages of the resurrected Emperor, Governor Beltane introduced the X-1 Viper in the hopes of freeing his people from Imperial rule.

- SD-9 and SD-10
- X-1 Viper ("Automadon")

Corellian Engineering Corporation

Corellian Engineering Corporation (CEC) is one of the galaxy's three largest starship manufacturers and arguably the most respected. In addition to blockade runners and light freighters, CEC manufactures the droid-based StarHauler cargo barge. Though the company has taken steps to prevent it, many of their products are stolen by criminals and refitted into deadly robot ramships.

- Drone Barge
- Robot Ramship

Corporate Sector Authority

The Corporate Sector Authority (CSA) is the ruling administration in the Corporate Sector, a free-enterprise profit center that was nominally controlled by the Empire during Palpatine's reign. Since the rise of the New Republic the CSA has remained aloof and reluctant to form political alliances. The region is a thriving and diverse manufacturing center, exporting thousands of new and innovative products to the greater galaxy each year.

- CD-2 Harvester
- Firefighting Robo

Cybot Galactica

One of the two largest droid manufacturers in the galaxy—Industrial Automaton is the other—Cybot Galactica is a major force in the galactic economy and a significant influence throughout the Core Worlds and Corporate Sector. Famous for the 3PO protocol series, Cybot is also responsible for an extraordinary array of droid models ranging from simple labor units to advanced security sentinels.

- Binary Load Lifter
- Guardian Droid
- Imperial City Maintenance Droid
- LE Repair Droid
- LIN Demolitionmech
- M-3PO Military Protocol Droid
- PD Lurrian Protocol Droid

- Robo-bartenders
- 3PO Protocol Droid
- WED Treadwell

Geentech

A small, quiet medisensor company, Geentech was casually run out of business by the much larger Genetech Corporation in a string of heavy-handed and highly expensive lawsuits. Claiming Geentech's similar name infringed on their own copyrights, Genetech forced their competitor into bankruptcy and, though these allegations have never been proven, might even have offered Imperial prosecutors a lucrative trade inducement to ensure their victory. Geentech's sole success story, the 2-1B Surgical Droid, was subsequently bought out by Industrial Automaton.

- 2-1B Surgical Droid

Genetech Corporation

One of the older and larger droid manufacturers, Genetech Corporation started out as a pharmaceutical firm. The company pioneered the concept of using droids to streamline the manufacturing process, which earned them a great deal of ill-will—and fueled the antidroid movement—when thousands of assembly workers were fired from their jobs. Genetech's first droids were medical units, but the company has since branched out into accounting, administrative, and bookkeeping models.

- Systems Control Droid
- 3D-4X Administrative

Go-Corp/Utilitech

Go-Corp/Utilitech is based on Etti IV and makes vehicle droids for sale throughout the Corporate Sector. Go-Corp produces the actual speeder carriages, while its subsidiary Utilitech manufactures and programs the more intricate droid brains. Apart from the widespread robo-hack, the company's products are not often encountered outside the Corporate Sector's borders.

- Robo-hack

Holowan Mechanicals

A public inquiry for more information about "Holowan Mechanicals—The Friendly Technology People" will reveal a bland corporate statement and a list of obscure industrial products. The shocking truth is much harder to come by. Holowan was a front corporation for the Imperially funded development of the IG-series assassin droid, an experiment that ended in disaster when the prototype units escaped from the laboratory and murdered nearly all of the design staff.

- IG Assassin Droid

Imperial Department of Military Research

During his decades-long reign, Emperor Palpatine conscripted many of the galaxy's best scientists and theorists for the purpose of creating genocidal implements of war. The Empire's top-secret Department of Military Research produced a number of inhuman inventions, from siege weapons such as the orbital nightcloak to murderous automatons such as the Dark Trooper.

- Dark Trooper
- Human Replica Droid
- Imperial Mark IV Sentry Droid
- IT-O Interrogator
- Shadow Droid

Industrial Automaton

The other half of the "Big Two," Industrial Automaton (IA) is a massive and influential droid corporation formed long ago through the merger of Automata Galactica and Industrial Intelligence. Known for its high-precision merchandise and deep discounts, the company's crowning glory is the universally accepted R series of astromech droids. IA continually battles Cybot Galactica for the credit accounts of consumers and offers an equally diverse product line.

- Asp
- Decon Droid
- Elegance Message Drone
- MD Medical Specialist
- FLR Logger ("Lumberdroid")
- LOM Protocol Droid
- Hound-W2 SPD
- MN-2E General Maintenance Droid
- P2 and R1 Astromechs
- R2 Astromech
- R3 and R4 Astromechs
- R5 Astromech
- R6 and R7 Astromechs
- SE4 Servant Droid
- Q9-X2

LeisureMech Enterprises

Based in the Corporate Sector, LeisureMech Enterprises produces high-quality recreational, entertainment, and luxury droids for sale to businesses and wealthy consumers. One subsidiary branch of LeisureMech was so successful at producing security droids that it was spun off to form the Ulban Arms company.

- Automated Sabacc Dealers
- C5 Robo-bartender

Les Tech

Les Tech is a small, privately owned business in the Core Worlds that specializes in exploration droids. Particularly notable is the fact that for years the company has determinedly—and so far, successfully—fought off a takeover attempt by the much larger Cybot Galactica. Most of Les Tech's droids were employed by Imperial frontier scouts, a reliance that financially crippled the company when the Emperor curtailed most exploration during the Galactic Civil War. To make up for the loss, Les Tech made a number of sales to the Rebel Alliance.

- M38 Explorer
- MULE Droid

Loronar Corporation

"All the finest, all the first." Beneath a cheery slogan, Loronar Corporation is one of the galaxy's largest and most diverse conglomerates—and also one of the most corrupt. Under its Loronar Defense Industries imprint the company produces blaster artillery, turbolasers, and immense Imperial military craft such as *Strike*-class cruisers and torpedo spheres. Charges of rights abuses in the Gantho system and elsewhere have dogged the company for years, but it took a Loronar-backed revolutionary uprising in the Meridian Sector to bring about substantial legal penalties and official New Republic condemnation. Loronar's largest droid manufacturing facility lies on the moon of Carosi.

- Fly Eye
- Synthdroid

Lovolan

The name Lovolan is synonymous with wealth, dignity, beauty, and exclusivity. Based in the Core Worlds, the company produces products that are astonishingly expensive and intricately ornamented, sometimes ostentatiously so. Lovolan's fortunes tend to rise and fall with the amount of disposable income in the galactic economy, but there are always enough affluent bureaucrats and self-important aristocrats to keep the company going during a lean year.

- R-10 Household Droid

Medtech Industries

A trailblazer in the medical field, Medtech Industries developed some of the earliest surgical-based automatons. Droids such as the FX were extremely successful in their day, but changing tastes and increased competitive pressures prevented Medtech from producing any new models. After the Battle of Yavin the company's corporate headquarters were relocated to the Deep Core, but all cost-cutting measures were in vain. Medtech filed for bankruptcy shortly before the Battle of Hoth.

- FX Medical Assistant

MerenData

A frequent beneficiary of Imperial contracts, MerenData specializes in security systems, military target drones, and a variety of droid products—some sinister, some benign. Efforts to establish a working relationship between MerenData and the New Republic government have been disappointing.

- EV Supervisor Droid
- Positronic Processor
- RM-2020 Espionage Droid

PowerPost

PowerPost is a small office supply company responsible for the SCM-22 Stenographer. Initially the SCM-22 was sold only in PowerPost authorized retail outlets, but the unit's success has prompted the company to expand its distribution channels.

- SCM-22 Stenographer

Publictechnic

A relatively new company serving the industrial-maintenance market, Publictechnic has achieved great success by tailoring their products to suit governments and large corporations. Publictechnic's main manufacturing plant is located on Sennatt, in Bothan space.

- 850.AA Public Service Headquarters
- Tree Feeder
- U2C1 Housekeeping Droid

Rebaxan Columni

A calamitous Chadra-Fan attempt to crack the galactic droid market, Rebaxan Columni was responsible for the much-despised "mouse droid." Though the company closed its doors long ago, its rodent-like product is likely to remain a military fixture for decades to come.

- MSE-6 ("Mouse Droid")

Rebel Alliance/New Republic Research and Development

When the ragtag Rebel Alliance couldn't beg, borrow, or steal the droids it needed for its war against the Empire, it was often forced to create them from scratch. Many of the early Rebel innovators later helped found the sophisticated New Republic Department of Research and Development.

- Foreign Intruder Defense Organism (FIDO)
- Scavenger Droid
- NR 1100 Slicer Droid

Roche

"Roche" is convenient shorthand for the name of the droid program operated by the insectoid Verpine species. The *correct* name, when translated into Basic, is Roche Hive Mechanical Apparatus Design And Construction Activity For Those Who Need The Hive's Machines. One of the most successful alien-owned droid corporations, Roche has suffered unfairly at the hands of its larger competitors, forcing it to resort to limited distribution channels in the Roche Asteroid Belt and on traveling Ithorian herdships.

- 8D8 Smelting Operator
- 11-17 Miner Droid
- J9 Worker Drone

Serv-O-Droid

Serv-O-Droid is an ancient droid manufacturing corporation responsible for some of the earliest construction and heavy labor automatons. In its later years the firm branched out into scientific, bookkeeping, security, military, and domestic models, but none of the new droids could prevent a slow, but inexorable, slide into bankruptcy. Technically Serv-O-Droid is no longer in business, but its name survives through a successful remainder house on Elshandruu Pica and millions of hardworking droids that have remained functional for decades.

- CZ Secretary Droid
- TT-8L ("Tattletale")
- Wrecker Droid
- ZZ-4Z ("ZeeZee")

Sienar Intelligence Systems

A powerful arm of Santhe/Sienar, which manufactures the Empire's ubiquitous TIE fighter, Sienar Intelligence Systems specializes in government contracts with an emphasis on filling Imperial orders. In this arena they compete with Arakyd Industries and, to a lesser degree, MerenData. Sienar's products are not sold in stores and can only be purchased by direct commission.

- E522 Assassin Droid
- Scarab Droid

SoroSuub Corporation

The volcanic planet Sullust is dominated by SoroSuub Corporation, an enormous manufacturing conglomerate with its fingers in the communications, foodstuffs, mining, armaments, starship, and droid industries. SoroSuub was a staunch ally of the Empire despite the Rebel sympathies of many Sullustan citizens. It took years of negotiations to convince the company to throw its support behind the Rebel Alliance, but SoroSuub is now one of the New Republic's most loyal friends. Its droid products are as varied as one might expect from such a diverse corporation.

- Memory Droid
- Scout Collector and Surveyor Package
- 12-4C-41 Traffic Controller
- Unit Zed

Telbrintel

Telbrintel is a specialist firm known for its highly accurate scientific droids, which are common sights in universities and military research laboratories. The company is based in the Core Worlds and has recently expanded its product line with paramedic and information-collating droids.

- TT-40 Library Droid

Trang Robotics

A family-owned business with a long and respected history, Trang Robotics is best known for the highly regarded Duelist Elite fencing trainer. The company's lavish headquarters and master-craftsman workshops are located on the inhabited moon of Drewwa in the remote Almanian system.

- Duelist Elite

Ulban Arms

An unlikely extension of LeisureMech Enterprises, Ulban Arms is a recently formed Corporate Sector company specializing in military and security designs. Ulban's first success was the Class I Defense Droid, an infantry unit based on—some would say *stolen from*—a set of Imperial blueprints. Since the fall of the Empire the company has produced several new products for sale outside the Corporate Sector's borders.

- Red Terror
- S-EP1 Security

Veril Line Systems

Veril Line Systems is a venerable corporation with a long history of superior industrial products. Its boxy, black Power Droids are used almost everywhere, while its forty-story Construction Droids have helped make Imperial City the metropolis it is today. Veril's main offices are located on Coruscant.

- Construction Droid
- EG-6 Power Droid
- Gyrowheel 1.42.08 Recycling Droid

Historical Droids

Ranging from the decades-old Arkanian revolution to the pre-Republic era of Xim the Despot more than 25,000 years in the past, the droids produced by early conquerors hold a special fascination for modern scholars. Regrettably, much of the original data on these battle machines is missing since the groups that produced them are no longer viable companies.

- Basilisk War Droid
- Gorm the Dissolver
- Krath War Droid
- Xim's War-Robot

Inventors

All droids are the products of inventors to some degree; the droids listed here are unique in that all of them were designed by a single individual, manufactured by a highly select group, and produced in extremely small numbers. One notable inventor, Simonelle the Ingoian, was said to have developed the first human replica droid, but recently declassified reports regarding the Imperial Department of Military Research and engineer Massad Thrumble have thrown Simonelle's folk-hero status into dispute.

- B'omarr Brain Walker
- Em Teedee
- Fromm Tower Droid
- Human Replica Droid
- Widget

Miscellaneous Alien Species

Besides the few established companies such as Roche, most alien species lack the resources and sales channels to market droids widely. This discriminatory fact was even more pronounced during the bigoted rule of Emperor Palpatine, though the New Republic has taken steps to reverse the Emperor's unjust legacy. Many alien droid products are produced by the homeworld government in question. Information on Vuffi Raa's creators and the bizarre technology of the Ssi-ruuk is still sketchy due to inadequate intelligence data from the Unknown Regions.

- C2-R4 Multipurpose Unit
- 8t88
- Rodian Hunter Trainer
- Ssi-ruuvi Security Droid
- Vuffi Raa
- X10-D Draft Droid

ASTROMECH
P2 AND R1

The P2 and R1 models were Industrial Automaton's first stabs at creating a new line of consumer-market astromechs. Though both droids were modest hits in their day, with the benefit of hindsight they appear as awkward baby steps compared to the giant leap forward that was the R2.

The P2 was an astromech prototype, sold exclusively to the Old Republic merchant fleet on a trial basis. Massive, cumbersome, and sluggish, it nevertheless showcased many of the sleek design features that would become common with later models in the R series. The droid had three wheeled legs, a rotating head dome, and retractable manipulator arms that folded into a cylindrical armored hull.

Sporting a primitive version of the Intellex ship-configuration computer, the P2 made a capable maintenance unit for bulk cruisers and container vessels, while its buzzsaw and laser welder helped it perform simple repair jobs. But the droid was clumsy, slow to learn, and could only communicate through its video display screen or a computer link.

Most captains, however, were pleased with the units. IA was finalizing plans to publicly release the P2 when they were slapped with a technology infringement lawsuit. Though the case was eventually dropped, legal delays and bad publicity killed the P2 line. IA was forced to start fresh.

The R1 was a natural evolution of the P2, despite its unconventional appearance. To save costs during its draining courtroom battles, IA reused the tall, black body shells from its Mark II Reactor Drone series. This gave the R1 natural shielding against the most intensive radiation.

Each R1 possessed an advanced Intellex III computer, containing a detailed catalog of 500 starship configurations. Furthermore, the droid was the first IA astromech with the ability to calculate navigational coordinates for a single hyperspace jump.

Due to their size, most R1s were stationed aboard Capital warships and large freighters. Their array of retractable tools turned them into adequate technicians, but many buyers complained about the droids' obstinate personalities and lethargic method of locomotion—a treaded unipod, which frequently broke down and stranded the unit in one spot. IA promised to address these concerns in their next model.

One major breakthrough introduced with the R1 was the beeping, whistling electronic language known as Droidspeak. This information-dense vernacular allowed R1s to communicate efficiently with other droids and data networks and would soon be recognized as a distinctive and endearing hallmark of the entire R series.

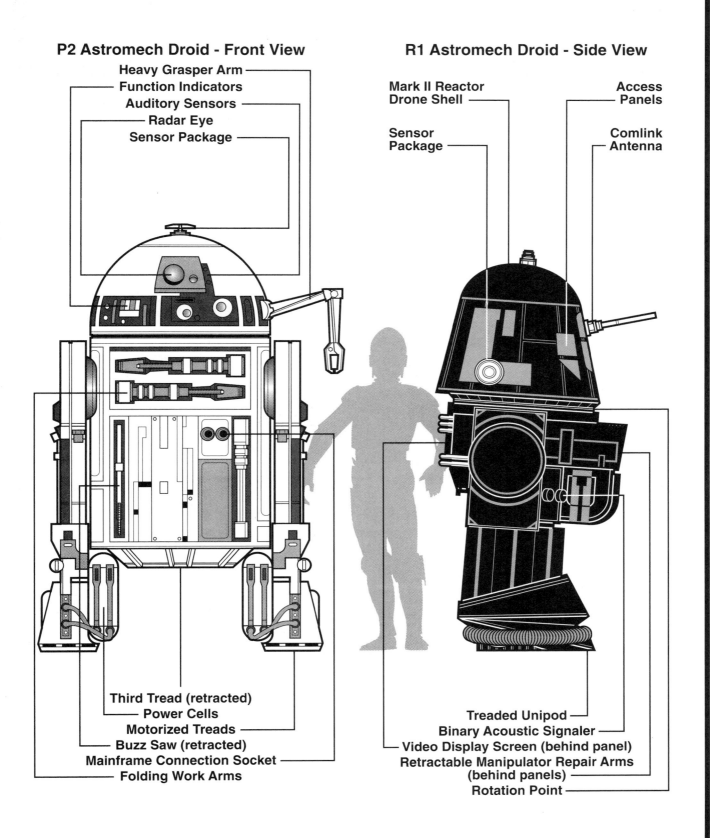

P2 Astromech Droid - Front View

- Heavy Grasper Arm
- Function Indicators
- Auditory Sensors
- Radar Eye
- Sensor Package

- Third Tread (retracted)
- Power Cells
- Motorized Treads
- Buzz Saw (retracted)
- Mainframe Connection Socket
- Folding Work Arms

R1 Astromech Droid - Side View

- Mark II Reactor Drone Shell
- Sensor Package
- Access Panels
- Comlink Antenna

- Treaded Unipod
- Binary Acoustic Signaler
- Video Display Screen (behind panel)
- Retractable Manipulator Repair Arms (behind panels)
- Rotation Point

ASTROMECH

R2

NO JOB IS OVER THIS LITTLE GUY'S HEAD.

—Ad slogan from the R2 product launch

With those bold words, the R2 unit moved from risky design concept to record-breaking phenomenon, dominating the small-droid market like a bantha at an Ewok picnic. Everyone, it seemed, wanted an R2, and for a time Industrial Automaton could do no wrong. As *MechTech Illustrated* put it, the new product was "one of the most versatile, multitalented droids we've ever seen. The R2 unit can do it all."

Like its forerunners, the R2 was designed to work in and around space vessels as a diagnostic and repair unit. But unlike the clunky P2 and R1, this waist-high droid fit perfectly into the standard astromech socket of a military starfighter. This was a radical move—previously, all such droids had been dedicated government models. The R2 quickly became as popular with Old Republic fighter jocks as it was with the public at large.

When plugged into the rear of a Y-wing or X-wing, an R2 unit monitors flight performance, pinpoints and fixes technical problems, and boosts power from the shipboard systems. It can store up to ten sets of hyperspace coordinates in active memory, and many have the intelligence to perform engine startup and pre-flight taxiing. Each R2 operates flawlessly in the vacuum of interstellar space.

The Intellex IV computer features over seven hundred different spacecraft configurations. The R2's sensor package is equally impressive, incorporating a full-spectrum transceiver and electromagnetic, heat, motion, and life-form detectors. The droid can also inspect small, enclosed spaces with an extendible—and fully maneuverable—video sensor.

Since the outer shell was streamlined, buyers were overwhelmed when they discovered the array of tools tucked away beneath the chassis. Standard equipment on an R2 includes two manipulator arms, an electric arc welder, a circular saw, a holographic projector, an internal cargo compartment, and a fire extinguisher. In addition, IA made the droids easy to adjust and upgrade—modified R2s have sported such diverse items as underwater propellers, laser pointers, zero-gee maneuvering jets, remote sensor limpets, and inflatable life rafts.

The R2's personality is obliging, quick-witted, and sincere. If the droids go too long without memory wipes they sometimes develop headstrong self-reliant streaks, but many owners actually prefer to have companions willing to offer candid second opinions.

Sales of the R2 certainly haven't been hurt by the fact that the famed R2-D2 has become one of the most famous figures in the Galactic Civil War. So far, IA has not played up Artoo-Detoo's heroics in its advertisements—to avoid alienating New Republic leaders—but the R2 line remains the only vintage astromech series still in active production.

Side View

Front View

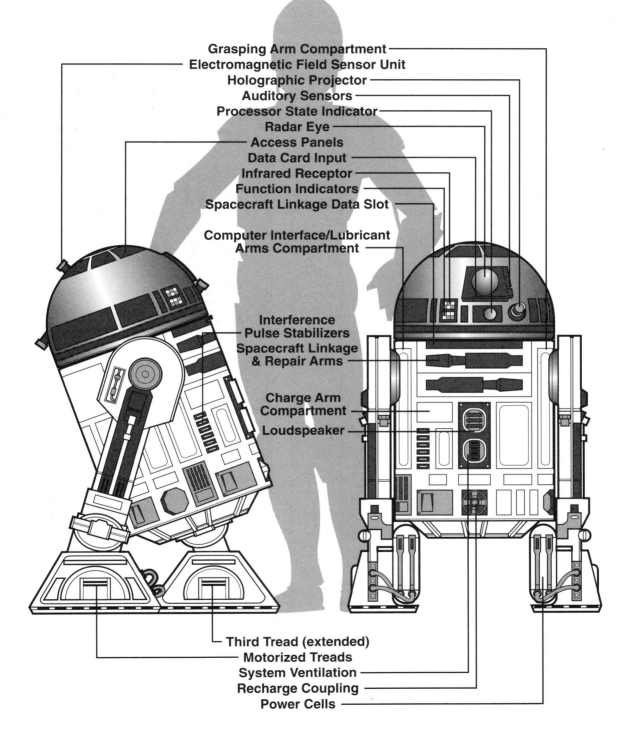

Grasping Arm Compartment
Electromagnetic Field Sensor Unit
Holographic Projector
Auditory Sensors
Processor State Indicator
Radar Eye
Access Panels
Data Card Input
Infrared Receptor
Function Indicators
Spacecraft Linkage Data Slot

Computer Interface/Lubricant
Arms Compartment

Interference
Pulse Stabilizers
Spacecraft Linkage
& Repair Arms

Charge Arm
Compartment
Loudspeaker

Third Tread (extended)
Motorized Treads
System Ventilation
Recharge Coupling
Power Cells

ASTROMECH
R3 AND R4

Flush with the staggering success of the legendary R2, Industrial Automaton scrambled to capitalize on their new-found dominance. The R3 and R4 lines were specialty models tailored for two wildly disparate markets—high-tech government agencies and low-income urban consumers.

Outwardly, the R3 aped its popular predecessor, right down to the brightly colored trim on its white metal chassis. The most obvious difference was its head, a clear dome of durable plastex. The transparent hemisphere gave the internal sensor package greater range and proudly showed off the R3's claim to fame—a newly updated Intellex V computer system.

The Intellex V contained an impressive database with detailed statistics on every vessel in the Old Republic navy. Armed with this information, the R3 worked effectively with gunnery crews, security troopers, and naval chiefs of operation aboard large-scale Capital warships. Though not primarily designed as a starfighter plug-in, the unit could still hold up to five hyperspace jumps in active memory.

Due to the specialized and sensitive nature of the R3's programming, sales of the high-priced model were restricted to recognized government militaries. The Old Republic purchased 125 million of the droids during IA's first production run, and the Empire later used R3s aboard its Star Destroyers and Death Star battle stations.

The R4 was a successful attempt to capture a new market prospect—the Outer Rim city-dweller who might not have an X-wing parked in her back lot, but who could really use a hand with her souped-up landspeeder. Accordingly, the R4 was simpler, tougher, and cheaper than previous R-series models.

To save money on production, items such as the video display screen and miniature fire extinguisher were omit-ted. The droid's Intellex VI computer was advanced, but geared toward common repulsorlift designs and specs for com-mercially available space trans-ports. The R4 was almost never used as a starfighter astromech—a good thing, as it could only hold coordi-nates for a single hyperspace jump in active memory.

The droids were rugged and able to shrug off the nicks and dents common to a working garage environment. IA was pleased to discover that, with regular maintenance checks, the R4 outlasted its design parameters for operational life, weather endurance, and time elapsed between recharge sessions.

Mass-market buyers liked the R4, as did the freedom fighters of the Rebel Alliance. The model's low cost and knowledge of general-purpose vehicles were appreciated by the resource-poor Rebels, and soon the droids' conical heads were familiar sights in Alliance bases and Mon Calamari hangar bays. A few R4s, rigged with nonstandard magnetic fault sensors, were used by the Empire to detect flaws and weaknesses in the Death Star's atmosphere containment fields.

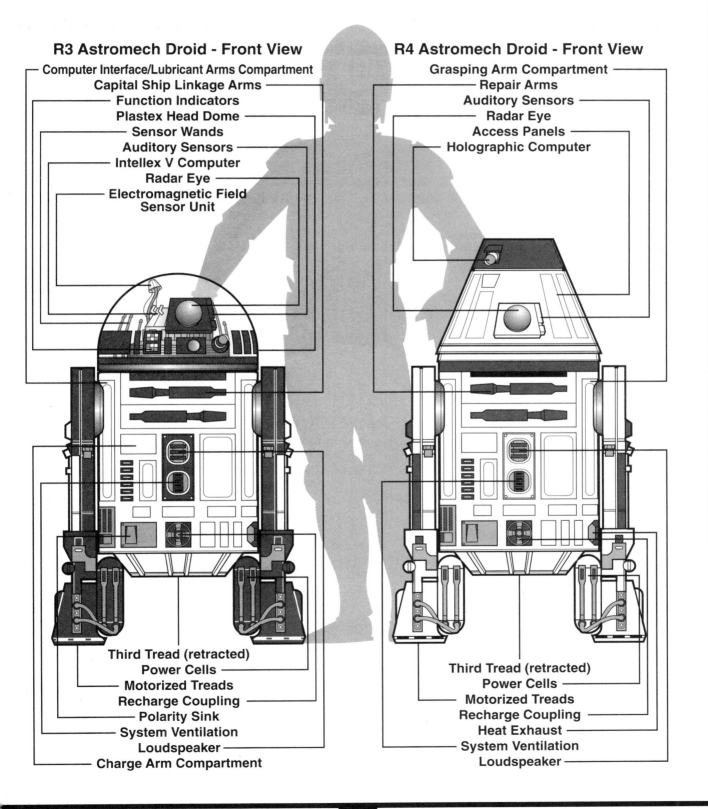

R3 Astromech Droid - Front View

- Computer Interface/Lubricant Arms Compartment
- Capital Ship Linkage Arms
- Function Indicators
- Plastex Head Dome
- Sensor Wands
- Auditory Sensors
- Intellex V Computer
- Radar Eye
- Electromagnetic Field Sensor Unit

- Third Tread (retracted)
- Power Cells
- Motorized Treads
- Recharge Coupling
- Polarity Sink
- System Ventilation
- Loudspeaker
- Charge Arm Compartment

R4 Astromech Droid - Front View

- Grasping Arm Compartment
- Repair Arms
- Auditory Sensors
- Radar Eye
- Access Panels
- Holographic Computer

- Third Tread (retracted)
- Power Cells
- Motorized Treads
- Recharge Coupling
- Heat Exhaust
- System Ventilation
- Loudspeaker

ASTROMECH
R5

How do you fix what isn't broken? Answer: you don't. Industrial Automaton tried anyway with the R5, resulting in its first true astromech flop.

The R5 was commissioned with no specific market or function in mind, and IA's insistence on cutting corners left the model bereft of the R2's "do anything" versatility. The company had created a new droid not because customers wanted one, but simply because they could. Dismal first-quarter sales figures were a bracing wake-up call to Industrial Automaton and a warning bell to the rest of the industry.

One word described the R5: *cheap.* That simple word, however, was interpreted quite differently by dealers and consumers. The former pointed out that the R5 was the least-expensive astromech in the marketplace; the latter responded that a shoddy, shabby, inferior droid like the R5 wasn't worth half that price even on its best day.

It didn't help matters that the model's behavioral circuitry matrix was prone to unwelcome glitches over time, causing many R5s to acquire caustic and disagreeable personalities. Buyers also reported problems with chronic overheating, jammed servos, loose bearings, and blown motivators. After a few lamentable sales seasons, each one worse than the last, IA quietly retired the R5 line.

Like most other astromechs in the R series, the R5 featured a heavy grasper arm with a twenty-five-kilo lifting capacity and a fine manipulator arm with less than one-micrometer placement accuracy. It moved about on three wheeled legs and was outfitted with a holographic projector, arc welder, circular saw, and fire extinguisher. A row of three tiny photoreceptors and sensors replaced the large radar eye found on earlier models.

While the droids could be purchased in bulk for next to nothing, their one-jump hyperspace capacity made them nearly useless as starfighter counterparts. Undaunted, the Rebel Alliance did some serious installing and reprogramming on their large stable of R5s. When they were finished, the modified units could hold six, seven, even ten sets of navigational coordinates in active memory.

But the droids' personality problems remained, and a few pilots didn't like the larger target profile their "flower-pot" heads offered to an enemy's laser cannons. Trusty R2s remained the combat droid of choice. Wedge Antilles, legendary commander of Rogue Squadron, used R5-D2 ("Mynock") as his X-wing's astromech during the bloody Battle of Borleias. Mynock's terrified screeching grew so annoying, however, that an irritated Wedge soon had him memory wiped and renamed R5-G8 ("Gate").

Side View

Front View

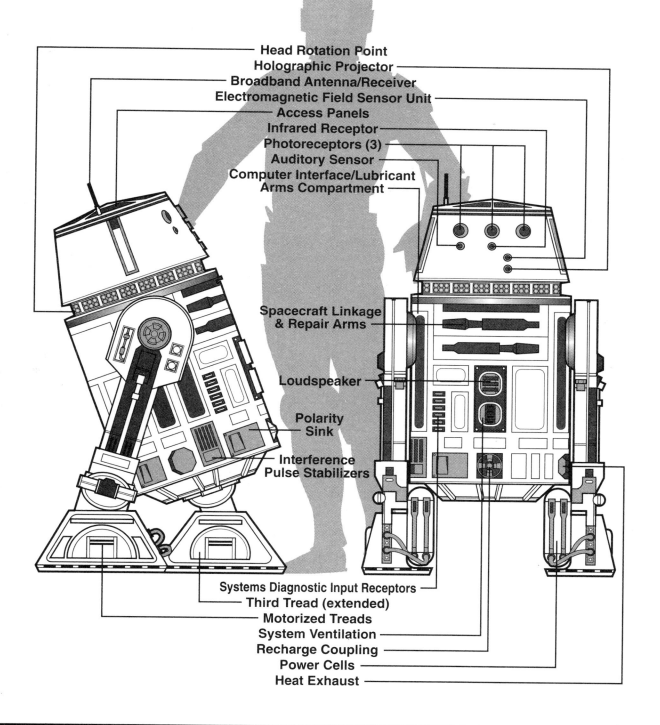

Head Rotation Point
Holographic Projector
Broadband Antenna/Receiver
Electromagnetic Field Sensor Unit
Access Panels
Infrared Receptor
Photoreceptors (3)
Auditory Sensor
Computer Interface/Lubricant
Arms Compartment

Spacecraft Linkage
& Repair Arms

Loudspeaker

Polarity
Sink

Interference
Pulse Stabilizers

Systems Diagnostic Input Receptors
Third Tread (extended)
Motorized Treads
System Ventilation
Recharge Coupling
Power Cells
Heat Exhaust

ASTROMECH
R6 AND R7

The Battle of Endor radically shifted the political balance of power. With the Emperor dead, the second Death Star destroyed, and the Imperial fleet in disarray, the citizens of the galaxy made a fresh start under the banner of the New Republic. Industrial Automaton seized the opportunity to buff up their corporate image, still tarnished by the failure of the R5.

First, the company approached the Republic's leaders and hammered out a lucrative military contract. IA agreed to design and build a new state-of-the-art astromech for exclusive use in a proposed starfighter called the E-wing. Unfortunately, the project would take several years to complete. To fill the gap, the R6 unit was released to the general public with widespread distribution and an inescapable advertising campaign.

The R6 had been on the drawing board for years, and IA engineers had solved all the bugs that had made its predecessor such a headache. The new droid perfectly replicated the R2's pleasant personality and array of hidden gadgets. Its processor was a significant step up, capable of storing up to twelve hyperspace jumps in memory. Finally, the unit was priced to move—though more expensive than the R4 or R5, it actually cost less than the original R2. Consumers bought them in droves, until the brilliant campaign of Grand Admiral Thrawn shattered a brief stretch of peace and prosperity.

On the heels of Thrawn came the unstoppable armies of the cloned Emperor Palpatine, and the R7 was suddenly needed more than ever. Industrial Automaton, working closely with the E-wing designers at Frei-Tek, Inc., had nearly completed their dedicated military droid. But before final testing could be completed, the units were pressed into active service fighting the Emperor's World Devastators at Mon Calamari.

The R7 is the most sophisticated astromech available anywhere. It performs multitasking operations at blinding speed and can hold an incredible fifteen sets of hyperspace coordinates in active memory. The droid is fully armored against power surges and can withstand a near-direct hit from a class-one ion cannon. It sits behind the cockpit of an E-wing fighter in a sealed compartment and greatly augments the ship's flight performance.

This is perhaps the R7's greatest weakness as well—designed specifically for the E-wing, the droid works poorly with other starfighters. IA fully anticipated this, but considered skill to be an acceptable trade-off for versatility.

Jedi Master Luke Skywalker briefly owned an E-wing and its astromech counterpart, R7-T1. He never felt comfortable with either the vessel or the droid, and ceased using both following the crisis in the Koornacht Cluster.

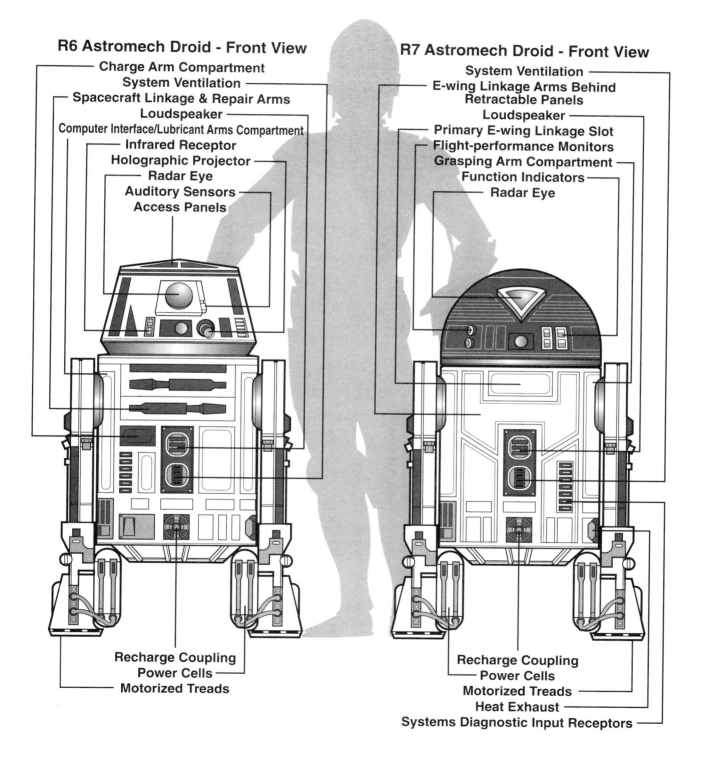

R6 Astromech Droid - Front View

Charge Arm Compartment
System Ventilation
Spacecraft Linkage & Repair Arms
Loudspeaker
Computer Interface/Lubricant Arms Compartment
Infrared Receptor
Holographic Projector
Radar Eye
Auditory Sensors
Access Panels

Recharge Coupling
Power Cells
Motorized Treads

R7 Astromech Droid - Front View

System Ventilation
E-wing Linkage Arms Behind
Retractable Panels
Loudspeaker
Primary E-wing Linkage Slot
Flight-performance Monitors
Grasping Arm Compartment
Function Indicators
Radar Eye

Recharge Coupling
Power Cells
Motorized Treads
Heat Exhaust
Systems Diagnostic Input Receptors

PROTOCOL

3PO PROTOCOL DROID

Cybot Galactica's 3PO protocol droids are among the most humanlike automatons ever developed—a triumph, one might think. Unfortunately, human beings can be nervous, flighty, and borderline neurotic.

Some 3POs are all that and more, thanks to the highly advanced neural network of the SyntheTech AA-1 Verbobrain. This superior cognitive module doesn't just allow for intense content parsing or number crunching, though it performs those functions with ease. The Verbobrain, designed to produce flawless interpreters and impeccable diplomats, permits a droid to develop genuine emotions and a surprisingly original personality. Cybot Galactica was actually forced to install creativity *dampers* in their 3PO units to ensure unembellished translations, and they recommend regular memory wipes to iron out any unexpected quirks.

The standard TranLang III communications module features over six million languages, including obscure dialects, trade vernaculars, security codes, and droid communications. The vocabulator speech/sound system allows the 3PO unit to reproduce nearly any sound it hears with the proper intonation and timbre, though the droid's humanoid construction limits its ability to duplicate nuances of alien sign language, such as the subtle *lekku* tics of Twi'leki. By analyzing speech construction and noting repeating patterns, 3POs can often translate previously unknown languages, making the droids invaluable tools for anthropologists and linguistic researchers.

3PO units are widely used by ambassadors, politi-

cians, consuls, and members of royalty as personal attachés in diplomatic or social settings. In a galaxy with thousands of alien species and millions of distinct cultures, no senator wants to trigger war with the Kian'thar, for example, by accidentally twisting a simple greeting into a personal insult. Not only are 3POs unrivaled in speaking alien tongues, but they are experts in etiquette, decorum, customs, posture, religious rituals, and table manners.

3POs stand 1.7 meters tall and are encased in a glittering, burnished body shell of gold, silver, white, and a handful of other hues. They possess photoreceptors, auditory pickups, broadband antenna receivers, microwave detectors, and olfactory sensors. The primary circuit breaker—a master on/off switch—can be accessed at the back of the neck. The droids require frequent oil baths to keep their joints and couplings in prime working condition.

Cybot Galactica has made 3PO droids in one form or another for over a century. Recently they have introduced a similar line of protocol units, the C series. Whether this line was commissioned to cash in on the fame of New Republic personality C-3PO is speculated, but officially denied. These new droids have been produced exclusively on the factory moon of Telti, and their model numbers range from C-1 to C-9.

Front View

Rear View

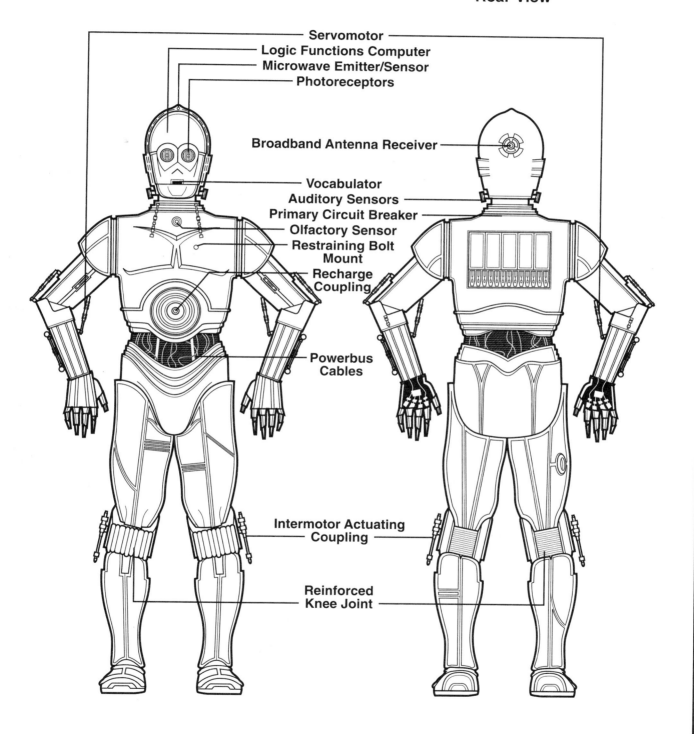

Servomotor
Logic Functions Computer
Microwave Emitter/Sensor
Photoreceptors

Broadband Antenna Receiver

Vocabulator
Auditory Sensors
Primary Circuit Breaker
Olfactory Sensor
Restraining Bolt Mount
Recharge Coupling

Powerbus Cables

Intermotor Actuating Coupling

Reinforced Knee Joint

PROTOCOL
M-3PO MILITARY PROTOCOL DROID

The M-3PO military protocol unit is a small but important subset of Cybot Galactica's total 3PO output. In the years since their introduction, the martial experts have become increasingly common in planetary garrisons and starfighter bases, much to some soldiers' dismay. The droids might *look* different from their diplomatic counterparts, the disgruntled grunts complain, but they're no less *annoying*.

Despite their "military" designation, M-3PO units aren't built for combat. Instead, the droids are administrative organizers acquainted with the rules, regulations, and procedures of over six million military and paramilitary organizations both past and present, including honor codes, ceremonial protocols, and historical military doctrines.

M-3PO units often specialize in equipment requisitioning, barracks billeting, duty roster planning, and personnel file management. Though they never shirk their duties, they are notorious sticklers for paperwork and going through "proper channels." Since most military bureaucracies are hopelessly sluggish, a simple order for two dozen blaster rifles can take a regiment's M-3PO *weeks* to fill.

The droids have standard 3PO bodies painted black, and clamshell-shaped heads appropriated from Cybot Galactica's discontinued KW traffic controller line. Two red photoreceptors glow from the dark cavity between the upper and lower

halves of the head where most of the communication and sensor equipment is stuffed. M-3POs are susceptible to all the physical shortcomings of the 3PO series, including stiff joints and poor balance.

The quartermaster of Rogue Squadron during the New Republic's fight to capture Coruscant was an M-3PO unit nicknamed "Emtrey." Years earlier, the droid had been cobbled together at Echo Base on Hoth with parts from three junked M-3POs. This radical rebuild allowed his assemblers to make some unique modifications to Cybot Galactica's basic design.

Emtrey was programmed with commodities-brokering software and given a second "scrounging" personality, allowing him to engage in bribery, bartering, and black-market transactions. Furthermore, upon hearing a verbal code phrase, Emtrey slumped into an inactive wait-state so that his memories and trade files could be accessed remotely. The only way to rouse him from this stupor was to depress the red reset button hidden at the top of his neck post.

Emtrey fulfilled a dual role, executing the squadron's day-to-day administrative duties while simultaneously keeping an eye on Tycho Celchu, a suspected Imperial pawn, at the behest of New Republic General Airen Cracken. Following Celchu's exoneration, Emtrey stayed on with the squadron and served with distinction for many more years.

Front View

Side View Head Detail

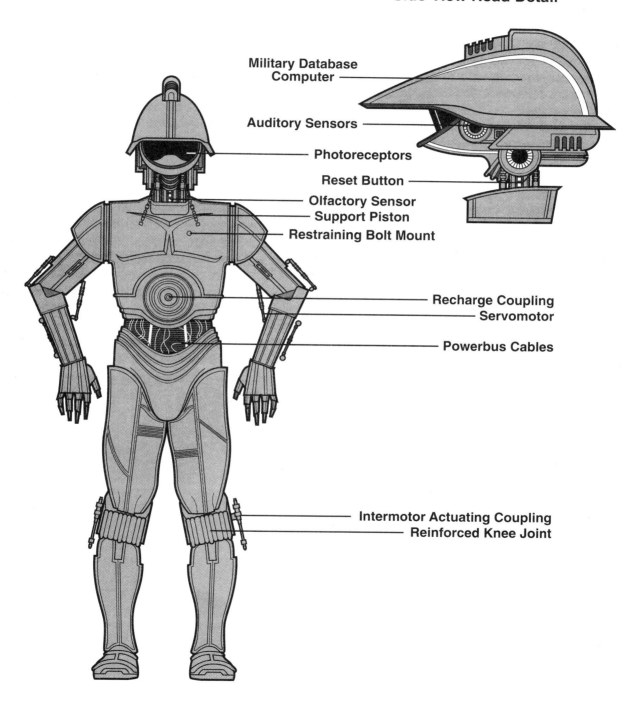

Military Database
Computer

Auditory Sensors

Photoreceptors

Reset Button

Olfactory Sensor

Support Piston

Restraining Bolt Mount

Recharge Coupling

Servomotor

Powerbus Cables

Intermotor Actuating Coupling

Reinforced Knee Joint

PROTOCOL
EM TEEDEE

"Greetings. I am a Miniaturized Translator Droid specializing in human/Wookiee relations. I am fluent in over *six* forms of communication."

These formal, precise words greet the user who switches on the tiny computing device known as Em Teedee. And if the prim tones sound familiar, it's no coincidence—Em Teedee was programmed by none other than C-3PO, one-half of the most famous droid duo in the New Republic.

When Lowbacca the Wookiee decided to attend Luke Skywalker's Jedi academy on Yavin 4, his uncle Chewbacca foresaw a problem. Wookiees can't vocalize Basic speech, and few humans can understand the barking, growling language of Shyriiwook. To spare his nephew frustrating miscommunications, Chewbacca and C-3PO collaborated to build a compact, self-aware translation module.

Using the finest components from the Thikkiiana fabrication facility on Kashyyyk, Chewie assembled a metallic silver oval slightly longer than his hand. Flat on the back and rounded on the front, the device was studded with sensory inputs that resembled a crude face.

Twin yellow photoreceptors provided visual data and could adjust to different light wavelengths and magnifications; they could also provide adequate illumination to light up a dark passageway. Between the eyes, a rough protuberance covered an array of specialized sensors including olfactory and temperature receptors. A perforated, oval vocoder grille completed the facial features and gave the droid an open-mouthed, surprised appearance.

See-Threepio took great pride in programming his tiny new counterpart. Due to his small size, Em Teedee could hold only a few of the knowledge patterns contained in C-3PO's AA-1 Verbobrain, but they were sufficient. The miniature droid was given complete glossaries of Shyriiwook, Basic, and a few other languages, as well as information on Wookiee customs and traditions.

Realizing that Em Teedee could be useful in other capacities as well, Chewbacca made sure to install limited databases on planetary geology, starship repair, and hyperspace navigation. The small droid could link to any computer network via an interface port. Lowbacca could also switch off Em Teedee with a multiposition circuit breaker on the droid's back.

Lacking locomotors of any kind, Em Teedee initially relied on others to get him from place to place. Lowbacca firmly affixed him to a belt of syren-fibers he wore around his waist, though the droid's outer casing was built to withstand sudden shocks should he be accidentally dropped.

Eventually Em Teedee was fitted with a maneuverable array of microrepulsor jets that allowed him to fly through the air like a seeker ball.

Em Teedee's success as a miniaturized translator has sparked industry interest. There are unconfirmed rumors that Cybot Galactica plans to mass produce a similar design for the consumer market.

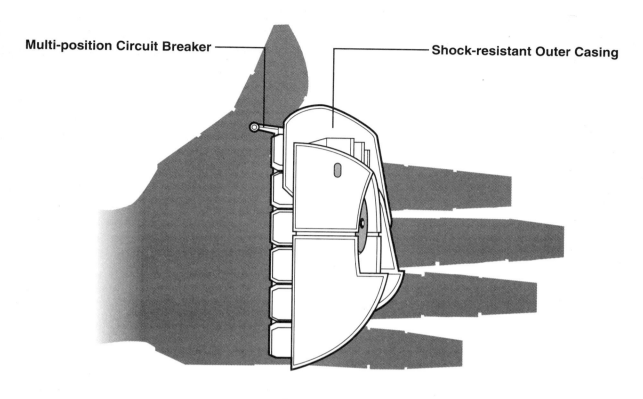

Multi-position Circuit Breaker

Shock-resistant Outer Casing

Side View

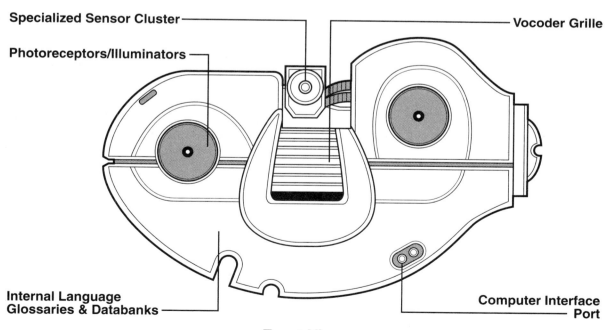

Specialized Sensor Cluster

Vocoder Grille

Photoreceptors/Illuminators

Internal Language
Glossaries & Databanks

Computer Interface
Port

Front View

PROTOCOL
3D-4X ADMINISTRATIVE DROID

Faced with Cybot Galactica's overwhelming dominance in the protocol market, many smaller companies attempted to mirror their competitor's success with their own entries. Those that tried to duplicate the 3PO precisely met with failure—without specific hardware such as the AA-1 Verbobrain, the droids couldn't match the newly defined industry standard. Wisely realizing that one-on-one competition with Cybot Galactica was beyond their abilities, Genetech Corporation developed a limited protocol unit with an emphasis on systems administration instead of interstellar diplomacy.

The 3D-4X administrative droid is most often employed as a personal assistant for businesspeople who require a traveling aide with the built-in initiative to handle many tasks on its own. Unlike outwardly comparable models such as Serv-O-Droid's CZ secretary droid, the 3D-4X is highly intelligent, meticulously precise, and endowed with a distinctive personality that somehow manages to be both aloof and deferential at the same time.

The droid's internal database of nearly two and a half million forms of communication, combined with an exhaustive library of business, financial, and administrative issues, allows it to communicate effectively with executives from any number of planets and commerce systems. Frequently, 3D-4X units are used by their owners to initiate preliminary trade negotiations with a compet-

ing corporation or merchant house, though the droid lacks the authority to finalize a deal.

Its humanoid frame is covered with thick plating of silver chromite, buffed and polished to a blinding sheen. Under focused lighting, the droid glistens like a landing beacon; when outdoors under a hot sun, the droid is blistering to the touch. The unusual head is shaped like the blunt end of a test tube and contains a vocabulator and a single photoreceptor. A laser pointer is built into the right index finger, while a sophisticated comm unit hangs from the neck. Various storage compartments lie concealed beneath sliding body panels.

Genetech utilized the factory world of Mechis III for the production of the 3D-4X, where one of the units was appropriated by then-administrator Hekis Durumm Perdo Kolokk Baldikarr Thun. Administrator Hekis allowed Fourex to run most of the day-to-day operations, and pressed the droid into menial service as a personal waiter, ordering it to deliver three hot meals to his office each day and an order of stim-tea at the top of every hour. Perhaps chafing under such rudimentary duties, Threedee-Fourex gladly accepted modified programming when the assassin droid IG-88 arrived on Mechis III and conscripted the entire mechanical population into his service. Immediately after, Threedee-Fourex delivered something unexpected along with the daily production summaries and status reports—his master's death.

Front View

Rear View

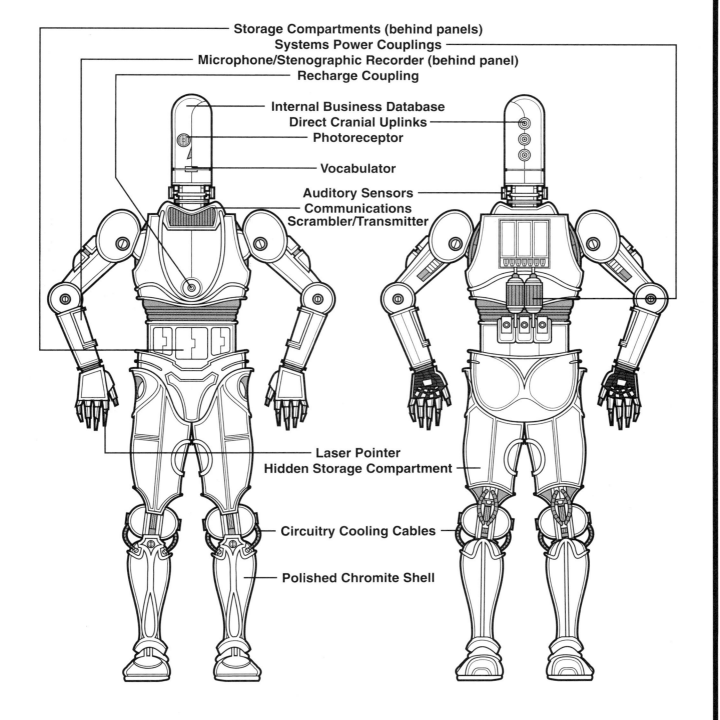

Storage Compartments (behind panels)
Systems Power Couplings
Microphone/Stenographic Recorder (behind panel)
Recharge Coupling

Internal Business Database
Direct Cranial Uplinks
Photoreceptor

Vocabulator

Auditory Sensors
Communications
Scrambler/Transmitter

Laser Pointer
Hidden Storage Compartment

Circuitry Cooling Cables

Polished Chromite Shell

PROTOCOL
PD LURRIAN PROTOCOL DROID

The PD series was an embarrassing and costly disaster for Cybot Galactica, though not through any fault of its own. Rather, the company was blindsided by the vagaries of the market and the capriciousness of Imperial lawmakers.

Niche marketing can generate big payoffs when done correctly, and Cybot Galactica had a ripe target. The alien Lurrians were innate geniuses at genetic manipulation and had amassed an ample treasury. Unfortunately, their frozen homeworld's harsh climate was tough on droids, and the automatons had never caught on as a consumer product among the inhabitants of Lur. Cybot's engineers decided to design a new protocol droid specifically for the Lurrian market.

The Lurrians were humanoid, so a stock protocol unit was used as a base. The exposed stomach wires, common to the 3PO series, were tightly shut behind plasteel plating, and all joints and seams were treated with weather-resistant industrial sealant. The shock-proof outer casing was produced in three bright colors—red, yellow, and orange—for better visibility against the snow.

The head was replaced with a new design, with stylized features more familiar to the wide-eyed Lurrians. Additionally, a jutting brow ridge prevented falling snow from obscuring the oversized photoreceptors. A standard AA-1 Verbobrain served as the droid's intelligence bank, with sixty percent of the language programming removed in favor of an extensive library on genetics and DNA resequencing.

But the most innovative change was dictated by Lur's steep terrain. The Lurrians inhabit warrenlike cities bored into snowy ravines and glacier peaks by genetically engineered *asgnat* swarms. Since Lur's gale-force winds can buffet a repulsorlift vehicle straight into a cliff face, many of the natives traverse their vertical environment via primitive hook and line.

The PD's delicate hands were exchanged for heavy servogrips, allowing it to cope with the terrain. Fully detachable, the hands could be fired with a controlled burst from rockets located at the wrist joints. A line of thin, but strong, cable spooled out from a reel in each forearm and could easily pull the droid up to a new perch once the hands had secured a firm hold.

The Lurrians expressed strong interest in the PD design, and thousands were produced—only to go unsold when the Emperor quarantined the entire planet to keep Lur's genetic scientists under his thumb. With no market, Cybot Galactica sold the entire production line to a major wholesaler at a loss.

Despite their highly specialized environmental adaptations, the PD models are still perfectly serviceable protocol units, particularly if their buyer has an interest in genetics. Zorneth the Ithorian, codeveloper of the mind-altering savorium herb, kept a crimson PDA6 as his personal assistant aboard his herdship.

Front View

Side View

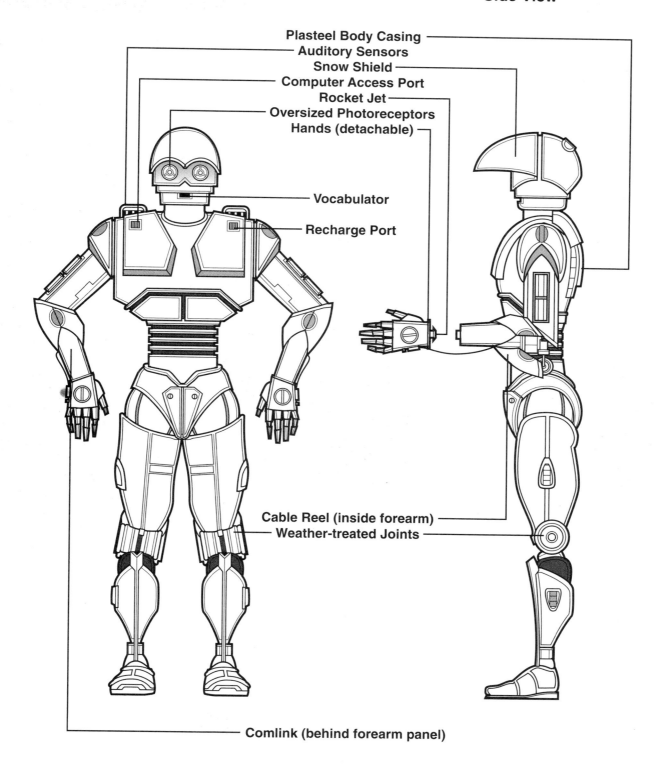

Plasteel Body Casing
Auditory Sensors
Snow Shield
Computer Access Port
Rocket Jet
Oversized Photoreceptors
Hands (detachable)

Vocabulator

Recharge Port

Cable Reel (inside forearm)
Weather-treated Joints

Comlink (behind forearm panel)

PROTOCOL

LOM PROTOCOL DROID

The corporate rivalry between Cybot Galactica and Industrial Automaton is legendary. No case better illustrates their boardroom backstabbing and petty mudslinging than the development of the controversial LOM protocol series.

Cybot Galactica has long been the overwhelming leader in the protocol market, a position that Industrial Automaton wanted to challenge. Realizing they couldn't afford to struggle with Cybot's dominant 3PO model for the all-important human consumer, IA decided instead to get their feet wet by releasing a droid tailored for niche alien species. If sales met or exceeded expectations, IA had plans to produce a human-based protocol series within two years.

Work on the LOM project was swiftly approved and initiated. Mindful of the disaster their competitor had suffered with the Lurrian PD series, IA made sure not to define their buyers too narrowly. Their target market encompassed most insectoid aliens, such as the Brizzit, Verpine, Xi'Dec, and Yam'rii, and the LOM's features were sculpted to look generically "insectlike" to comfortably suit a wide variety of species phenotypes.

If things had stopped there, Cybot Galactica might have ignored the new product. But the LOM was a test bed for a future humanoid droid, and IA was determined to sink the 3PO by offering a comparable model for a better price. Their designers approached parts suppliers such as SyntheTech and, through some crafty deal-mak-

ing, obtained many *identical* technical and peripheral components. The net result? From the neck down, the droid could easily be mistaken for a 3PO.

Like its rival, the LOM possessed an AA-1 Verbobrain and a TranLang III communications module packed with millions of galactic languages. Despite the bulbous compound eyes, internal photoreceptor pickups were keyed to the human visual spectrum. The droids were as intelligent and cultured as 3POs, but seemed less jumpy and more prone to passivity and well-mannered altruism.

Cybot Galactica was furious. The use of trademark hardware like the Verbobrain enraged them even more than the obvious cosmetic duplications. Within a day, an army of their best copyright attorneys were on the case.

A snarl of lawsuits followed, forcing IA to put their future protocol plans on hold. The LOM sold well in limited release, but then a second headache arose. The droid 4-LOM, working as a valet aboard the cruise liner *Kuari Princess,* suddenly became a master thief and one of the galaxy's most lethal bounty hunters. Cybot was quick to point fingers at IA's "shoddy craftsmanship," while IA blamed the *Kuari Princess*'s shipboard computer for causing the mysterious programming glitch. Either way, it was a public-relations fiasco and it effectively buried the LOM series.

Front View

Rear View

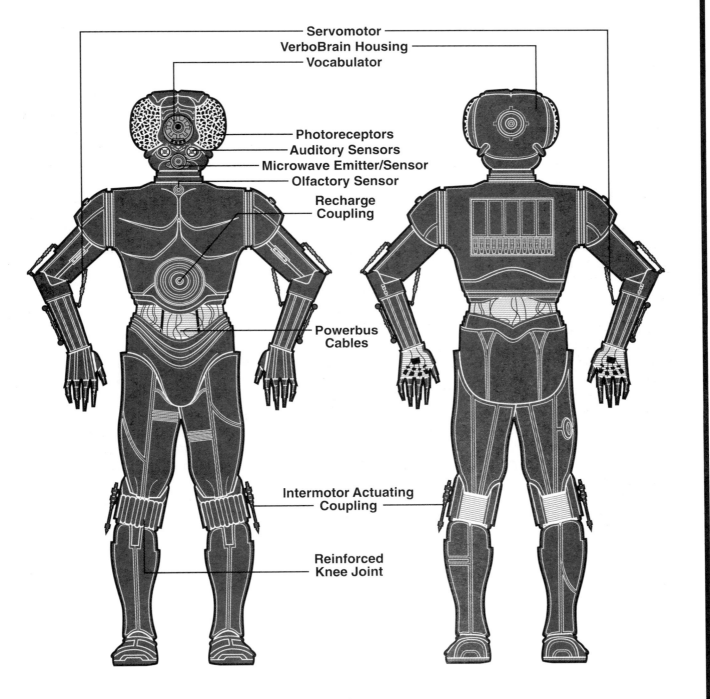

Servomotor
VerboBrain Housing
Vocabulator

Photoreceptors
Auditory Sensors
Microwave Emitter/Sensor
Olfactory Sensor
Recharge
Coupling

Powerbus
Cables

Intermotor Actuating
Coupling

Reinforced
Knee Joint

MEDICAL
2-1B SURGICAL DROID

The 2-1B surgical droid was a joint venture between Industrial Automaton and a small medisensor company called Geentech. The droids were an instant hit and are now found in nearly every major clinic, emergency ward, and roving hospital ship.

Droids possess several inherent advantages over organic surgeons—their hands are always steady, their minds are always clear, and they never forget a preprogrammed procedure. But previous surgical models met with only modest success, since their limited intellects couldn't deal with sudden complications or foresee unpleasant side effects. Additionally, many close-minded patients refused to be operated on by droids.

Geentech could do nothing about the latter concern, but addressed the former quite handily. The 2-1B is an extremely intelligent unit, equipped with an advanced analytical and diagnostic computer. After the prototype knowledge matrices were completed, they were sent to the State Medical Academy on Rhinnal, where some of the finest physicians in the galaxy further refined their programming.

The 2-1B can diagnose impending cardiac arrest in a hibernating Pui-Ui, recall that the species possesses a fatal allergy to perigen, and deal with an enzyme eruption in the patient's third heart by inserting an Intravenous Access Unit catheter or administering a mixed dose of Iotramine and Clondex. This level of sophistication was previously unheard of in any surgical model.

The droid's gunmetal-gray body is unremarkable, even a bit ugly, but the 2-1B wasn't built for looks. Many of its internal components are visible through a translucent torso sheath. Each arm is long, delicate, and perfectly balanced. The gripping claws at the end of each limb are deceptively gentle for holding laser scalpels and other medical instruments. In some operating rooms, these hands are removed altogether and replaced with hypodermic injectors or cutting saws.

Each 2-1B comes with a five-meter computer interface tether that plugs into a chest-mounted access port. When the cable's other end is attached to a medical mainframe, the droid can instantly download detailed historical data or search through patient archives. The earliest 2-1Bs were designed to be hardwired into place like heavy appliances, but newer versions can move about on two long legs.

Although all 2-1Bs share a common knowledge base, some have since become specialists in fields such as neurosurgery, cybernetic limb replacement, and alien biology. The vain and wealthy even employ them to resculpt their sagging faces and burn away unsightly pockets of body fat.

Several years after the introduction of the 2-1B, Geentech was run out of business by the larger Genetech Corporation, who filed a copyright-infringement suit based on the smaller company's suspiciously similar name. The successful surgical line continues to be manufactured under the aegis of Industrial Automaton.

Front View

Rear View

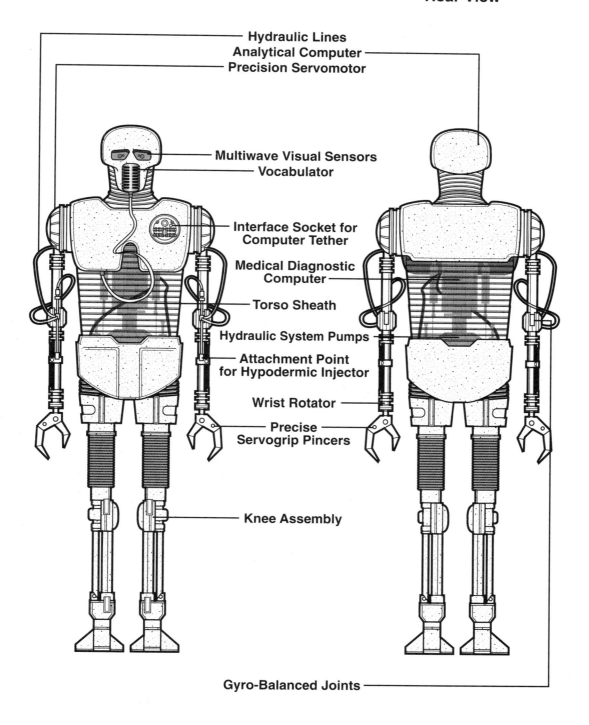

Hydraulic Lines
Analytical Computer
Precision Servomotor

Multiwave Visual Sensors
Vocabulator

Interface Socket for
Computer Tether

Medical Diagnostic
Computer

Torso Sheath

Hydraulic System Pumps

Attachment Point
for Hypodermic Injector

Wrist Rotator

Precise
Servogrip Pincers

Knee Assembly

Gyro-Balanced Joints

MEDICAL

MD MEDICAL SPECIALIST

2-1Bs might be the most *advanced* medical droids in the galaxy, but the various models in the MD series are by far the most *common*. Introduced decades ago, original Emdees are still in widespread use, and new units are produced every day on the factory moon of Telti.

The familiar body style is reminiscent of the newer Too-Onebee, which isn't surprising considering Industrial Automaton's ownership of both products. Key differences in the MD units include more humanlike hands and the use of an insulated sheath to protect delicate mechanisms. They also are more dependent on mainframe computers for data and generally don't function as well outside a hospital bay. All Emdees look largely alike, but each type has specialized attachments depending on its model number. Currently, there are ten models.

MD-Os are diagnostic units that examine symptoms and identify possible ailments from an internal database. Their dexterous hands sport two opposable thumbs, and they are equipped with thermometers, X-ray scanners, magnetic resonance imagers, and diagnostic gauges. On occasion, Emdee-Ohs are fitted with cognitive matrix analysis packages for analyzing psychological disorders.

Emdee-Ones serve as laboratory technicians for governments or large genetic research corporations. Programmed with advanced inquiry patterns, they isolate pathogens, detoxify poisons, and develop vaccines, usually under the supervision of an organic physician.

Emdee-Twos are anesthesiologists. Their hands are modified breath masks, and they are experts in alien biological susceptibility to various anesthetic gasses. They also dispense epidural perigen and localized numbing agents.

Emdee-Threes work as pharmacists, measuring proper medicinal dosages and filling prescriptions. Some Hutt crime lords keep Emdee-Threes busy preparing their private stashes of glitterstim, lesai, and other illegal narcotics.

Emdee-Fours perform microsurgery, though they have since been supplanted in popularity by the more versatile Too-Onebee. Their fingertips contain near-microscopic extensions for careful, precise work.

Emdee-Fives, the most common Emdees, are general practitioner units advertised by IA as the "country doctors of space." Ideal for extended freighter missions, they can capably treat most injuries but lack the sophistication for cyborging or intensive surgery. Smaller, repulsorlift-driven variants of the Emdee-Five are used aboard cramped voyages where space is at a premium.

Industrial Automaton hasn't let their distinguished MD line die off. Emdee-Sixes were built exclusively for the Empire. Emdee-Sevens, experts in emergency trauma, and two successive models were sold only as prototypes in limited sectors. Emdee-Tens were introduced only recently, but are looking to be a breakout success. With each Emdee-Ten a specialist in a particular field such as cardiology, neurology, obstetrics, or dentistry, IA has endeared itself to niche practitioners and ensured the future of the MD series.

Front View

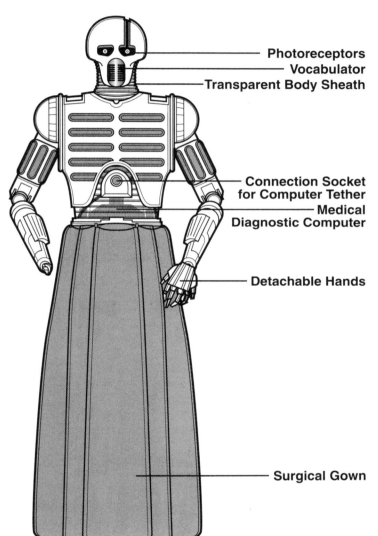

Photoreceptors
Vocabulator
Transparent Body Sheath

Connection Socket
for Computer Tether
Medical
Diagnostic Computer

Detachable Hands

Surgical Gown

**Emdee Series
(Basic Stock Model)**

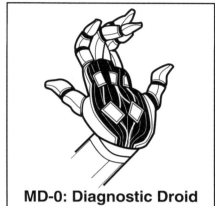

MD-0: Diagnostic Droid

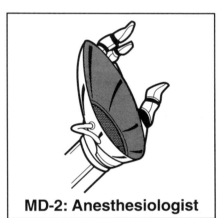

MD-2: Anesthesiologist

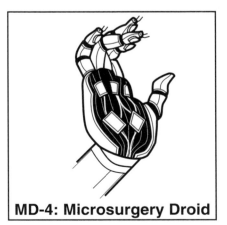

MD-4: Microsurgery Droid

MEDICAL
FX MEDICAL ASSISTANT

Now obsolete, Medtech Industries' FX series was developed to serve as a nursing assistant for organic physicians. While a doctor intently lasers open an ailing patient's chest cavity, the FX unit administers anesthesia, monitors vital signs, and hands over scalpels and sponges. But the sky-rocketing success of all-in-one surgeon droids, including Geentech's 2-1B, cut the legs out from under the medical-aide market.

The FX droids, standing 1.7 meters tall, were designed for maximum utility. Cylindrical and essentially symmetrical on all sides, they bear no resemblance to the standard humanoid form. Mobility was not a key concern for Medtech's conceptual engineers—if a standard FX needs to get from one place to another, it has to be physically dragged.

Folded close against the body are twenty precise manipulator arms on a rotating base. Some are capped with grippers, some with medical tools, and all can be customized to suit a particular task or surgical procedure. The limbs are lightweight and quite fragile, but since FXs are rarely subjected to rough conditions, this is not a significant drawback. When not in use, each arm lies flat in its protective torso groove.

Just above the delicate appendages is the droid's primary grasping arm. This telescoping limb is much stronger than the rest and is used for heavier, everyday work. It can extend nearly one meter.

The FX's head can rotate 360 degrees and is fitted with visual sensors and other scanning devices. The limited vocoder is capable of communicating only in droid or computer languages. Several monitor screens on the head and upper body can display printed information in Basic, or show charts, graphs, and schematics.

All FXs have an analytical computer and a respectable medical diagnostic package. If their scomp-link port is connected to a surgeon droid or a hospital mainframe, the FX operates with a much shorter lag time.

FXs are good droids—during their entire production run, Medtech Industries received astonishingly few complaints. But Too-Onebees and the newer Emdees are superior in almost every respect. FX units lacked the intelligence and the hardware to compete, and Medtech retired the line years ago. They are still common, however, on thousands of planets throughout the Expansion Region and Outer Rim, and the cash-strapped Rebel Alliance was quite fond of the droids. With the proper programming, Effexes make superior bacta-tank operators; despite their antiquity, many are owned by the Xucphra and Zaltin bacta conglomerates on Thyferra.

Front View

Fine Manipulator Arm (detail)

Front View   Side View

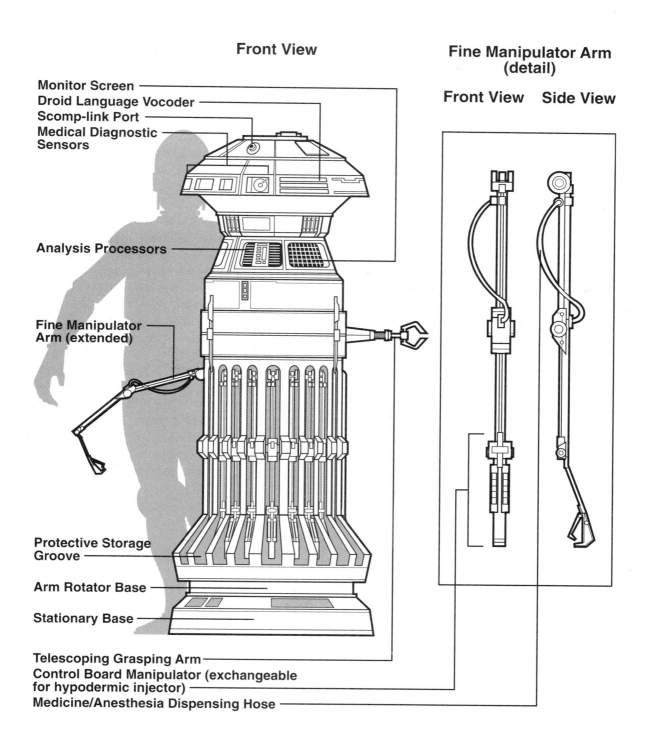

Monitor Screen
Droid Language Vocoder
Scomp-link Port
Medical Diagnostic Sensors

Analysis Processors

Fine Manipulator Arm (extended)

Protective Storage Groove

Arm Rotator Base

Stationary Base

Telescoping Grasping Arm
Control Board Manipulator (exchangeable for hypodermic injector)
Medicine/Anesthesia Dispensing Hose

STAR WARS

HOUSEHOLD SERVICE

TDL NANNY DROID

Infants and children need round-the-clock supervision, but work schedules frequently don't allow parents to stay at home. For those with credit accounts big enough to afford one, Accutronics' TDL nanny droid is the next-best alternative.

By nature, droids are methodical, patient, and tireless, attributes that would seem to make them excellent choices for dealing with children. However, the earliest attempts to market nanny droids were widespread failures. "Sure," consumers complained, "the droid obeys orders and keeps a tight schedule. But where's the *warmth*?"

The TDL nanny droid was designed from the start to address these concerns. Standing 1.9 meters tall, the silvery automaton sports a torso and multiple arms sheathed in soft brown synthskin. This artificial flesh is kept at normal human body temperature to comfort infants, and to ease the transition between natural mother and surrogate. A few deluxe TDL models can be customized to exude the mother's familiar scent and pheromone pattern.

Each droid is equipped with four arms, making it easy to hold a baby while performing additional tasks. An internal basin holds 2 liters of refrigerated milk or formula—when needed, the fluid is pumped through a warming unit and into one of the four arms, where it passes into a detachable tube/bottle assembly.

The TDL features a limited AA-1

Verbobrain with a TranLang communications module, allowing it to understand millions of languages—though this feature is rarely utilized to its fullest. It is an expert in child-rearing techniques from thousands of alien cultures, although the Accutronics company chose not to model the droids to resemble particular alien species. The droids possess datalogs crammed with the most advanced theories on cognitive and social development. Nanny droids also make excellent school tutors for preadolescents.

Their vocabulators produce a firm but gentle voice that is often described as "grandmotherly." All corners, seams, and edges on the body are rounded off to prevent any accidental injury to the child.

The XL-Lioness version of the standard TDL contains a deadly surprise—behind the removable hands on the lower pair of arms are two blaster cannons. This model is marketed for politicians and celebrities who think their children are possible kidnapping targets.

Chief of State Leia Organa Solo purchased a Lioness TDL to protect her children at a secret base on Anoth, but had her technicians modify it beyond its original specs. The new version had *four* concealed blasters, one in each arm, and an unfolding laser screen to shield her charges from enemy fire. Sadly, the droid was destroyed in the line of duty while trying to protect Anakin Solo from an Imperial abduction attempt.

Front View

Rear View

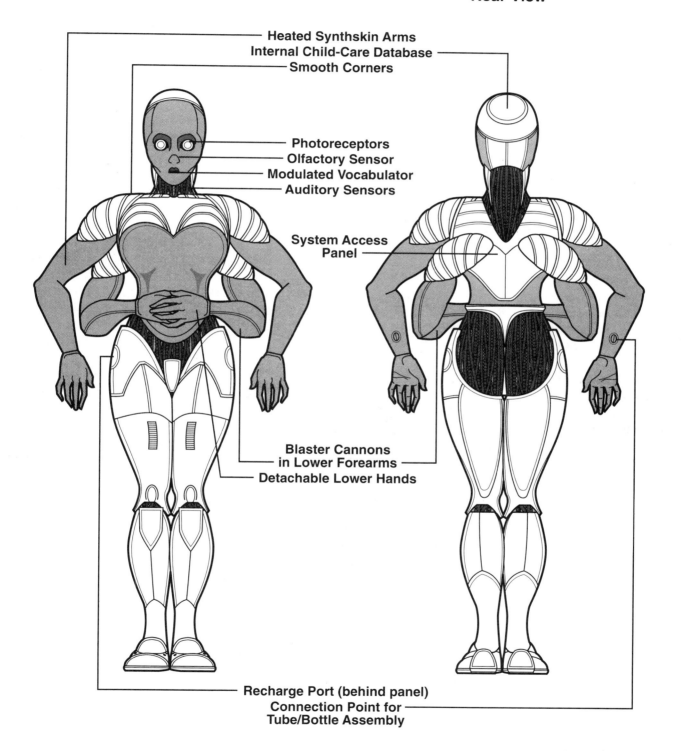

Heated Synthskin Arms
Internal Child-Care Database
Smooth Corners

Photoreceptors
Olfactory Sensor
Modulated Vocabulator
Auditory Sensors

System Access
Panel

Blaster Cannons
in Lower Forearms
Detachable Lower Hands

Recharge Port (behind panel)
Connection Point for
Tube/Bottle Assembly

STAR.WARS

HOUSEHOLD SERVICE

MODEL E

Designed by Accutronics to interact with young children as playmates and secondary caregivers, the Model E has performed with distinction for well over a century. The line has long been out of production, but a few vintage units are still in use, watching the children and grandchildren of the adults whom they first helped raise.

Most Es saw service in schools and childcare centers. Some were stationed in recovery wards of pediatric med-centers, and still others used by psych-counselors for putting traumatized children at ease. And of course, more than a few were purchased by wealthy parents as presents for their privileged heirs.

Regardless of their background, no child can resist falling in love at their first sight of a Model E. The droids are designed to look as nonthreatening as possible. Standing under one meter tall, the humanoid frame is smooth, rounded, and appealing. The plastic-coated durasteel shell can easily withstand an errant smashball pitch or a lofty tumble from a tree limb. Es were manufactured in a variety of bright colors, including yellow, red, green, blue, orange, and pink.

Large, alert photoreceptors stare from an oversized head that protects a cube-shaped primary personality matrix. While not particularly sophisticated, the matrix accomplishes its programming quite admirably.

Es are programmed to make friends

and are highly skilled at reading the emotions of organic beings. Their voices are carefully modulated to sound mellow and genial. They can sing dozens of songs from numerous alien cultures and produce simultaneous musical accompaniment with their vocabulators. The droids' databanks are filled with thousands of children's sports, hobbies, and games, from Alderaan's Arch to zizzledy box, and they will readily lead a group of youngsters outside for an exercise walk, a nature lesson, or a spirited round of Hound the Hawk-bat. Model Es are also equipped to handle feedings, diaper changes, and emergency medicine, though their programming in these areas cannot compare to the complexity of the TDL Nanny Droid.

Over time, most children become emotionally attached to their Model E, which is why the droids seldom receive memory wipes. When several Es serve together for extended periods, they frequently become inseparable.

This loyalty can be exploited for personal gain. On the planet Kalarba, a weapons manufacturer once tried to coerce Q-E, 2-E, and U-E to assemble illegal blasters. The trio had operated the town nursery for nearly four generations, but were forced to obey when U-E's body was blasted to scrap. Fortunately, thanks to a resilient cognitive module, U-E was successfully reinstalled in the body of a freight droid once the criminal's plan was foiled.

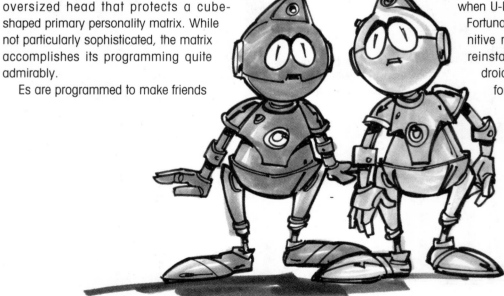

QE Head Variation

Front View   **R2 Astromech**   **Rear View**

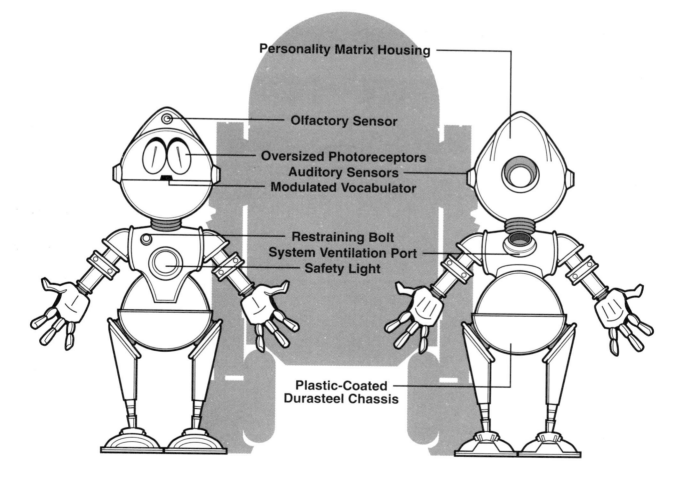

Personality Matrix Housing

Olfactory Sensor

Oversized Photoreceptors
Auditory Sensors
Modulated Vocabulator

Restraining Bolt
System Ventilation Port
Safety Light

Plastic-Coated
Durasteel Chassis

HOUSEHOLD SERVICE

GUARDIAN DROID

Cybot Galactica, famous for its protocol units, decided to blaze a new market niche with the creation of the GV/3 Guardian droid. The gleaming plasteel canine was designed from the earliest concept sketches to be the ultimate protector, companion, and friend.

Four-legged domesticated guard animals are common on countless inhabited planets. The Guardian's similarity to these watch creatures is no accident. Its personality programming is on par with that of a particularly bright beast; it cannot speak, but instead communicates a wide range of emotions through growls, roars, and yips. The droid can understand most simple commands if they are delivered in Basic.

The GV/3's metal body is heavyset and powerful. Hydraulic leg muscles allow it to easily outrun a fleeing burglar, or to pin a luckless intruder to the floor. The Guardian is strong enough to carry a standard human on its back. An array of solar collection panels allows the droid to store reserve energy throughout the day, dramatically reducing the amount of time wasted during repowering sessions.

As a terrifying attacker that is also a loving children's pet, the Guardian must take special care never to accidentally injure its charges. Its twin rows of razor-sharp, serrated incisors are fully retractable, snapping into place only when danger threatens. Its blaster is concealed in a sealed belly compartment, and it is usually set for stun in households—though this is seldom the case in industrial facilities.

At four thousand credits new, Guardian droids are appropriate units for any number of jobs. Wealthy landowners buy them to protect their estates from trespassers. Scientists and military types use them to guard installations and research laboratories. And indulgent parents purchase them as full-time companions for their offspring. In all of these situations, the GV/3's preprogrammed loyalty imprint ensures its everlasting devotion. In fact, the tenacious droid will always sacrifice itself rather than relinquish whatever item it has been told to defend.

The product line has benefited from strong sales and favorable word-of-mouth. The children's market caught fire after a Guardian was featured in the popular holo-series *Revella's Journey: A Story of a Girl and Her Droid*. Families now constitute the largest segment of GV/3 buyers.

Recently, a new use has been discovered for the Guardian droid: search and rescue. In a widely publicized incident, an SAR squad on Corellia used a GV/3 to save a team of four spelunkers trapped in the notorious Keen's Grotto catacombs. Cybot Galactica, mindful of the good press, is currently developing a modified version of the droid featuring enhanced detection sensors, an emergency transponder, a spotlight, and a weatherproof packet of survival gear.

Front View

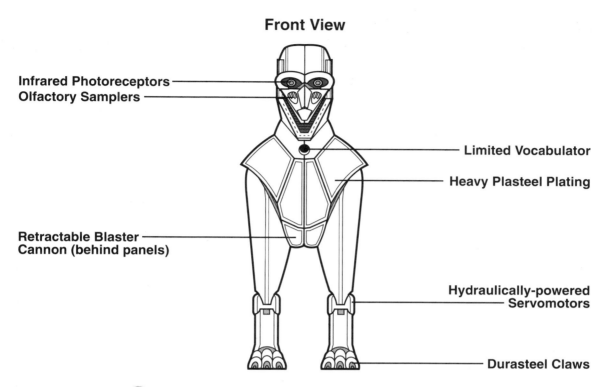

Infrared Photoreceptors

Olfactory Samplers

Limited Vocabulator

Heavy Plasteel Plating

Retractable Blaster
Cannon (behind panels)

Hydraulically-powered
Servomotors

Durasteel Claws

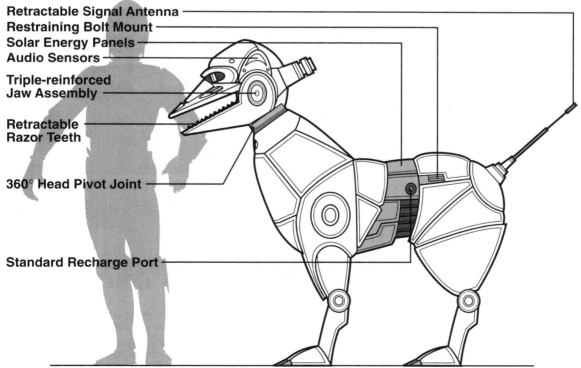

Retractable Signal Antenna

Restraining Bolt Mount

Solar Energy Panels

Audio Sensors

Triple-reinforced
Jaw Assembly

Retractable
Razor Teeth

360° Head Pivot Joint

Standard Recharge Port

Side View

HOUSEHOLD SERVICE
ZZ-4Z ("ZEE ZEE")

Once, butler droids were all the rage. Blue bloods and aristocrats, anxious for new ways to flaunt their good fortune, snapped up the toys and showed them off at receptions and dinner parties. When their interest faded, so did the market. The only butler droids still functional today are centuries-old models like ZZ-4Z, nicknamed "ZeeZee."

ZeeZee is a JV-Z1/D unit, manufactured by Serv-O-Droid during the heyday of the butler fad. Like his long-vanished lotmates, ZeeZee is outfitted with all the necessary tools to attend to his master's every domestic whim.

The JV-Z1/D is humanoid in shape, with a short stature and intentional slouch meant to imply subservience. Though ZeeZee has grown rusty and pitted over the years, the original models were coated with a burnished veneer of silver chromite. The droid's head contains an infrared lintscope, a genteel-sounding vocabulator, and an internal database packed with highbrow minutiae such as the proper way to fold an Oseoni greatcoat.

Butler droids are endlessly patient, unfailingly polite, and impeccably cultured. They are equipped to supervise entire household staffs of chefbots, cleaning robos, and chauffeur droids, and, while they can be quite snippy to their mechanical underlings, are obsequiously civil to their masters and invited guests.

ZZ-4Z has had a long and checkered career as a domestic steward. Generations ago, he was willed to the dean of the Military Academy of Carida by a wealthy donor "in the hopes that the deans may never forget the civility

that all citizens must hold dear." Stationed in the administrative annex at Cliffside, ZeeZee served as office secretary and personal valet for seventeen successive deans and was quite popular with the cadets, who could always count on the droid to relate amusing anecdotes highlighting the deans' private foibles.

One of ZeeZee's friends was Cadet Mako Spince. When Spince was expelled for destroying Carida's "mascot moon" with a gram of stolen antimatter, he took the butler droid with him to the blighted undercity of Nar Shaddaa. The ubiquitous squalor and filth pushed poor ZeeZee's tidiness circuits past their redline limits. Mako, tired of his carping, intentionally lost the droid in a sabacc game to a young Han Solo.

When Han left the Smugglers' Moon, he left ZeeZee behind. Sadly, the droid was neglected for more than a decade. But six years after the Battle of Endor, ZeeZee finally saw his master again, and was proud to announce the latest house guest: a curious gentleman named Boba Fett.

Unfortunately, the ensuing blaster fight tore him to pieces. It remains to be seen whether some enterprising being will repair ZZ-4Z.

Front View

Rear View

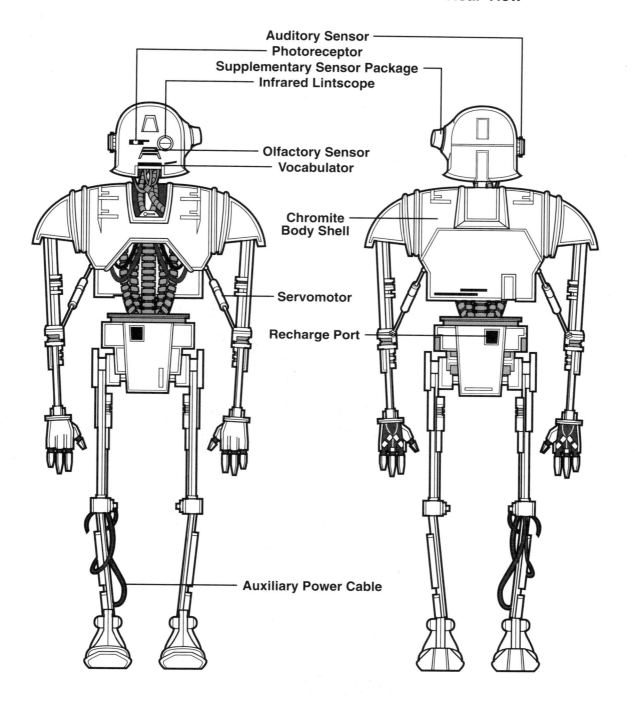

Auditory Sensor
Photoreceptor
Supplementary Sensor Package
Infrared Lintscope

Olfactory Sensor
Vocabulator

Chromite
Body Shell

Servomotor

Recharge Port

Auxiliary Power Cable

HOUSEHOLD SERVICE
U2C1 HOUSEKEEPING DROID

The U2C1 housekeeping droid is a cheap but efficient model popular with hotel managers and janitorial services. Despite its vaguely sinister appearance, the droid is a common enough sight that it attracts scant notice, a trait that has been exploited by an increasing number of thieves and gangsters.

Manufactured by Publictechnic, the U2C1 was designed from the drawing board for commercial, not consumer, applications. As a result, attractive styling and pleasant personality programming were jettisoned in favor of simple utilitarian functionality. This helped keep costs down and allowed Publictechnic to maintain a decent profit margin while selling the droids as discounted "fleet sales" to medium-sized businesses.

Each U2C1 has a flimsy bare-bones humanoid frame cast from hardened blue plastic. Its hunched-over head contains an optical slot, audio sensors, and a vocabulator capable of speaking Basic. All the behavioral and performance circuitry is contained in the head and neck; the droid's torso consists of an internal waste-storage bin. Debris is expelled from the bin via a hinged ventral discharge hatch.

Both arms are made of black flex-tubing and are used as powerful vacuum sweepers. The right arm features a vacuum attachment for cleaning upholstery, while the left contains a stiff wire brush for

removing persistent stains. Most U2C1s work as robotic maids and janitors and perform the same duties night after night. They require little direct supervision.

Until recent years, Publictechnic's problems with the U2C1 were minimal. The droids' external parts snapped off easily, but replacement units were dirt cheap and serious user complaints were rare. Unfortunately, some enterprising criminal minds soon discovered that Publictechnic's housekeeping software was very easy to subvert. In one subsequent instance, a U2C1 was programmed to enter hotel rooms and suck up jewelry and credit vouchers. In another, a droid vacuumed a timer bomb into its belly and exploded outside the office of a Corporate Sector executive as it passed by on its way to buff the lobby floor.

Lady Valarian, the Whipid crime boss of Tatooine, used a U2C1 to keep tabs on her chief rival Jabba the Hutt. The little droid acted as spy, informant, and courier, using its status as the Hutt's palace housekeeper to deliver covert messages, while using the noise of its vacuum arms to prevent others from listening in. The U2C1 passed secret information to the Whipid hunter J'Quille, among others, but the droid's fate following Jabba's death is unknown.

Front View

Side View

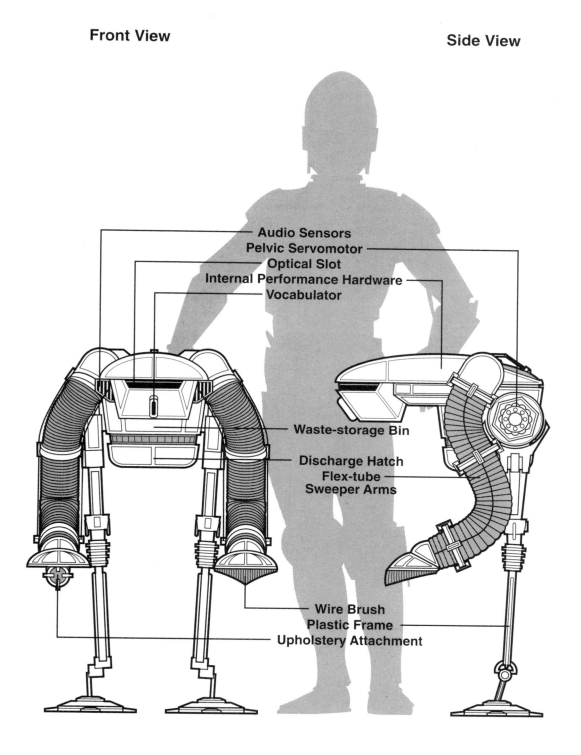

Audio Sensors
Pelvic Servomotor
Optical Slot
Internal Performance Hardware
Vocabulator

Waste-storage Bin

Discharge Hatch
Flex-tube
Sweeper Arms

Wire Brush
Plastic Frame
Upholstery Attachment

HOUSEHOLD SERVICE

SE4 SERVANT DROID

When dining on bruallki, don't use a three-pronged fork. Always remember to crack the shell of a boiled suuri to release trapped steam pockets. And *never* serve plicto steak with chilled Algarian wine. After all, your guests might not even notice, but your SE4 servant droid will likely switch off its central processor and clatter to the floor in stunned horror.

Some wags have joked that the SE4 was designed for those who think protocol droids are too *relaxed*. Meticulous, persnickety, and fretful in the extreme, the automatons are nevertheless quite skilled at arranging large banquets and performing domestic duties in the dining room and beyond.

The SE4 is one of the oldest lines produced by Industrial Automaton. It has proven surprisingly resilient to the eccentricities of the economy and the quirky tastes of consumers. Like the similar 3PO units sold by IA's arch-rival Cybot Galactica, as long as they keep making them, people keep buying them.

Each droid possesses a shining humanoid frame and stands a bit short at 1.6 meters. Its joints are stiff and its posture flawless. The face, which looks slightly vacant, features two photoreceptors, two auditory sensors, and a vocabulator, all in human ranges. The SE4's olfactory detector is quite sensitive, and it even has simulated taste buds lining the inside of the left index finger.

Without these devices, proper preparation of recipes would be impossible.

Servant droids come hardwired with certain knowledge matrices, making them inherent experts at party planning, home economics, and the culinary arts. Their base behaviors are then modified with the installation of secondary skill modules, which can provide additional information on the local cuisine or detailed maintenance standards for a fifty-room palatial estate.

Some owners use their SE4s as household handymen. With programming and experience, they can easily unstick a cabinet door or scrub l'lahsh stains from a woven carpet, but anything more complicated—say, taking apart and reassembling a sputtering fusion furnace—is well outside their capacity and best left to a WED Treadwell. In a pinch, the droids can even serve as translators, since their intelligence units contain nearly one hundred of the most common galactic languages.

The current market value of a new SE4 is about twenty-six hundred credits. Since the units can remain in active service for generations, picking up new dining tips and banquet customs with each passing year, most consumers feel they easily get their money's worth.

Front View

Rear View

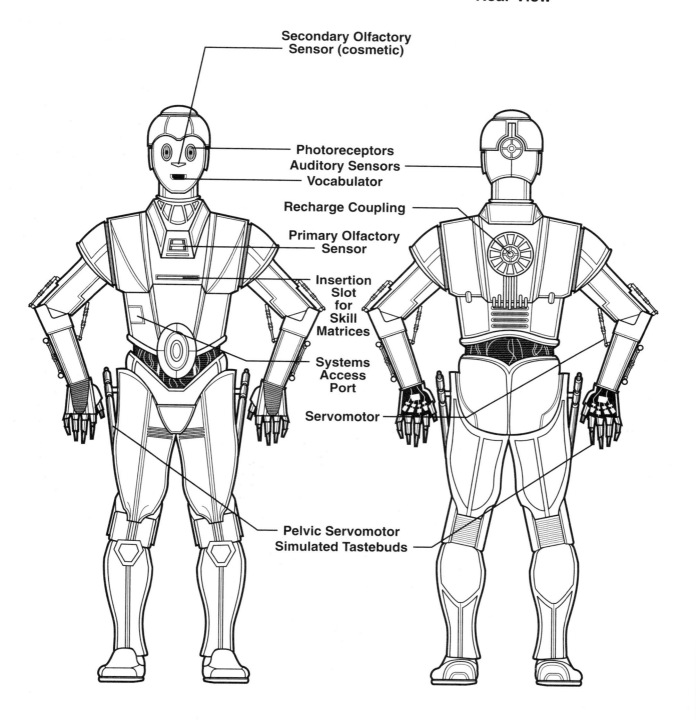

Secondary Olfactory
Sensor (cosmetic)

Photoreceptors
Auditory Sensors
Vocabulator

Recharge Coupling

Primary Olfactory
Sensor

Insertion
Slot
for
Skill
Matrices

Systems
Access
Port

Servomotor

Pelvic Servomotor
Simulated Tastebuds

HOUSEHOLD SERVICE
R-10 HOUSEHOLD DROID

Engineered by the careful craftsmen of Lovolan, the R-10 household droid is a smoothly unobtrusive party waiter and drink server for the obnoxiously rich. The fact that the R-10 so often goes unnoticed—despite its jewel-encrusted design—is testament both to its quiet efficiency and to the ostentatious surroundings in which it usually operates.

Lovolan's first R-10s were produced at the request of Emperor Palpatine for use in the glittering pleasure palaces of the resort moon Hesperidium in the Coruscant system. The squat automatons were decorated with antique brass fittings, green bronze plating, polished greel-wood panels, and inset corusca gems—*imitation* gems, but quite dazzling nonetheless. The droids fit perfectly into Hesperidium's elaborate fantasy environment of zero-gee fountains and singing warbleflowers, though some found their superfluous stylings too over-the-top.

Lovolan followed up the Hesperidium model with a more subdued unit designed for the affluent consumer. Done in tasteful black marble with a decorative brass rail, the newer R-10 met with great success among the wealthy, particularly with the aristocrats in the Senex and Tapani sectors.

All R-10 units move about on four wheels and have a ventral droid-brain package that perceives the area in front of it through a single photoreceptor. Upon purchase, each R-10 is programmed with the complete blueprints of its owner's mansion or villa, especially the loca-

tions of the kitchen, pantry, dining room, and wine cellar. Though the R-10 lacks a Basic-capable vocabulator, it is perfectly able to understand verbal commands.

The droid's marble serving tray sits 0.72 meters off the floor, the perfect height for a guest to casually pick up a frosted glass of narcolethe as an R-10 slowly trundles by. The tray is electronically charged, which helps "grip" glasses in place and prevents accidental spillage. If needed, additional trays can swing up from the body and create a larger serving area for drinks or appetizers.

Retractable manipulator arms are located at the front and rear of the droid. Each hand has two fingers and a padded velvet palm, which is slightly sticky for delicate adhesive traction. A brush-tipped cleaning arm and a vacuum hose remain hidden behind forward compartments until needed, though accidents are very rare. R-10s come with a hardwired programming module that makes it nearly impossible for them to mistakenly spill a bottle or drop a goblet.

Roganda Ismaren, a former Emperor's Hand who attempted to use the *Eye of Palpatine* against the New Republic, kept several R-10s in her personal dwelling on Belsavis. Her son Irek possessed a cybernetic implant that allowed him to use the Force to control machinery, and he frequently practiced his skills by forcing his mother's R-10s to disobey their primary programming.

Front View

Side View

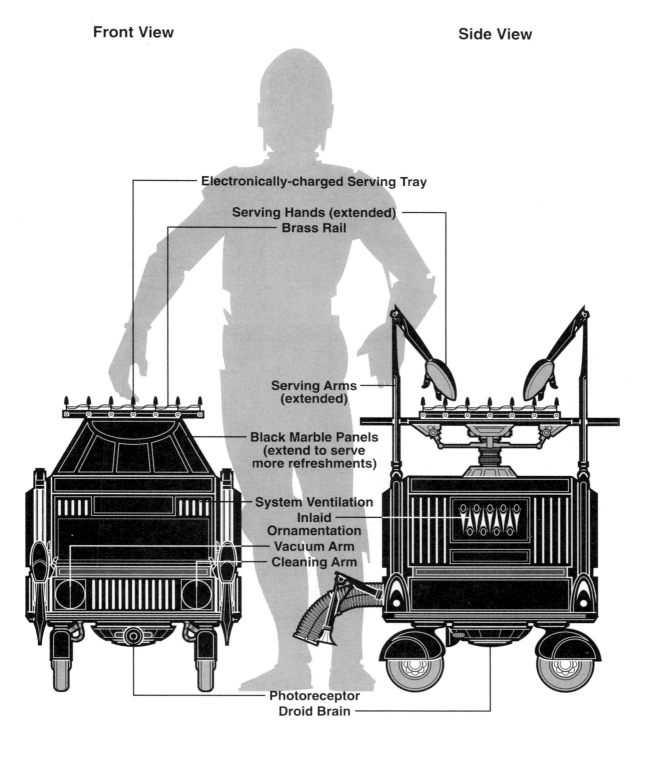

Electronically-charged Serving Tray

Serving Hands (extended)
Brass Rail

Serving Arms
(extended)

Black Marble Panels
(extend to serve
more refreshments)

System Ventilation
Inlaid
Ornamentation
Vacuum Arm
Cleaning Arm

Photoreceptor
Droid Brain

HOUSEHOLD SERVICE
TT-8L ("TATTLETALE")

Serv-O-Droid's TT-8L, originally sold to the gentrified rich as a discreet vestibule snoop, makes a capable threat scanner and surveillance system. More than one dozen variants have been produced over the generations, from the slightly menacing Y7 to the gilded, bauble-trimmed XSS.

The TT-8L, little more than an eye on a stalk, quickly earned the nickname "tattletale." The droid remains in a single fixed position throughout its operational life, typically someplace near a main doorway. An approaching visitor's footfalls trigger the unit's audio sensors, whereupon it peers carefully through a hidden peephole, matches the guest's physical parameters to its internal database, and announces the newcomer's arrival to its master, who can either admit the visitor or request further observation.

The obvious objection—that this job could be easily performed by a nonintelligent security holocam for much less money—explained why Serv-O-Droid initially marketed the TT-8L to wealthy nobles accustomed to servants and hirelings. This elite sales strategy eventually reached its gaudy pinnacle in the fabulously ornate XSS.

Equipped with a snakelike body stalk cast from antique brass, the TT-8L/XSS is bolted to the floor but allowed a limited range of movement through its multiple joints. Its blue-tinted glass optical lens functions much like a pair of macrobinoculars and is protected by a bronze shutter when inactive. Its vocabulator is carefully modulated to deliver mellow and courteous diction. The droid's entire 2.5-meter length

is a showcase for intricate scrollwork designs, sparkling silver adornments, and inlaid synthetic gemstones. A large number of XSS units were obtained by the Emperor's personal staff and set up on the resort moon of Hesperidium.

The Y7 model was developed when Serv-O-Droid realized their observation machine had many potential uses beyond simple nosiness. Criminals, recluses, and paranoids had great need for a device that could interrogate suspicious callers and scan them for weapons. Instead of meekly secretive, this new model was directly confrontational.

A TT-8L/Y7 is designed for direct installation in a door, door frame, or entranceway alcove. Its rigid body stem lacks the serpentine fluidity of the XSS frame, possessing only a single socket joint at the base of the trunk. For obvious reasons, all unnecessary ornamentation has been omitted in favor of a basic black shell of resilient durasteel.

The Y7's central eye, shielded by a retractable blind, is capable of low-light surveys, spotlight illumination, and scanning sweeps in the ultraviolet and infrared ranges.

Since the droid's unremarkable intelligence matrix wasn't always enough to please the truly distrustful, Serv-O-Droid installed a remote-activation subroutine that allowed the Y7 to be directly controlled by a security guard at any time. One of the units watched over the foreboding entrance to Jabba the Hutt's palace on Tatooine until Han Solo blasted it to tiny bits during the momentous Darksaber crisis.

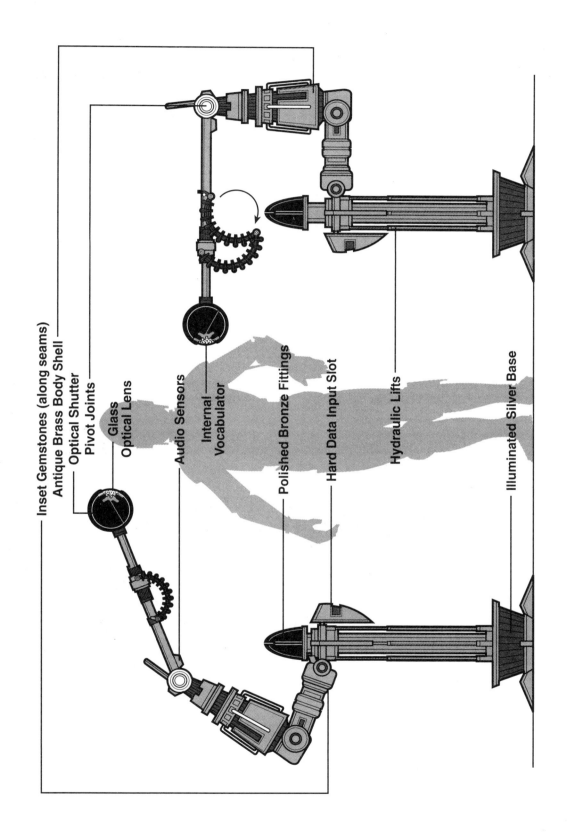

Inset Gemstones (along seams)
Antique Brass Body Shell
Optical Shutter
Pivot Joints
Glass Optical Lens
Audio Sensors
Internal Vocabulator
Polished Bronze Fittings
Hard Data Input Slot
Hydraulic Lifts
Illuminated Silver Base

COMMERCIAL SERVICE

AUTOMATED SABACC DEALER

Learning sabacc is easy. The game is played with sixty cards in four suits—sabers, staves, flasks, and coins—and sixteen face cards. Each card has a positive or negative value. The first player to reach a point total of twenty-three is the winner.

Mastering sabacc is a bit trickier. Knowing when to stand, when to fold, and when an opponent is bluffing are skills that can take a lifetime to master. The cards randomly shift values during play, requiring players to have quick reflexes and sharp minds. It is this beguiling combination of simplicity and intricacy that has made sabacc the most popular pastime in the galaxy and spawned a host of mechanical spin-offs like LeisureMech Enterprises' automated sabacc dealers.

While some casino owners still stick with organic dealers for that "personal touch," droid dealers are cheaper to operate since they don't earn an hourly wage. In addition, because most players don't tip droids, more of their money is wagered—and lost—at the gaming tables. Finally, droids have high-speed photoreceptors and sophisticated processors to keep track of every card that has been dealt and put into play, making them experts at spotting cheaters.

High-class establishments such as Cloud City's Trest Casino use only the most decorous and genteel automated dealers; squalid dives such as Coruscant's grossly misnamed Crystal Jewel employ something considerably rougher—LeisureMech's RH7 CardShark.

The entire CardShark assembly is bolted to the ceiling, directly above the gaming table. The droid dealer, suspended in the center of the metallic saucer base, can raise and lower itself to a maximum extension of 1.5 meters. The dealer possesses specialized sensors, two skillful manipulator arms, and a "mouth" orifice where it can store sabacc decks.

When play begins, the dealer announces the house rules and the sabacc variant—Bespin Standard, Empress Teta Preferred, etc.—that will be played. The droid then shuffles the deck, passes out cards, and initiates the first round of betting. As play continues, the CardShark unit emits random electronic pulses that cause all cards not placed in the table's interference field to fluctuate in value.

Six surveillance eyes keep a close watch on everyone's hand. If a player is discovered with an illegal "skifter" cheat card, he or she is forcibly ejected from the game with two heavy grasper arms. Force pikes, modulated to deliver moderate stun shocks, can extend to keep other patrons away from the cheater or to protect the dealer until bouncers can arrive.

Just like organic dealers, droids are occasionally ordered to cheat the customers to ensure a house victory. Owners who routinely engage in this practice play a risky game, since force pikes won't stop a blaster bolt—and droid dealers are expensive to replace.

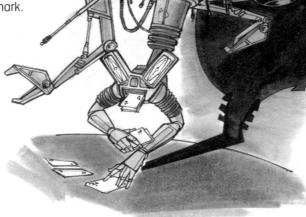

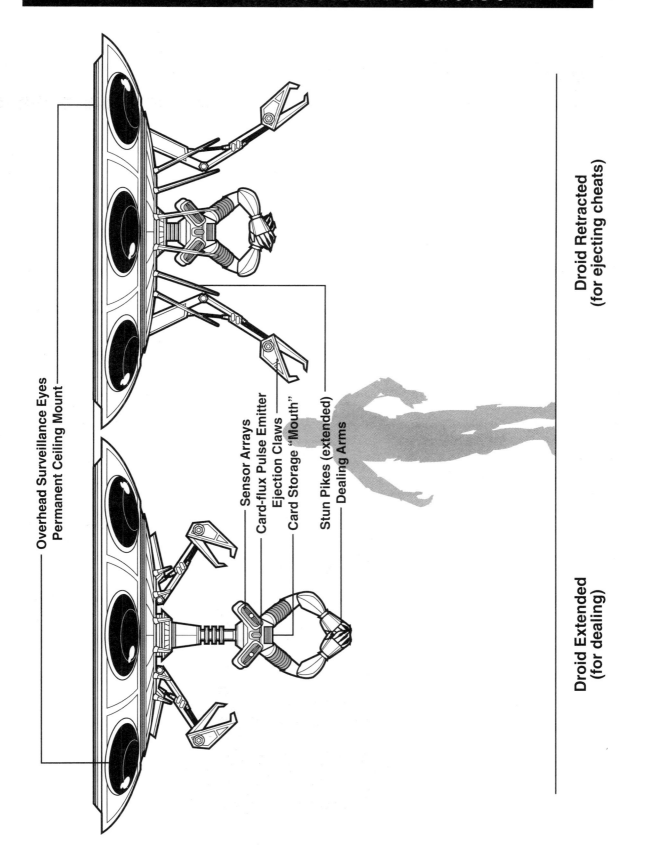

Overhead Surveillance Eyes
Permanent Ceiling Mount

Sensor Arrays
Card-flux Pulse Emitter
Ejection Claws
Card Storage "Mouth"
Stun Pikes (extended)
Dealing Arms

Droid Retracted
(for ejecting cheats)

Droid Extended
(for dealing)

ROBO-BARTENDER

"Setting 'em up and knocking 'em back" is how most rough-and-tumble freighter pilots prefer to spend the interminable stretches of downtime between cargo hauls and charter flights. If a starport's cantina is situated amidst a high-tech urban zone or anywhere in the cosmopolitan Corporate Sector, it's a good bet that the barkeep is a droid.

Automated drink mixers, commonly known as robo-bartenders, are in use wherever efficiency takes precedence over atmosphere. Droids can't empathize with a crestfallen customer over his lost love and have no interest in the local shockball team's win/loss record. On the other hand, they can whip up complicated concoctions in a twinkling and never forget an order.

This trade-off explains why robo-bartenders are usually found in busy starports. The proprietors of these establishments care little for customer loyalty, since dozens of new passenger ships arrive daily. Robo-bartenders are a cheap and effective way to move patrons through the doors as quickly as possible.

Cybot Galactica's MixRMastR is the most common bartender on the market, followed closely by LeisureMech Enterprises' C5. The MixRMastR, less than 1 meter tall, is designed to be bolted directly to a table or countertop. Tubes extend through

the base of the unit and into the floor, where they connect to drums of soda water and common alcohols. The droid's speedy processor takes drink orders, finds their matches in its extensive library of libation recipes, and siphons the appropriate ingredients into a glass. Drinks are dispensed, and money collected, through a retractable tray at center front.

Not every business owner can afford to place a robo-bartender at every table. For them, Cybot Galactica offers a mobile version of the MixRMastR. This droid comes equipped with a tiny repulsorlift unit and two manipulator arms for fixing and carrying beverages. A rudimentary vocabulator and auditory sensor allow it to perform simple interactions with customers. Because of the automaton's small size and 3.5-meter flight ceiling, it can easily navigate the busiest barroom.

Electronic sabotage is a constant headache for droid-dependent tavern owners. Unscrupulous slicers can reprogram robo-bartenders to delete their bar tabs or give them endless rounds "on the house." Pranksters have also been known to override the droids' safeties and order fictional cocktails with ingredients that are chemically incompatible. The subsequent explosions are always met with roars of approval from the inebriated crowd.

Front View

Side View

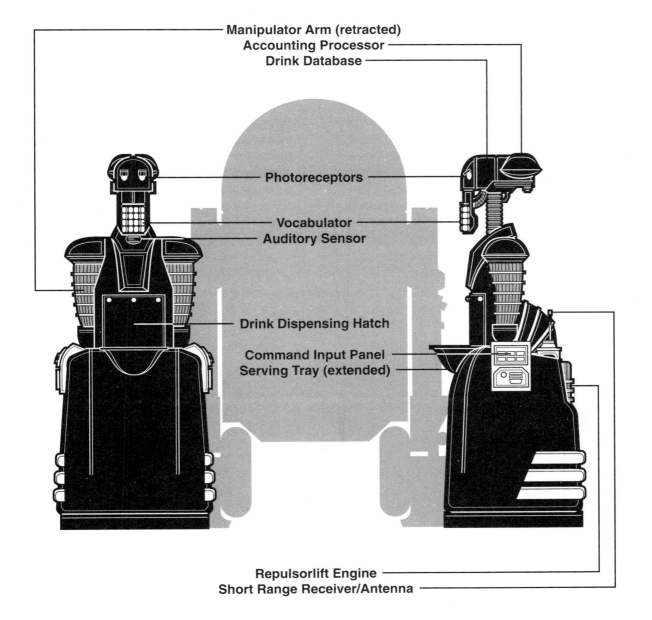

Manipulator Arm (retracted)
Accounting Processor
Drink Database

Photoreceptors

Vocabulator
Auditory Sensor

Drink Dispensing Hatch

Command Input Panel
Serving Tray (extended)

Repulsorlift Engine
Short Range Receiver/Antenna

COMMERCIAL SERVICE
C2-R4 MULTIPURPOSE UNIT

Not every droid is made by a massive conglomerate like Cybot Galactica, or even an antiquated fading star like Serv-O-Droid. Some are slapped together by teams of eccentric inventors and anxious investors, who share a dream of hitting the big time by working outside the system.

Sadly, close to 95 percent of these rollouts are failures, and even the lucky survivors are usually bought out by large corporations or their subsidiaries. The C2-R4 Multipurpose Unit falls into the former category—it was a colossal flop from day one.

Years ago, a colony of Squibs decided the space detritus they'd been collecting for the Squib Merchandising Consortium could easily be assembled into functional automatons. Their excitement at creating something new was exceeded only by their anticipation of fervently haggling with consumers over the final retail price. With typical Squib enthusiasm, they set to work building a product that everyone would want. With typical Squib shortsightedness, they neglected to decide on a single overriding function or give any thought to aesthetic appeal. The result was a cobbled-together monstrosity only its creators could love.

The C2-R4's chassis was a scrapped R-series astromech shell. Welded onto either side were jutting collections of household appliances joined by snaking power cells and elec-

tronic leads. The body and head were studded with secondhand sensors, blinking diodes, and unidentifiable gizmos, and looked like the losing entry in a primary-school science fair.

The Squibs grabbed whatever programming matrices they could get their paws on, resulting in a schizophrenic mishmash of function and ability. The C2-R4s "specialized" in catalytic fuel conversion, enzymatic breakdown, chemical diagnostic programming, and bacterial composting. Furthermore, their appliances made them into mobile blenders, toaster ovens, and bang-corn air poppers. The upshot was that, when a C2-R4 fed trash into its sharp, grinding maw, it could produce a presentable four-course dinner for two.

But no one, not even Gamorreans, wanted meals made out of garbage. The disastrous washout of the C2-R4 line was a disappointment to the Squibs, but they enjoyed haggling with the bill collectors and remainder houses.

One unit ended up on Tatooine, where it was taken in by Wuher, gruff bartender of the Mos Eisley cantina. After the novice bounty hunter Greedo was fatally blasted by Han Solo, Wuher converted the C2-R4 into a makeshift distillery. He then fed the unlucky Rodian's stiffening corpse into the droid's shredder, piece by piece. Allegedly, the resulting cocktail was exquisite.

Side View

Front View

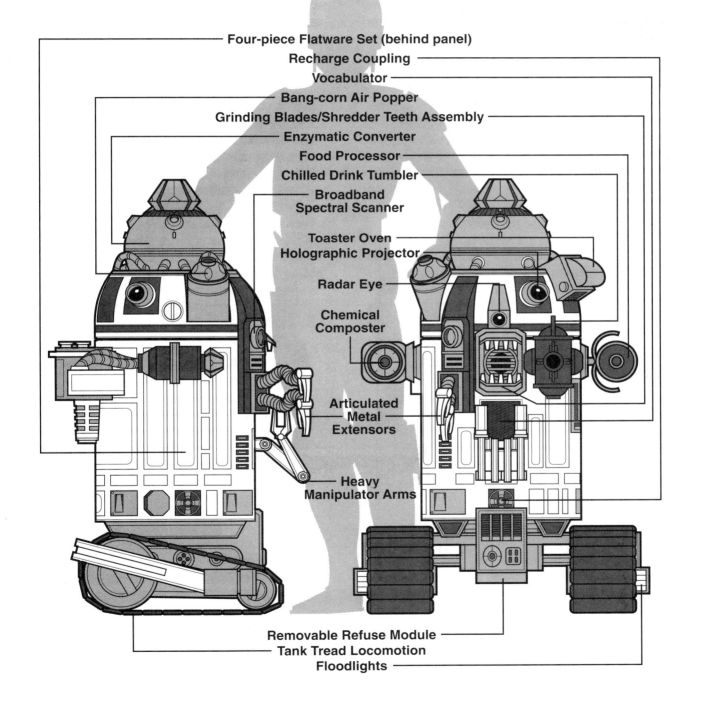

Four-piece Flatware Set (behind panel)
Recharge Coupling
Vocabulator
Bang-corn Air Popper
Grinding Blades/Shredder Teeth Assembly
Enzymatic Converter
Food Processor
Chilled Drink Tumbler
Broadband
Spectral Scanner

Toaster Oven
Holographic Projector

Radar Eye

Chemical
Composter

Articulated
Metal
Extensors

Heavy
Manipulator Arms

Removable Refuse Module
Tank Tread Locomotion
Floodlights

MUNICIPAL

SYSTEMS CONTROL DROID

Genetech Corporation's string of highly successful supervisory and administrative units hit a snag with the PIP/2 systems control droid, a big-budget failure that briefly caused the company to return to its medical-supply roots.

Market research prodded Genetech to exploit a relatively untapped niche—control-board operation. Although a few modern computer systems are completely automated through artificial intelligence and microprocessors, many networks rely on old-fashioned central switchboards and keyboard input panels. The reasons for the latter setup are many, ranging from cost to security to convenience, but the humans and aliens who run the control boards are almost universally overworked. Inevitably, this leads to accidental goofs and anxiety-induced foul-ups.

The PIP/2 was rushed into development to replace these flawed workers with a fast and foolproof droid. For reasons unclear, Genetech invested a huge number of production credits in the line's creation, despite the fact that the droid could only be sold to a relatively small market. Numerous logistical delays compounded their problem. Before long, the company and its stockholders had an enormous stake in the PIP/2—if it didn't sell in record numbers, the fiscal year would be a disaster.

No droid model could be expected to fulfill such high expectations, but the PIP/2 failed in an extraordinarily spectacular fashion. Genetech advertised the unit as "glitch-proof," even going so far as to offer money-back guarantees to municipal and corpo-

rate buyers. To the company's horror, glitches seemed to be all the new droid was capable of.

The PIP/2's droid brain handled simple tasks with ease, but quickly became overtaxed when subjected to excessive stimuli—alarm bells and warning lights, for instance. The stressed unit would either switch itself off or punch the wrong buttons in a vain effort to keep up. In one case, a systems control droid cross wired a habitation sphere's sewage drains with its water-flow piping, resulting in 1,013 cases of severe intestinal distress.

Genetech was quick to respond to complaints, recalling as many units as possible and installing new programming patches. These modified droids operated almost perfectly—their optics-covered heads could scan every section of the control board simultaneously, while their eight jointed limbs punched keys with enviable speed and precision. Unfortunately, the damage was done. The systems control line continued for two dismal years until its merciful discontinuation, while a chastened Genetech refocused its sales efforts on its core medical market until the public's memory of the PIP/2 had faded.

Occasionally, a galactic citizen might see one of the outdated droids still in use. The Holographic Zoo of Extinct Animals on Coruscant used a PIP/2 to control the holographic dioramas and keep visitors moving through the exhibit halls. When Han Solo's children became lost in the museum, the droid had a distinctly unpleasant encounter with an enraged Wookiee named Chewbacca.

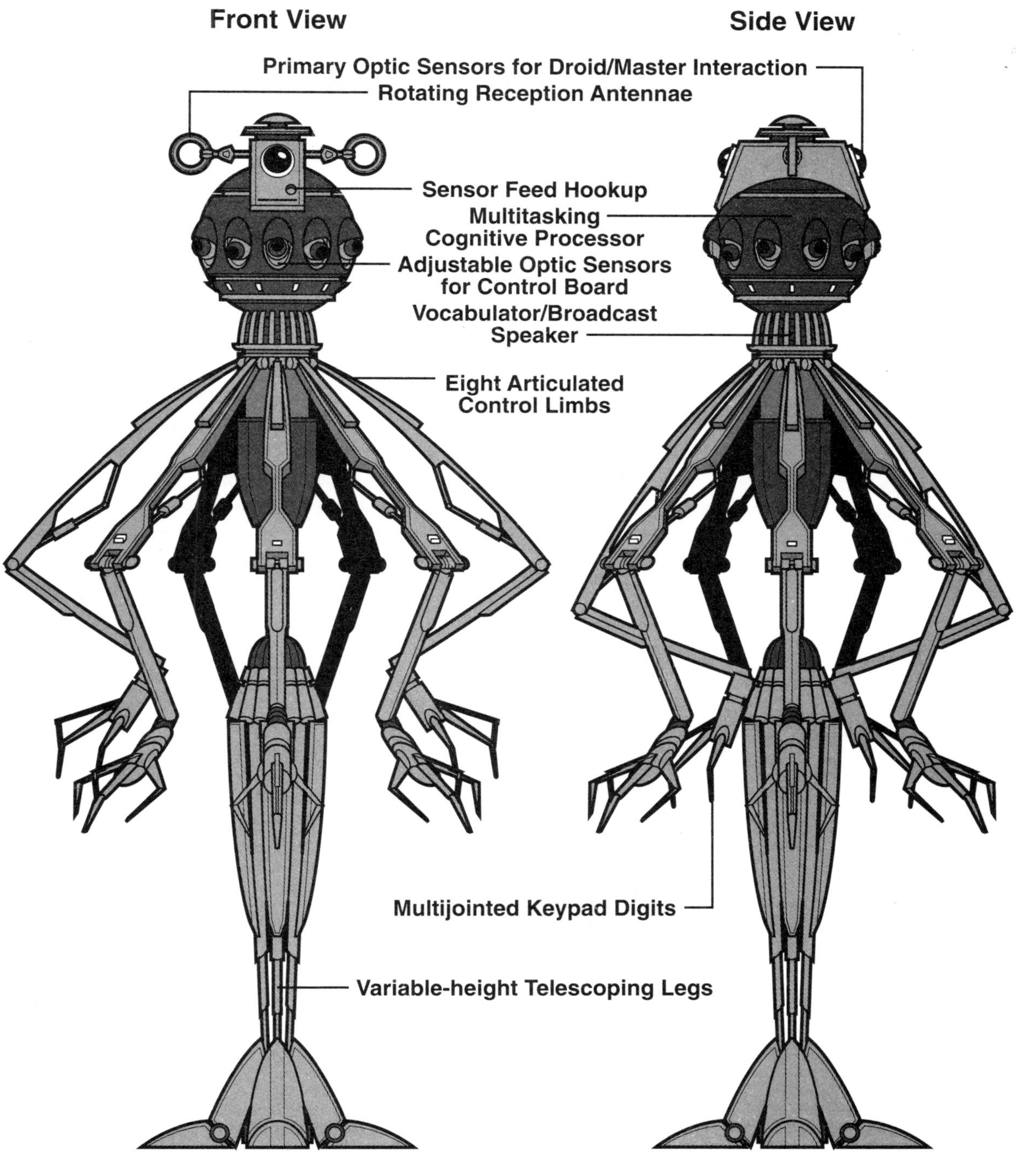

Front View

Side View

Primary Optic Sensors for Droid/Master Interaction

Rotating Reception Antennae

Sensor Feed Hookup

Multitasking
Cognitive Processor

Adjustable Optic Sensors
for Control Board

Vocabulator/Broadcast
Speaker

Eight Articulated
Control Limbs

Multijointed Keypad Digits

Variable-height Telescoping Legs

MUNICIPAL 12-4C-41 TRAFFIC CONTROLLER

Space travel and air travel are universally accepted methods of transportation, but most planets don't allow ship pilots to just touch down wherever they desire. Whether it's a buzzing orbital docking platform or a simple dirtside landing strip, traffic controllers in observation towers perform the complicated task of directing vessels through a three-dimensional control zone and guiding them down to a safe anchoring berth.

For humans and most other organics, the job can be tedious and exhausting. Numerous companies have attempted to solve the fatigue problem with fully automated computer-controlled landing systems, but these have a history of dramatic failures. On Tala 9 two fully laden passenger liners collided in orbit when their old-model shipboard hardware misinterpreted a landing signal intended for upgraded systems only.

A viable alternative to both organics and computers is the traffic controller droid. Unlike living beings, SoroSuub Corporation's 12-4C-41 units don't suffer from bleary eyes and clouded minds. And unlike automated guidance systems, the droids are able to keep track of multiple ships and respond to unexpected situations with flexible thinking. Since over 90 percent of spaceport control towers are designed for biological workers, their bipedal mobility and standard humanoid frames make it easy for them to interface with existing equipment.

Each 12-4C-41 comes equipped with a sophisticated optic/recorder system capable of panoramic and macroscopic scans. The droid can pinpoint a wayward ship's position through kilometers of thick fog while simultaneously viewing dozens of glowing monitor screens and dumping all information into its multilayered cognitive processor. When the 12-4C-41 needs to access specialized databases—vehicle classes, landing codes, transit protocols, etc.—it can plug into standard mainframe access ports with a retractable data-probe in its left index finger.

The middle torso of the 12-4C-41 doubles as a landing beacon. Behind smoky translucent panes lies a powerful omnidirectional floodlight that can flash in preprogrammed patterns and cycle through a variety of colors. This feature was designed for emergency use in cases where the landing station had lost power due to generator failure or ion cannon attack. Managers of large orbital stations sometimes employ numerous 12-4C-41 units to jet through the vacuum, outlining approach vectors with their illuminated bodies and leading smaller ships to individual berths. For this purpose multiple "worker" units—labeled 12-4C-41/b—can be purchased with limited cognitive modules for a substantially reduced price.

Cloud City in Bespin is one of the many establishments that utilize 12-4C-41 traffic controllers. In an incident that occurred prior to the Battle of Hoth, the renegade supervisory droid EV-9D9 sadistically disassembled more than one-fourth of the city's automaton population. Wuntoo Forcee Forwun, a survivor from the traffic department, doggedly tracked the hateful killer to Tatooine and took his justifiable revenge.

Front View

Rear View

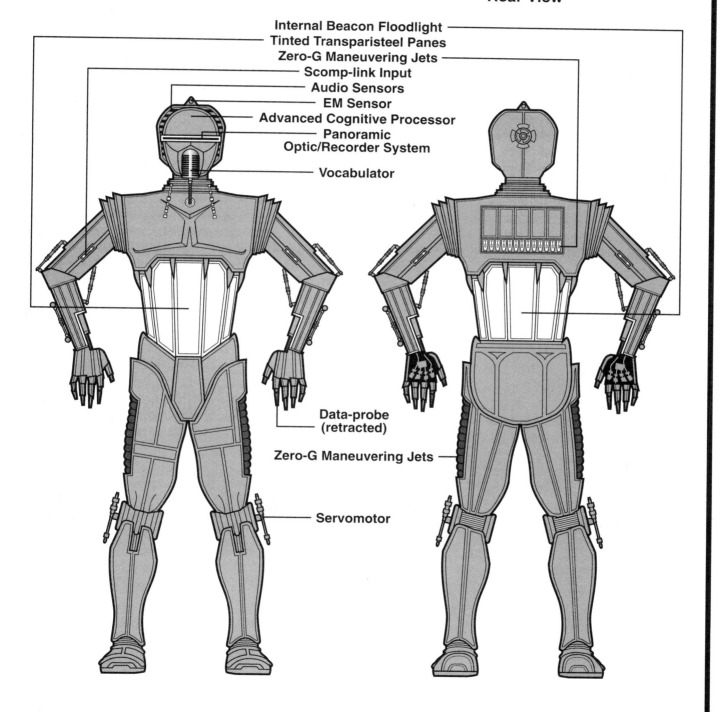

Internal Beacon Floodlight

Tinted Transparisteel Panes

Zero-G Maneuvering Jets

Scomp-link Input

Audio Sensors

EM Sensor

Advanced Cognitive Processor

Panoramic
Optic/Recorder System

Vocabulator

Data-probe
(retracted)

Zero-G Maneuvering Jets

Servomotor

MUNICIPAL

5T TREE FEEDER

Publictechnic's 5T Tree Feeder—a gigantic clattering metal spider with spades for feet and blades for arms—is an unsettling sight at first glance. But unless you're a plant-based Revwien badly in need of petal-pruning, you have nothing to fear from the docile automated gardeners.

The line has been in production for decades. The current model is serial-stamped RO/5T.N1, but the droid has always been better known as "Tree Feeder" despite the fact that it is capable of many tasks beyond simple nutrient spraying. Publictechnic manufactures the droids for large-scale government, municipal, and corporate use, so it is difficult to purchase new Tree Feeders in batches of less than fifty units. Private growers and landscapers often scour used-droid lots to pick up individual Tree Feeders for home applications.

The droids are fairly intelligent, but that aptitude is focused exclusively into gardening and caretaking techniques. Tree Feeders care little for events that occur outside their patch of cultivated territory, and they will become irritated at anyone who picks a blossoming T'iil flower or errantly wanders off a flagstone pathway onto freshly clipped grass.

The droid moves about on six pointed limbs, which connect to a dorsally mounted support rod. The arachnid body hangs underneath and is packed with retractable cutting and grooming tools. Blinking yellow lights and sensory nodes are arrayed around the rim of the body, while two independently mounted turret photoreceptors can zoom in to examine insect damage on a leaf or the delicate root structure of a seedling.

A Tree Feeder comes equipped with an articulated hose and an adjustable sprayer nozzle for dispensing fertilizer, organic pesticides, and water; a large water tank makes up the droid's abdomen. Other implements include twin manipulator arms, a combination edger/trimmer, pruning shears, probes for testing the pH and moisture content of soil, and a specialized appendage for weeding and for plucking fruit.

The droids' daily duties are routine but can be fairly elaborate. Each Tree Feeder is acquainted with over one million of the most common decorative and edible plant species and will make every effort to protect its charges from harm, including laying down mulch bedding and running complex pollination programs if the environment lacks local insect carriers.

Beautiful, well-manicured worlds such as Kuat and Hesperidium rely heavily on Tree Feeders, but the droids are common enough to be found in out-of-the-way spots like the Plawal rift on Belsavis. There, the Mluki government employs them to maintain the local shalaman and podon orchards. When Roganda Ismaren arrived on Belsavis, her son Irek occasionally forced the Tree Feeders to run wild in a prankish test of his budding Force abilities.

Front View

Side View

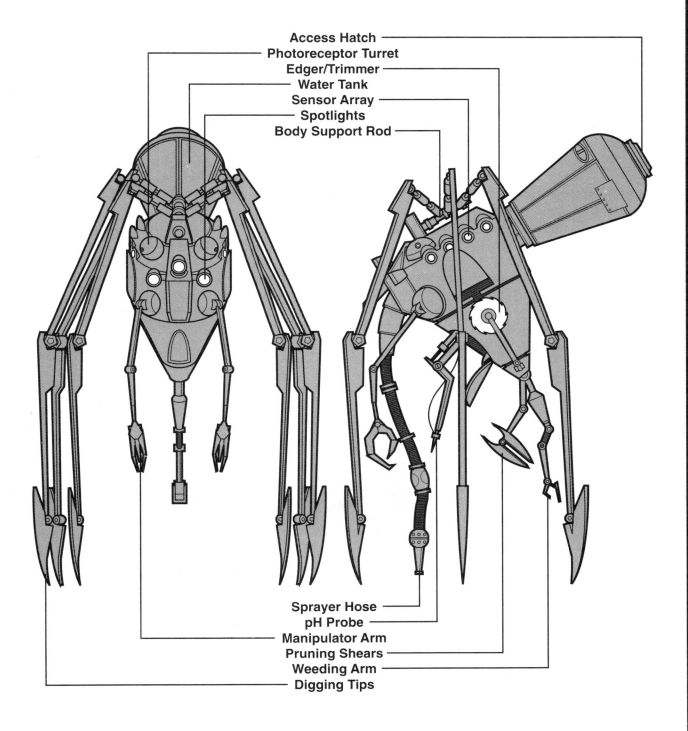

Access Hatch

Photoreceptor Turret

Edger/Trimmer

Water Tank

Sensor Array

Spotlights

Body Support Rod

Sprayer Hose

pH Probe

Manipulator Arm

Pruning Shears

Weeding Arm

Digging Tips

MUNICIPAL
INFERNO FIREFIGHTING ROBO

One of the greatest advantages of droids is their ability to operate in environments that would cripple or kill organic beings. The firefighting robo is a perfect example, capable of surviving blistering temperatures to douse a burning warehouse or rescue a stranded child.

The Corporate Sector Authority's modular Inferno units are among the most original and versatile emergency droids ever devised. Quick and maneuverable, Infernos can link together to fight fires in teams or split up and use their antigravity repulsors to attack a blaze from different elevations. Whether deployed on their own or in conjunction with organic rescue squads, the droids are becoming increasingly common in both governmental and privately funded fire stations.

A complete CSA Inferno system consists of one "host" carrier unit and four smaller firefighters. When an alarm is raised, the host unit races to the scene with its military-grade repulsorlift engine—in a large-scale crisis, multiple hosts are ferried to the site aboard cargo transports. Upon arrival the individual robos detach from their parent and speed into the conflagration.

These small units are protected by tough armor and a heat-resistant alloy coating. The ventrally mounted spray nozzle releases a high-pressure stream of fire-retardant foam that is effective against most electrical and chemical blazes. A small laser cutter works well for slicing through doors and flaming wreckage. Two heavy gripper arms were originally designed to manipulate machinery, but are more often used to drag unconscious victims to safety. A compact "head" on the droid's left side contains an infrared photoreceptor, an echolocation scanner, a high-intensity searchlight, and a loudspeaker used to broadcast evacuation instructions or siren whoops.

The droids can snap together atop one another like children's building blocks. Although dozens of robos are capable of forming a formidable firefighting tower, a more familiar configuration consists of two units facing front and back, spraying foam in both directions as they streak through the heart of a burning edifice. When their supplies of chemical froth are exhausted, the Inferno units return to their host unit for replenishment. The host's central body is one large tank of compressed foam, and it dispenses the mixture to its thirsty droids through eight articulated fueling hoses.

Outside the Corporate Sector the droids are still gaining popularity; within the Corporate Sector, they are ubiquitous. Even primitive backwaters like Ammuud have a full complement of Infernos stationed at the clan fortresses and at the starport landing field.

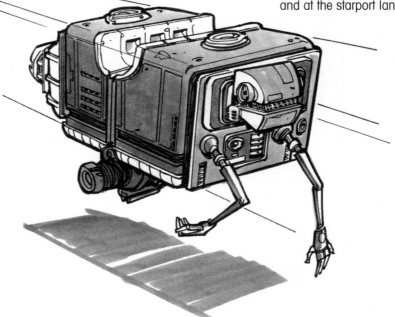

Firefighting "Team"

Firefighting Robo2 - Rear

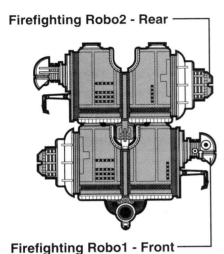

Firefighting Robo1 - Front

Host Carrier

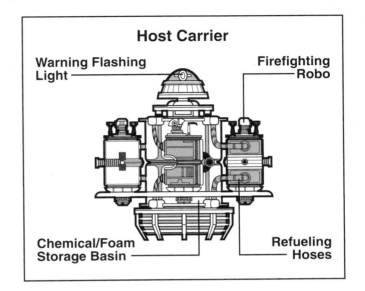

Warning Flashing Light

Firefighting Robo

Chemical/Foam Storage Basin

Refueling Hoses

Searchlight
Audio/Echolocation Scanner
Refueling Port

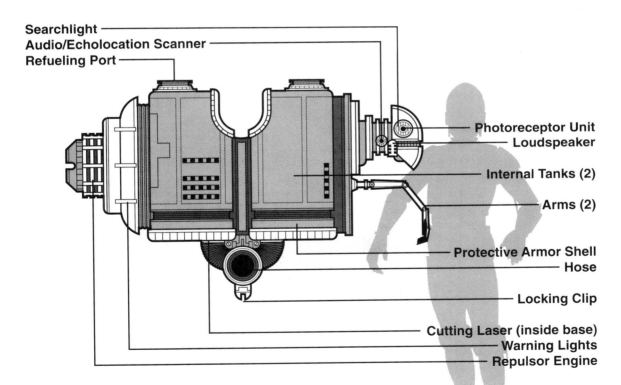

Photoreceptor Unit
Loudspeaker

Internal Tanks (2)

Arms (2)

Protective Armor Shell
Hose

Locking Clip

Cutting Laser (inside base)
Warning Lights
Repulsor Engine

Front View

MUNICIPAL
ROBO-HACK

Robo-hacks are automated taxis, guided by simple droid brains through crowded metropolitan streets and freeways. The battered, brightly colored vehicles are an inescapable sight on any industrialized planet from the Core to the Outer Rim.

The idea behind robo-hacks is simple—take a droid's intelligence module and install it in an already-existing passenger vehicle. The resulting creation is more efficient than an organic driver, and usually cheaper to operate as well. Other examples of this "vehicle droid" concept include drone barges and robot ramships.

A standard Go-Corp/Utilitech Metrocab is an enclosed landspeeder about six meters in length. Accommodations are spartan, consisting only of a back seat for one to four passengers, a pair of scratchy speakers playing a local music broadcast, and a snuff-pot for stubbing out used cigarras. Frequent users of robo-hacks become inured to the grime, the smell, and the torn upholstery.

When passengers enter, they announce their destination in the direction of the large auditory sensor embedded in the front wall. If further clarification is needed, the droid asks questions through an adjacent vocoder. This is usually the extent of conversation—few robo-hacks have the personality programming for idle chitchat.

Upon arrival, the customer pays by inserting a credit voucher into the data port or feeding the local currency unit into a change slot. If a passenger

tries to exit the vehicle without paying, some droids lock both doors and deliver the scofflaw to the nearest police precinct.

Behind the cabin divider, in the sealed forward compartment, is the droid's cognitive module and primary performance circuitry. All robo-hacks are equipped with complete maps of the local streets, as well as a Central Learning Chip (CLC) allowing them to learn shortcuts based on past experience. Some canny droids routinely defraud ignorant tourists by taking the longest, and therefore most expensive, route between two nearby locations.

On many planets, robo-hacks are allowed to access the municipal traffic control network for up-to-date information on weather conditions, vehicle accidents, and other roadway problems. Banks of sensors above the two forward headlights provide situational tracking data for high-speed lane changing. A panoramic optical sensor in the back acts as a rear view mirror.

When they were first introduced centuries ago, robo-hacks were often cornered and blown to pieces by street gangs eager to nab their locked credit repositories. Nowadays, the droids are manufactured with a resilient outer covering making them immune to even the most determined small-arms fire.

Front View

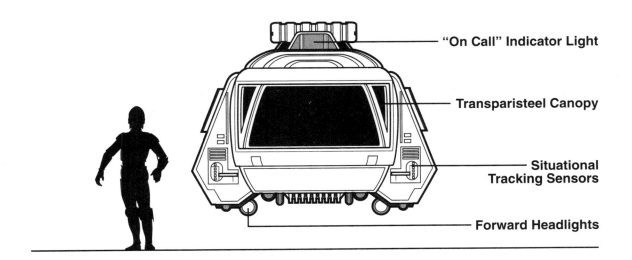

"On Call" Indicator Light

Transparisteel Canopy

Situational
Tracking Sensors

Forward Headlights

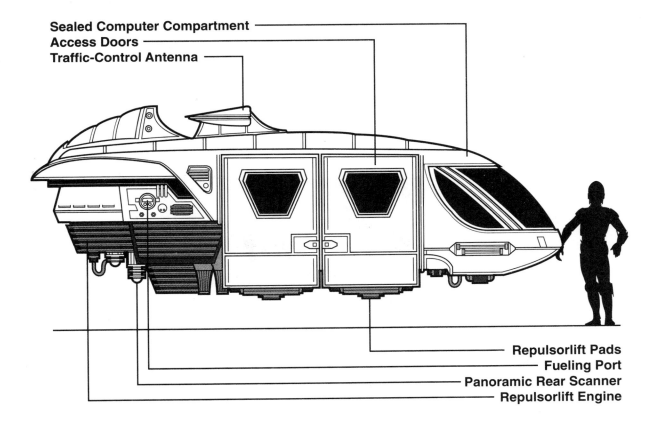

Sealed Computer Compartment
Access Doors
Traffic-Control Antenna

Repulsorlift Pads
Fueling Port
Panoramic Rear Scanner
Repulsorlift Engine

Side View

BUSINESS

SCM-22 STENOGRAPHER

The SCM-22 appears at first glance to be nothing more than a child's windup toy. The little egg-shaped droid, however, is a puny powerhouse packed with sensitive recording equipment. As a portable stenographer, its small size allows it to be carried in a pocket or to perch unobtrusively on the corner of a desk.

The SCM-22 is manufactured by PowerPost, a minor office supply corporation. Since PowerPost's product experience was previously limited to nonintelligent calculating machines and business datapads, the company licensed the necessary droid cognitive hardware from Industrial Automaton. The finished product is owned entirely by PowerPost. Despite better-than-expected sales figures, the company has no immediate plans to produce additional types of droids.

The SCM-22 was marketed to busy corporate executives who made frequent interplanetary business trips. Since human-sized personal secretaries like Serv-O-Droid's CZ series were too bulky to bring along on passenger starliners, the SCM was advertised as the perfect alternative. It was only after the first research studies were conducted that PowerPost realized many SCM-22 buyers were high-ranking military officers, who valued the droid's portability and secure encryption protocols. PowerPost adjusted their advertising strategy accordingly.

Each droid has a glossy black finish and two stunted, wheeled legs for limited mobility. A directionalized microphone receiver is built into the SCM's dorsal shell—it can record a normal speaking voice from a distance of fifteen meters and has a total playback capacity of over one hundred seventy hours. In addition, the unit can differentiate up to five simultaneous conversations, screen out background noises, and delete lengthy pauses and extraneous stretches of "dead time."

Miniature visual sensors and a high-pitched vocabulator permit the droid to interact with its owner. Its intelligence matrix is limited, so the SCM-22 responds best to simple, direct verbal commands. A "recorder" or "activate" order causes the unit to waddle over to a convenient listening distance, while "record" begins the dictation process. At any time, the droid can be ordered to save its logs, compress them into a single condensed file, and scramble the document for transmission by way of an advanced encryption code. The process takes less than five seconds.

After many years of PowerPost military-oriented advertising, the SCM-22 has become fairly common in the officers' cabins aboard New Republic warships. General Etahn A'baht frequently employed one of the ovoid droids during his hectic tour of duty near the Koornacht Cluster.

Front View

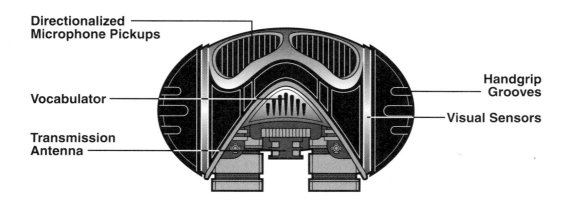

Directionalized
Microphone Pickups

Vocabulator

Transmission
Antenna

Handgrip
Grooves

Visual Sensors

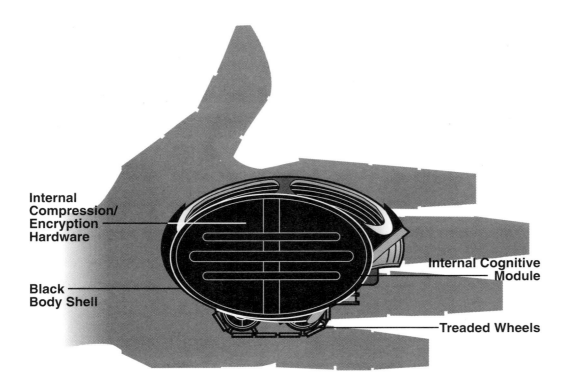

Internal
Compression/
Encryption
Hardware

Black
Body Shell

Internal Cognitive
Module

Treaded Wheels

Side View

CZ SECRETARY/COMM DROID

Outmoded and obsolete in the current market, the CZ droid was once a winning profit leader for Serv-O-Droid back in the days of the Old Republic. But even though newer models from Cybot Galactica have it beat cold for processing speed, the CZ still makes a more than adequate secretary and file manager for small businesses. Witness the sheer number of them in clerks' offices and bookkeeping bureaus throughout the Outer Rim, and you'll find it difficult to believe that there hasn't been a new CZ manufactured in over four decades.

The CZ uses the same familiar bipedal configuration adopted for most droids that work with humans or humanoid aliens. In the assembly plant, each unit received a truly head-spinning olive-and-peach paint job with bright yellow trim, to make it stand out from its competitors on the sales floor. The tactic certainly succeeded, but most consumers sprayed on a more sedate hue. Even those droids that weren't repainted have long since lost their original finishes to weather and wear.

Classified as both a secretary droid and a comm droid, the CZ has a number of methods for processing, storing, and transmitting information. Its built-in comlink has surface-to-orbit range and operates on a number of communication frequencies. The droid can randomly phase between frequencies to frustrate eavesdroppers and possesses a number of advanced scramblers, jammers, and encryption algorithms.

As a secretary, the unit has basic language programming, data processing skills, and knowledge of general business procedures. Furthermore, each CZ has an extensive storage cache for saving and organizing corporate files. While the cache's storage capacity pales next to the boundless information banks of a memory droid, the CZ's encryption algorithms make it extremely difficult for an unauthorized slicer to extract usable data without first obtaining a working passcode.

Since the information they carry is so secure, CZs make excellent couriers. Many individuals who have secrets they'd prefer to keep hidden—crime bosses, smugglers, corporate raiders, and the like—employ the droids to store their most sensitive information. Jabba the Hutt kept one unit, CZ-3, at his private townhouse in Mos Eisley. This droid, operated by Jabba's crack team of Nimbanese accountants, served as a repository for class-red intelligence data.

In order to trap a business rival, however, Jabba ordered his technicians to patch a remote surveillance rig into CZ-3's cognitive matrix. The new recording circuitry incriminated Jabba's competitor when he foolishly stole the unit, but it also exhausted the droid's overtaxed logic systems. The unit was discovered aimlessly wandering the streets of Mos Eisley when Obi-Wan Kenobi and Luke Skywalker booked their historic passage to Alderaan.

Front View

Rear View

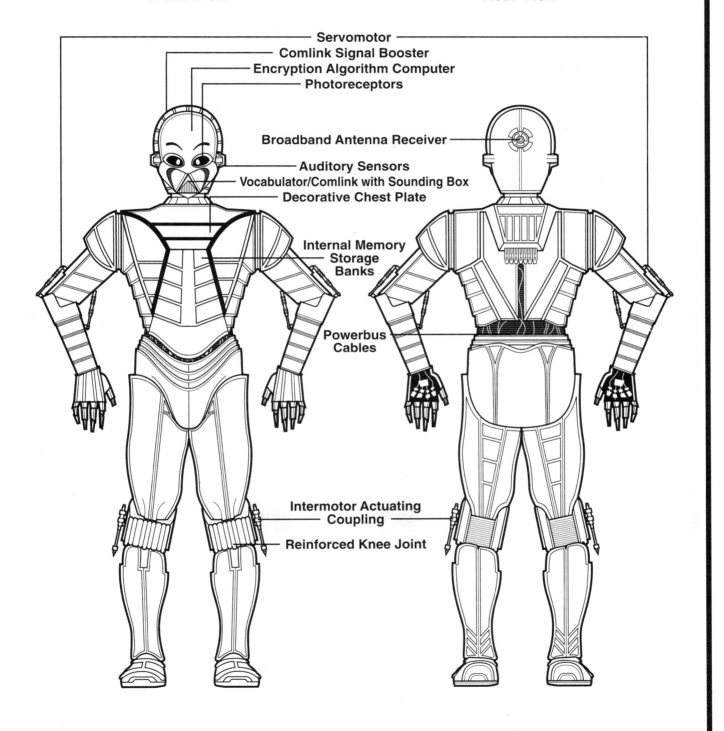

Servomotor
Comlink Signal Booster
Encryption Algorithm Computer
Photoreceptors

Broadband Antenna Receiver
Auditory Sensors
Vocabulator/Comlink with Sounding Box
Decorative Chest Plate

Internal Memory
Storage
Banks

Powerbus
Cables

Intermotor Actuating
Coupling
Reinforced Knee Joint

BUSINESS

TT-40 LIBRARY DROID

A relatively new product from the data-crunchers at Telbrintel, the TT-40 library droid is primarily an information retrieval system with little capacity for data storage and no facilities for file encryption. The droid works best as a permanent "information desk" in corporate lobbies, municipal kiosks, and public archives.

Rather than sitting behind a workstation, the TT-40 hovers on an antigravity repulsorlift and sports a 360-degree data terminal. The droid is typically installed at the center of a large open area so it can accept information requests from any direction. Users can either type their search parameters directly into the multiple keypads or interact with the droid verbally.

The main body of the TT-40 contains three data wheels with extendible probes that mesh with a proprietary Telbrintel switchboard. These oversized wheels, usually a blur of motion as they extend, retract, and spin from socket to socket, create incredibly fast links with their switchboard data device but are too specialized to plug into standard scomp-link access ports. Twin cables support the computer interface from the ceiling and contain protected data-filaments that link the TT-40 with the central mainframe of a city or corporation.

TT-40s excel at providing information quickly and accurately. Typical search-and-retrieval operations involve census figures, historical records, genealogical research, birth and death certificates, sales data, employee dossiers, profit/loss statements, and consumer survey results. Though quite expensive, the droids are usually subsidized by local governments or large businesses, and the use of their services is often free. Nominal fees are sometimes collected for particularly lengthy sessions or to draw data from restricted archives. Final search results can be delivered through the droid's vocabulator, printed out on a flimsiplast document, or downloaded into a user's portable datapad.

Personality-wise, the TT-40 is all business. It has no interest in subjects other than information retrieval and can come across as brusque and officious to those who don't phrase their requests in the proper bureaucratic patois. Telbrintel is considering future upgrades to the droid, such as faster processing speed, but the punctilious personality is unlikely to change.

Luke Skywalker briefly encountered a TT-40 library droid during the crisis in the Koornacht Cluster. While searching for the mysterious Fallanassi sect on the planet Teyr, Luke and his companion Akanah questioned the TT-40 known as "Recorder of Assignments and Transactions for the Supervisor's Committee" in the sleepy city of Griann. The droid's imperturbable character inspired Luke to nickname it "Chuckles," but its quick search of Teyr Central Directories allowed them to continue their search in the city of Sodonna.

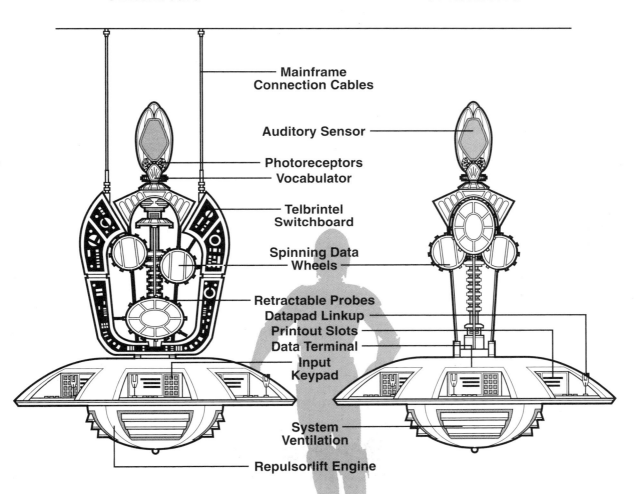

Docked Inside Switchboard

Droid Outside Switchboard

Mainframe Connection Cables

Auditory Sensor

Photoreceptors
Vocabulator

Telbrintel Switchboard

Spinning Data Wheels

Retractable Probes
Datapad Linkup
Printout Slots
Data Terminal
Input Keypad

System Ventilation

Repulsorlift Engine

BUSINESS

MEMORY DROID

Over the centuries, data storage has progressed to the point at which the complete technical readouts of the massive Death Star battle station can be stored on a flat disk no larger than a human's hand. But when that same data is decompressed, encrypted, and backed up, it can fill a floor-to-ceiling array of interlocked information banks. Most businesses and laboratories use permanent computer networks like these for their archiving needs.

Others don't have that luxury. On military installations, particularly those in contested space, all personnel could potentially be ordered to evacuate the base at a moment's notice. In years past, this required erasing all computer records with a mag-pulse device rather than allowing them to fall into enemy hands. With the advent of memory droids, however, such wasteful bridge-burning is now a thing of the past.

SoroSuub Corporation's memory droids possess an astonishing endowment for information storage. The average consumer has no need for such tremendous volume, but a large military base dealing with star charts, subspace monitoring reports, authentication codes, intelligence dossiers, historical archives, and encryption algorithms—and possessing multiple backup copies of all documents—can easily fill five or six memory droids to capacity.

The droids' most unique feature, and the only thing that truly separates them from storage computers, is their mobility. Within five minutes, a memory droid can be packed and placed onboard an airspeeder or starship for immediate evacuation. Repulsorlift pads at the base of the unit nullify its substantial weight, while hinges and seams along the body allow the data banks to be opened and disassembled if necessary. Two manipulator arms assist with this process.

Three black memory cores are arranged around the central equipment column. Each core is composed of writable memory boxes containing multiple Kraren XI Superprocessors and data-sifter filters. Chilled cooling tubes keep the internal temperature low and facilitate rapid transmission of byte streams from point to point. Monitoring screens and input keypads adorn the exterior of the droid, along with numerous computer interface ports.

The New Republic listening post on Utharis, which Luke Skywalker visited during the crisis in the Koornacht Cluster, is fairly typical of the type of installations that employ memory droids. The outpost consists of a silo-dome in the city of Taldaak packed with instrument stations and transceiver arrays. The base's three memory droids and its three-man staff mean that everything of value can be quickly evacuated in a simple six-place landspeeder.

Front View

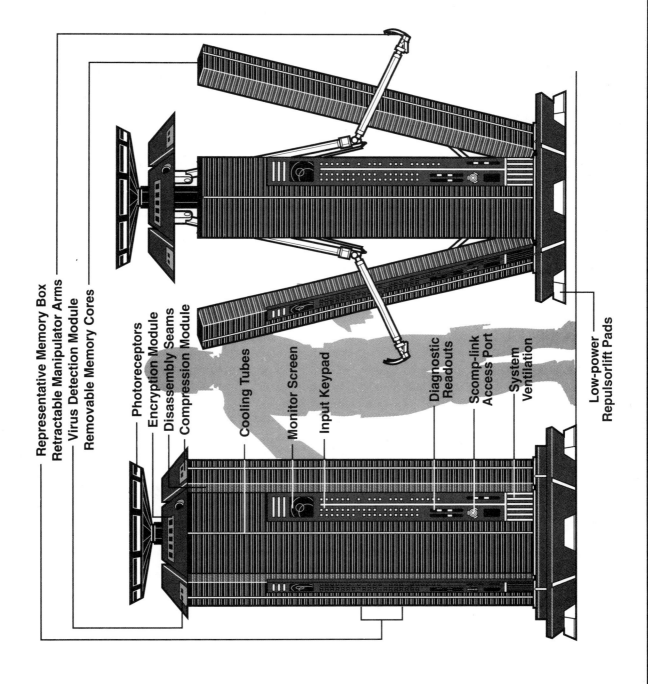

Representative Memory Box
Retractable Manipulator Arms
Virus Detection Module
Removable Memory Cores

Photoreceptors
Encryption Module
Disassembly Seams
Compression Module

Cooling Tubes

Monitor Screen

Input Keypad

Diagnostic Readouts

Scomp-link Access Port

System Ventilation

Low-power Repulsorlift Pads

HEAVY INDUSTRIAL

EVS CONSRUCTION DROID

Factories with legs, construction droids transform bombed-out building shells into shining towers of ferrocrete and transparisteel. Their pace is slow but unstoppable, and the atomic incinerators burning in their bellies have caused some to dub them "the Death Star's little brothers."

But unlike Imperial terror weapons, construction droids destroy only what is no longer needed, painstakingly recycling each part, and leaving newer, better structures in their wake. Due to their size and cost, gargantuan constructors like Veril Line Systems' EVSs are used exclusively on overdeveloped urban worlds such as Coruscant and Bonadan.

The EVS is a staggering forty stories tall and supports its considerable weight on two broad support pods. In a detailed construction project, the droid takes a single step forward every half-hour, but it can move much faster during simple razing jobs. Its optics-covered head constantly scans the edifice in front of it, analyzing the weak points and comparing the architecture to the master blueprints stored in its computer core.

Heavy shovel-arms plow down the structures that are no longer needed, scooping the useful wreckage into a cylindrical processor mouth for recycling. Worthless rubble is dumped into storage hoppers for disposal at a later date. Hundreds of other, smaller limbs, many of them retractable beneath the

droid's chassis, sport specialized destructive appendages, including implosion wrecking balls, plasma cutters, collector trowels, debris nets, and explosive electrical claws.

Inside the processor mouth, debris is carried by a conveyer belt into furnaces, smelting pods, and a devouring atomic incinerator. Raw materials are separated and conveyed to an adjacent factory that extrudes plasteel girders, transparisteel sheeting, and blocks of compressed duracrete. These components are ejected from the rear of the droid and assembled into polished new constructs by hundreds of fabricating arms. The waves of intense heat generated by the internal recycling and manufacturing plants are vented through a number of discharge stacks, but the ambient temperature is still high enough that the droid emits a faint glow under dark lighting.

The EVS has an outdated droid brain—once interrupted, it takes nearly three days to reprogram and reinitialize. Often, a small work crew remains onboard the constructor to ensure that such shutdowns are rare. Crew members park their airspeeders on a small dorsal landing pad and inhabit a cramped control cabin within the droid's head.

Construction droids were crucial to the New Republic's capture of Coruscant. The members of Rogue Squadron hijacked unit EVS-469, diverting its path to bring them up against a subsidiary computer center where they brought down the planet's defensive shields. Wedge Antilles later supervised EVS-6962, whose routine tear-down assignment inadvertently uncovered a secret Imperial Interrogation Center.

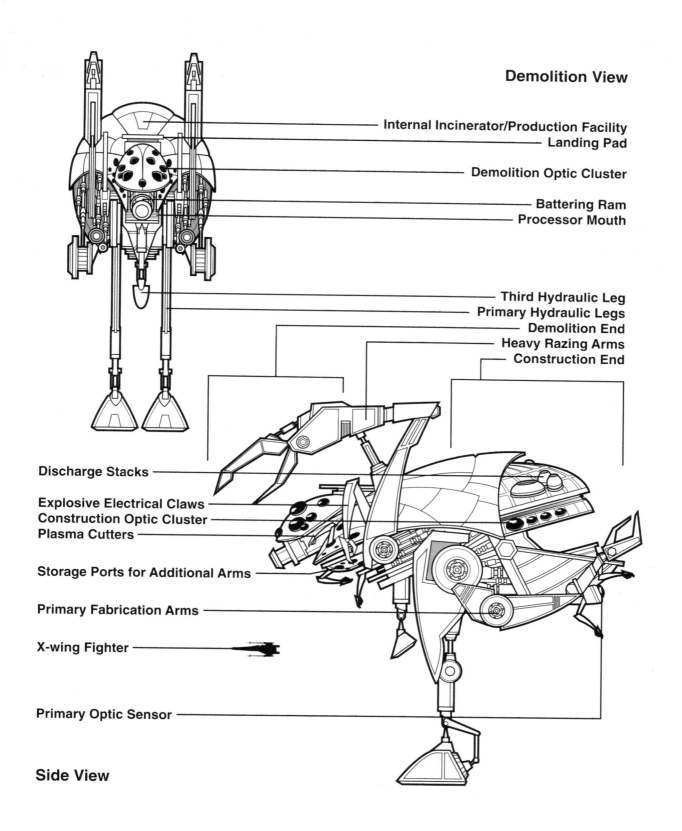

Demolition View

Internal Incinerator/Production Facility
Landing Pad

Demolition Optic Cluster

Battering Ram
Processor Mouth

Third Hydraulic Leg
Primary Hydraulic Legs
Demolition End
Heavy Razing Arms
Construction End

Discharge Stacks

Explosive Electrical Claws
Construction Optic Cluster
Plasma Cutters

Storage Ports for Additional Arms

Primary Fabrication Arms

X-wing Fighter

Primary Optic Sensor

Side View

HEAVY INDUSTRIAL
GRZ-6B WRECKER DROID

Wreckers are the opposite of construction droids—instead of carefully disassembling, they recklessly demolish; instead of erecting glittering high-rises, they produce heaps of rubble, dross, and slag.

In keeping with their job description, wrecker droids are hard-edged and ugly, built for functionality only. Size and configuration vary greatly from planet to planet, but the Serv-O-Droid GRZ-6B is a fairly typical representative.

The GRZ-6B looms six meters above the ground, stomping resolutely between job sites on hydraulically driven legs. Both metallic feet are splayed for better balance, for the droid is much too slow to catch itself should it begin to fall.

The squat, rectangular torso is plated with three layers of heavy durasteel, making it nearly impervious to heat, impacts, and minor explosions. The joints in the arms and legs are sheathed in flexible sleeves composed of plasteel bands and a polymerized coating.

Hinged, fire-blackened plates attached to the hands allow the droid to pick up objects; these crude fingers can be magnetized at will for ease in removing ferrous metals. An industrial-grade plasma torch is built into the left palm, a laser cutter into the right. Armed with these implements, the GRZ-6B can make mincemeat out of an abandoned building or decrepit space barge.

The wrecker's square face is dominated by a colossal maw consisting of two grooved shearing plates. When ground together with full force, the plates can snap a meter-thick structural cable like a toothpick. Those bits of scrap metal consumed by the wrecker fall directly into its internal fusion furnace and are instantly melted. After the droid has been shut down and allowed to cool, these alloys are removed for disposal or recycling.

The internal forge takes up nearly all of the droid's body cavity, leaving little room for electronics or circuitry. Fortunately, the GRZ-6B is a blessedly simple unit. All orders are entered through a rear access panel. The wrecker doesn't require direct supervision, but simple directional commands and an emergency cutoff signal can be broadcast from a handheld control, if desired.

Since the GRZ-6B has been out of production for over thirty years, most surviving units have been extensively rewired and jury-rigged.

Obviously, a maliciously programmed wrecker droid can be a menace. On Kalarba's Hosk Station, the criminal Olag Greck used a rampaging GRZ-6B to cover his theft of an ash-ore shipment. Fortunately, the station's Unit Zed constable thrust an electrified stun stick into its access panel. Circuits fried, the rogue wrecker pitched face forward into the dirt.

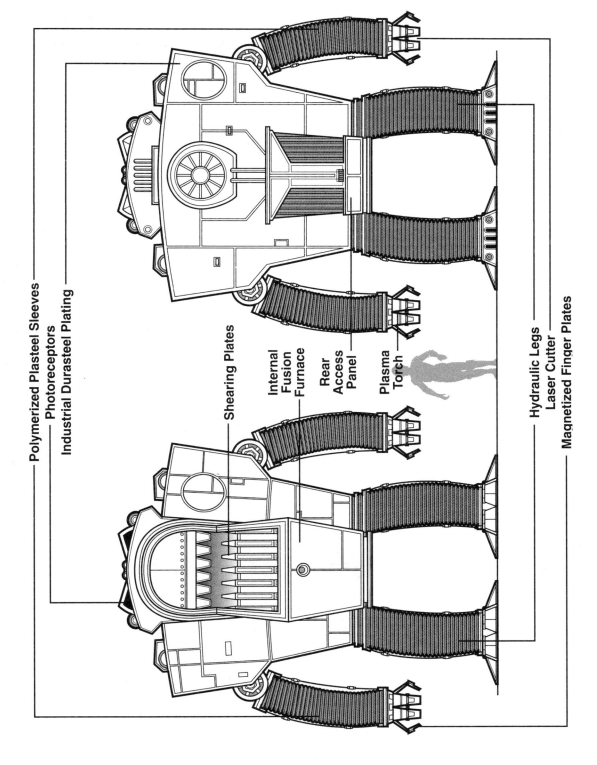

Rear View

Front View

Polymerized Plasteel Sleeves
Photoreceptors
Industrial Durasteel Plating

Shearing Plates

Internal Fusion Furnace

Rear Access Panel

Plasma Torch

Hydraulic Legs
Laser Cutter
Magnetized Finger Plates

HEAVY INDUSTRIAL
FLR LOGGER ("LUMBERDROID")

Industrial Automaton, under contract from the Greel Wood Logging Corporation, put considerable effort into the FLR Logger, matching the provided design specs to a tee. The fact that the specs were flawed to begin with, IA execs were happy to point out, wasn't *their* fault.

The Greel Wood Logging Corporation is a small but profitable company based in the Pii system. Pii 3 and Pii 4 are the only worlds in the galaxy with the proper ecosystems to support greel trees, and the crimson timber is in great demand as an expensive luxury item. Since the rolling terrain of Pii 3 is perfect for droids, the GWLC hired Industrial Automaton to produce a number of tree-felling machines.

The final blueprints, however, had too many people's fingerprints on them—IA was forced to construct a droid to please everyone, and consequently pleased no one. The FLR Logger was slow, prone to breakdown, and frustratingly difficult to repair.

But in every other respect, the Logger, nicknamed "Lumberdroid," was a perfectly respectable automaton. The boxy behemoth stood two meters high and ground forward on two widely spaced tractor treads. Its grasper arms were positively huge, sporting massive claws and possessing enough strength to heft the most titanic trunks.

Mounted under the left limb was the droid's primary cutting saw, a vibro-edged blade more than one meter long. Beneath the right arm hummed a smaller, lighter vibro-saw, used for clearing brush and scrub rather than slicing through greel boles.

The droid's square chassis was bulky by design—in case of an accident, it had to withstand the impact of a falling two-ton timber. Its sensitive video sensor could be retracted beneath its hull like the head of a Bonadanian tortapo, and both saws were protected by the mammoth sheltering arms. While almost nothing could rattle the Lumberdroid's tough armor, the unit was vulnerable to more insidious menaces such as moisture, extreme heat, and localized magnetic fields.

Each Lumberdroid sported a Fabritech communications array with a telescoping antenna, and a probability projection computer that could foresee where a severed tree would fall. In the unlikely event that the droid miscalculated, it possessed an emergency alarm siren to warn human workers to watch their heads.

Industrial Automaton hoped to sell the FLR series outside the Pii system, and programmed the units to recognize more than 150,000 commercially viable trees throughout the galaxy. But the idiosyncrasies of the Lumberdroid seem to have doomed it to a lifetime sentence at the greel wood harvest.

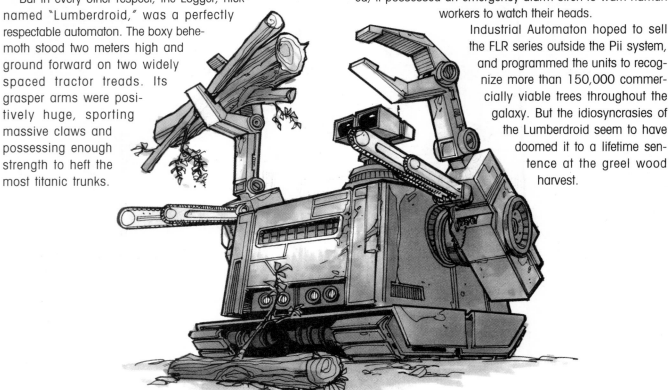

Side View

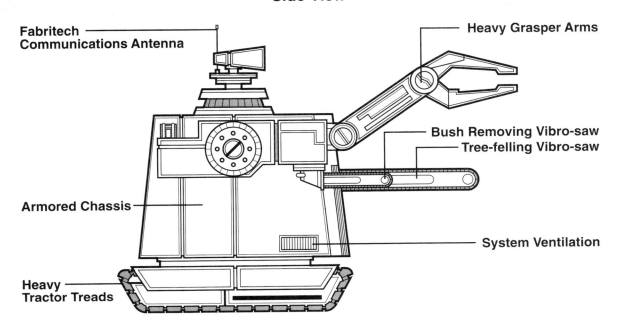

Fabritech Communications Antenna

Heavy Grasper Arms

Bush Removing Vibro-saw
Tree-felling Vibro-saw

Armored Chassis

System Ventilation

Heavy Tractor Treads

Front View

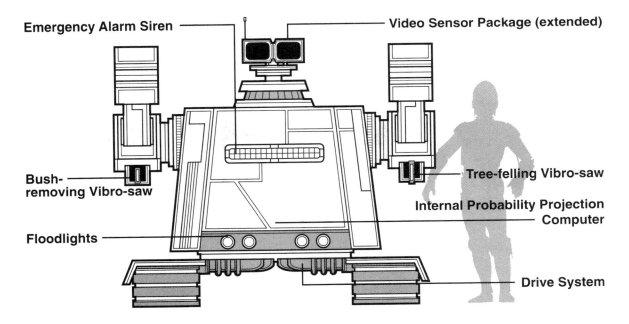

Emergency Alarm Siren

Video Sensor Package (extended)

Bush-removing Vibro-saw

Tree-felling Vibro-saw

Internal Probability Projection Computer

Floodlights

Drive System

LIN DEMOLITIONMECH

For laying mines and industrial explosives, few droids are better equipped than the LIN Demolitionmech. Sadly, a fluke tragedy triggered the recall of the entire line, sounding the death knell for an efficient and superior design.

Cybot Galactica built the LIN undercarriage with parts from their WED Treadwell series. The droid was fitted with twin tank treads for locomotion, each controlled by a set of five wheels. The sensitive innards were then covered with a protective dome of reinforced industrial durasteel. Unfortunately, the dome was quite heavy, and severely curtailed the planned five-speed drive impeller. The design team considered this sluggishness an acceptable trade-off for defense against accidental explosions and falling debris.

A large slot in the front of the ebony hemisphere provided egress for the LIN's retractable manipulator arm. During normal operation, the droid used this appendage to pluck timer mines from a spinning internal rack and gingerly place them in the area to be blasted. The entire dome, including the manipulator arm, was able to rotate 360 degrees, allowing the LIN to avoid laying charges in its own path.

Standard equipment on the Demolitionmech included a visual sensor and an acoustic signaler capable of vocalizing droid languages only. A pair of broadband antennae allowed the droid to send and receive orders through kilometers of rock; they telescoped beneath the protective metal housing when not in use.

The Demolitionmech was primarily intended for industrial and commercial use—to plant explosives for collapsing an abandoned structure or blasting a fresh spice tunnel. But the military soon realized the droid made a perfect—and expendable—mine-layer. Many LINs were refitted to seed battlefields with pressure bombs or antirepulsorlift grenades prior to an enemy ground assault.

Initially, the only performance complaints directed at Cybot Galactica concerned the Demolitionmech's susceptibility to breakdown under unusually damp conditions. Since many mining shafts are at least partially flooded, this bug was a serious concern for the Cybot tech team. But before they could devise a fix, a shocking story was broadcast across the newsnets—on Gosfambling, a detonite charge had gone off prematurely while a LIN unit was still holding it. The resulting explosion caused a cave-in and the suffocation deaths of 600 miners. Terrified of PR damage to their brand image, Cybot's board of directors overreacted by halting the entire Demolitionmech production line permanently.

A recall of existing units was initiated, but most owners were quite happy with their trusty LINs. Even today, years after the shutdown, Demolitionmechs are frequently seen in military bases, ore quarries, and droid auctions.

Side View (cutaway)

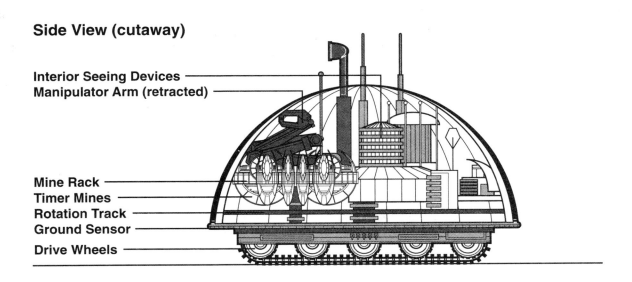

Interior Seeing Devices
Manipulator Arm (retracted)

Mine Rack
Timer Mines
Rotation Track
Ground Sensor
Drive Wheels

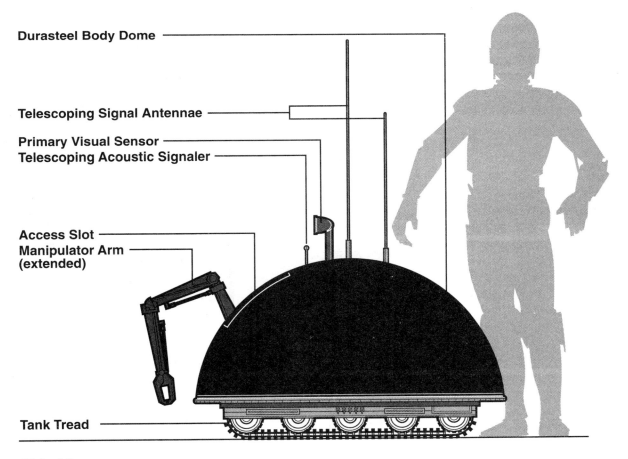

Durasteel Body Dome

Telescoping Signal Antennae

Primary Visual Sensor
Telescoping Acoustic Signaler

Access Slot
Manipulator Arm
(extended)

Tank Tread

Side View

HEAVY INDUSTRIAL
8D8 SMELTING OPERATOR

Tough, surly, crude, and slow-witted—8D8 units aren't exactly scintillating conversationalists. But if you spent your operational life locked in a superheated blast furnace, you'd develop a bantha-sized grudge, too.

Smelting factories are common on resource-rich outposts like Aridus, and on established industrial powerhouses like Balmorra. The factories' blast furnaces stand over thirty meters high, reach temperatures of 1,650 degrees centigrade, and operate round the clock every day of the year. There are several steps in metal processing that can be streamlined with the help of intelligent laborers, but the utter inhospitability of the working conditions have always dictated that those tasks be performed by automated robotic equipment.

That is, until the introduction of the 8D8 by the Roche hive. The Verpine, still smarting from the failure of their J9 Worker Drone, built the 8D8 to resemble humans rather than insects. The dour, long-faced look was quite distinctive, despite the fact that the units rarely interacted with organics once installed on the job. The droids' attenuated limbs and complicated leg joints remained telltale signs of Verpine manufacture.

Roche's greatest challenge lay in fireproofing the automatons; every 8D8 had to operate in an eternal oven, where furnace-feeding air blasts melted most alloys in minutes. Thus, each body part was cast from a unique proprietary metal—high-grade durasteel molecularly bonded with kevlex. The off-white substance had a melting point of over four thousand degrees centigrade.

For practical reasons, external adornments were kept to a minimum. Even the photoreceptors were small and protected, giving the 8D8 rather poor eyesight. While slow, the droids were remarkably strong and possessed astonishing stamina.

Under normal conditions, three 8D8 units are stationed outside the bosh, the lower portion of the blast furnace. One monitors the blast tuyeres, one drains the slag from the top of the melt, and one taps the furnace by forcing out molten metal approximately ten times a day. Two more 8D8s operate the skip hoists that dump raw materials into the bell hoppers and the furnace. Occasionally, a sixth unit oversees the control board and checks the condition of the firebrick refractory shell.

8D8s were designed with simplistic personalities, and they are just intelligent enough to know it. They often resent other droids with more accessories, better programming, and nicer-looking paint jobs than they have, and a few are mean-spirited bullies.

One notable 8D8 unit served as a laborer in Jabba the Hutt's palace. Although Atedeeate had been modified by his former master to perform complex starship repairs, his duties in Jabba's droid pool were menial and degrading. Atedeeate secretly despised his superior, EV-9D9, but nevertheless helped her torture and dismantle dozens of helpless droids.

Front View

Side View

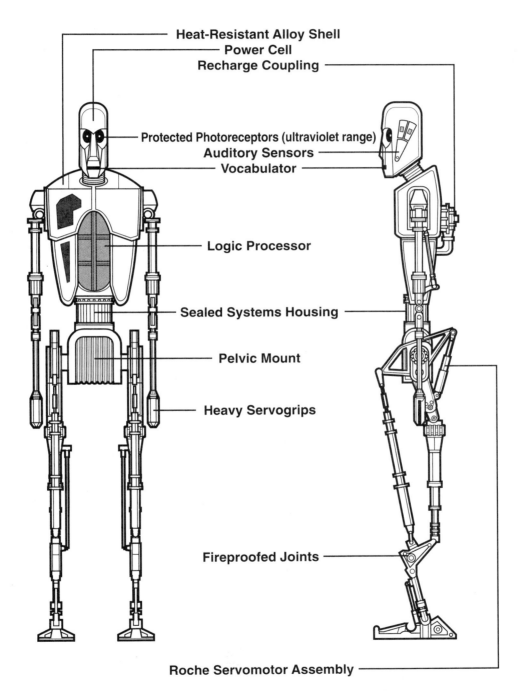

Heat-Resistant Alloy Shell

Power Cell

Recharge Coupling

Protected Photoreceptors (ultraviolet range)

Auditory Sensors

Vocabulator

Logic Processor

Sealed Systems Housing

Pelvic Mount

Heavy Servogrips

Fireproofed Joints

Roche Servomotor Assembly

HEAVY INDUSTRIAL
11-17 MINER DROID

The 11-17 miner droid was developed generations ago by Roche, in association with Slayn & Korpil, as an autonomous precursor to the successful Mole Miner design. Though the 11-17 has been out of production for years, it was built to last, and can still be found in industrial facilities and excavation quarries far from the Core Worlds.

Mining is a notoriously hazardous profession. Hearing stories of organic workers crushed by rockslides, drowned by tunnel floods, and asphyxiated by toxic gases, the hive executives at Roche finally approved their long-planned design for an independent, robotic miner. The 11-17 was the result.

Standing less than one meter tall, the compact droid is sheathed in a heavy layer of armor plating. This durasteel alloy is resistant to heat, moisture, and impacts, and adequately protects the sensitive inner circuitry. The 11-17 moves on two heavy tractor treads, protected from falling rocks—and a possible jam—by three additional armor plates jutting out from either side of the body.

The 11-17's main burrowing tool is a heavy plasma jet, mounted directly above the chassis. It can modify the diameter of the superheated beam from a needlepoint to a low-intensity cone 0.5 meters across. For major projects, several 11-17s work together to drill large shafts.

A buzz saw, mounted on a rotating, telescoping arm, is capable of cutting through metal and clearing many obstructions. On the opposite side of the chassis, another telescoping arm holds a blowtorch for burning out organic debris and weakening a target area prior to blasting.

Three high-beam, forward-mounted spotlights provide illumination in the darkest of tunnels, while a pair of retractable antennae—boosted to punch their signal through kilometers of diffracting ore veins—can receive and answer orders dispatched from other 11-17s or a central command center.

The 11-17's droid brain, securely packed beneath its shock-repellent hull, is simple and single-minded. The droid is not equipped to communicate verbally, only through transmissions or direct linkup. Though not particularly intelligent, the 11-17 seems to genuinely love its work, and long-time owners report the automatons develop a dogged loyalty to their masters over time.

The 11-17 was doomed as a commercial product when a market research study reported that buyers found individual droid brains to be an unnecessary expense. Since it was easier and cheaper to produce nonintelligent drilling machines, the Roche factories switched over to Mole Miners. Surviving 11-17s are still in service on Kalarba's Hosk Station and elsewhere.

Front View

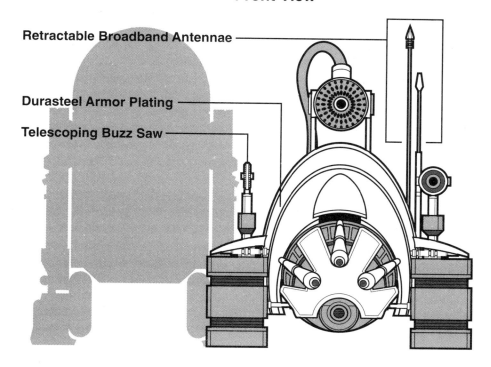

Retractable Broadband Antennae

Durasteel Armor Plating

Telescoping Buzz Saw

Side View

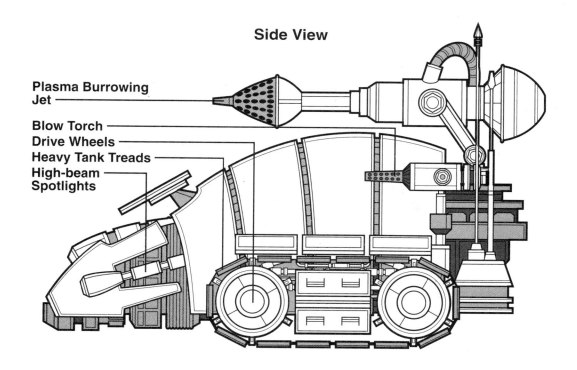

Plasma Burrowing Jet

Blow Torch

Drive Wheels

Heavy Tank Treads

High-beam Spotlights

AGRICULTURAL
CD-2 HARVESTER

As Old Republic settlers spread like nova blossoms across the galaxy, entire planets were industrialized to support the infrastructure of colonization. Worlds dedicated to ore mining or starship construction required a constant influx of foodstuffs to sustain life in a barren and hostile environment. Soon, thousands of fertile, temperate planets with year-round growing seasons, such as Ukio, Taanab, Salliche, and Dilonexa XXIII, were exporting billions of tons of agricultural products each year.

Agribots made it all possible. Simple automated machines programmed for tilling, planting, spraying, or harvesting were unleashed on endless hectares of fruitful farmland. The droids were primitive, but always reliable, and only a skeleton crew of biological overseers was required to supervise their progress.

The Corporate Sector Authority manufactures one of the best agribots: the CD-2 Harvester. This AT-AT-sized behemoth was designed to work on CSA grainworlds like Orron III, but tens of thousands have been sold to the Empire, New Republic, and various planetary confederacies.

The droid's strength lies in its versatility. The name "Harvester" is a bit of a misnomer, as the CD-2 can also perform soil preparation, planting, and yield expansion with the proper tools and programming matrices. The top one hundred cash crops grown on factory farms, from tallgrain

to denta beans, are usually maintained by a dependable stable of CD-2s.

Each Harvester rolls forward on four enormous treaded tires. Its visual sensor suite can perceive only the grain directly in front of it and often overlooks unexpected obstacles—such as a human wandering into the path of its spinning reaper blades. Each droid possesses a remote interface to shut it down in case of emergency, but tragic accidents have been known to happen.

Three huge tilling arms at the front of the CD-2 expertly break up soil to give the seedbed maximum aeration, moisture saturation, and root penetration. Removable nose attachments allow the droid to work as a furrower, fertilizer sprayer, or pellet dispenser for granular herbicides and insecticides. The most impressive feature is a shining twenty-meter array of durasteel cutting blades.

Grain harvested by the blades is drawn into an intake shaft, cleaned and separated, and bundled in internal load-carriers for later transport to a storage silo. Chaff and other debris is expelled through three rear discharge chutes.

Some crops requiring unique growing conditions can't be handled by a CD-2 Harvester. The reclusive Hapes Consortium, for instance, manufactures a small harvest droid—the HD-234-C—for plucking berries. That particular droid is nearly impossible to find outside the borders of the Hapes Cluster.

Front View

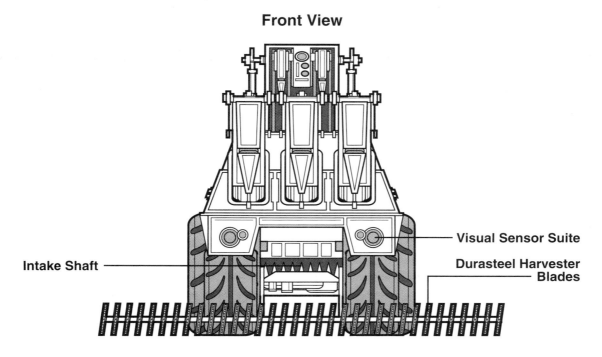

Intake Shaft

Visual Sensor Suite

Durasteel Harvester Blades

Bright Yellow Chassis
External Storage Hopper
(in retracted position)

Insulated Catwalks
Soil Tiller Arms

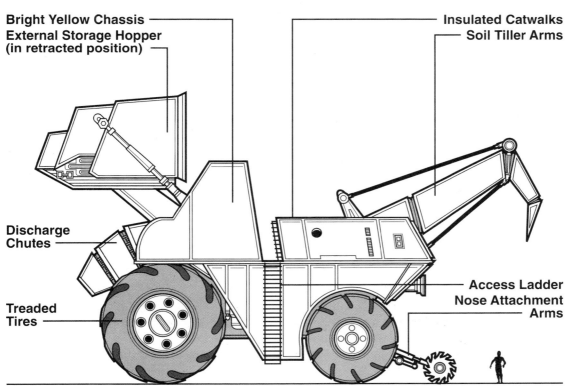

Discharge
Chutes

Treaded
Tires

Access Ladder
Nose Attachment
Arms

Side View

AGRICULTURAL

DECON III DROID

Not every planet boasts the rich, loamy topsoil of bread-basket grainworlds like Orron III or Ukio. When an environment is devastated by war, irradiated by chemical spills, or simply unfit for human habitation from the start, decontamination droids begin the long and laborious process of restoration.

"Decon" droids come in all shapes and sizes, including a small model that resembles a stunted Imperial probot, but the most common version is Industrial Automaton's Decon III. The squat, boxy units stand 1.3 meters tall and aren't much to look at. But if you see one in action, you'd better think twice before biting into that bowvine fruit you just plucked.

The presence of decon droids indicates a problem with the ecosystem, possibly a severe or life-threatening one. IA originally designed their machines for use on Old Republic colonization missions—the droids would supplement the terraforming process by filtering out harmful alien bacteria. In recent years, however, they have primarily been used by the Empire and New Republic for salvaging moribund planets despoiled by the Galactic Civil War.

A decon droid has a heavy front shovel for scooping up mouthfuls of dirt—about a quarter cubic meter with each "bite." The loose soil falls into the intake hopper and passes through a four-stage series of cleansing chambers that contain catalytic processors capable of removing most any foreign

contagion. The purified loam, now safe for planting, is expelled from a rear discharge chute. The speed of the process varies depending on the level of pollution, but most Decon IIIs can treat roughly three kilograms of top-soil per hour.

A variant design is often stored aboard long-range starships. In the event that the entire vessel is flooded with radiation, these droids deploy chemical spray hoses and coat the cabins, decks, and bulkheads with rad-absorbing foam. The poisonous froth is then scooped up and subjected to the same internal sterilization process as tainted soil.

Decon IIIs possess visual, infrared, and specialized analytical sensors. Their vocabulators are capable only of communicating in binary. Some move on treads, some on four stumpy legs, and all have a single retractable manipulator arm.

A large number of decon droids were used by the Empire in one of its most shameful deceptions—the "purification" of Honoghr. Imperial scientists seeded the remote world with a hybrid grass that choked off all other plant life, then gave the desperate Noghri modified Decon IIIs that cleared this grass at a ridiculously slow pace. After the downfall of Grand Admiral Thrawn, the New Republic brought proper droids to Honoghr, but the ecological damage is so far-reaching that a full recovery seems unlikely.

Front View

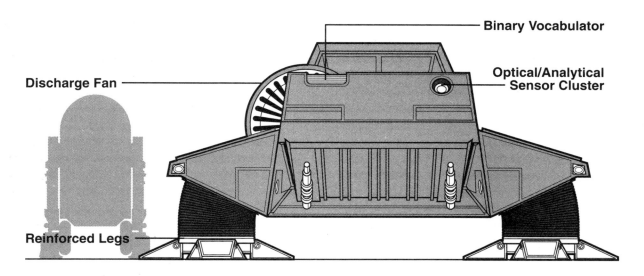

Binary Vocabulator

Optical/Analytical
Sensor Cluster

Discharge Fan

Reinforced Legs

Side View

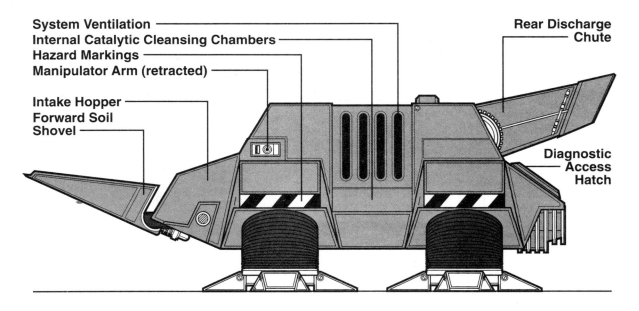

System Ventilation
Internal Catalytic Cleansing Chambers
Hazard Markings
Manipulator Arm (retracted)

Intake Hopper
Forward Soil
Shovel

Rear Discharge
Chute

Diagnostic
Access
Hatch

COURIER/TRANSPORT

MESSENGER DROID AND MESSAGE DRONE

There are many ways to get a message from place to place. You can transmit via subspace—slow; use the galaxywide HoloNet—restricted; or hire a mail delivery service like Core Couriers—known to have intentionally dumped their cargoes in the past. Given the choices, it's little wonder that those who can afford it rely on direct, point-to-point messenger droids.

The Arakyd Industries' Seeker AS-M12 is a fast and nearly foolproof dispatcher. Arakyd has taken the hyperspace pod from their popular probots and scaled it down to a more practical size. The pod makes a one-way hyperspace hop to its destination, lands, and discharges a small sphere that hovers above the ground on repulsorlifts.

This metal orb sports little exterior ornamentation—most of its tools stay tucked out of sight until needed. Its sole function is to locate its target and deliver its message as quickly and unobtrusively as possible. The droid has sensitive visual and audio sensors and can plug into public directories with a computer input jack. It can also open doors and operate turbolifts with a retractable manipulator arm.

Once the recipient is found, he or she must provide a verbal passcode before the droid can replay its missive. Visual data is displayed through a holographic projector/recorder, while voice-only notes are routed

through the droid's vocabulator. Luke Skywalker and Dash Rendar once encountered an Arakyd Seeker while staying at Obi-Wan Kenobi's hut on Tatooine.

While a new Seeker might be a bit on the pricey side—24,000 credits for the complete system—an Elegance message drone is grossly exorbitant. Worth at least a quarter million credits each, these nine-meter behemoths from Industrial Automaton are relics from a bygone era. Before the HoloNet was established, most governments relied on message drones almost exclusively for long-range communications. Even today, some remote Imperial outposts keep them as backups in case the local comm satellites are destroyed in an attack.

The Elegance is almost all engine. Its hyperdrive is unbelievably fast, but limited to one jump before it must refuel and five jumps before the entire motor is destroyed by wear. Upon arrival in a system, the drone broadcasts a beacon signal to attract the attention of ships or orbital stations. Since most Elegances were used to transport classified government or military data, they possess fail-safe self-destruct mechanisms. In the case of unauthorized tampering, two electrite crystal triggers snap together, vaporizing the drone with enough force to incinerate everything within six hundred meters.

In the aftermath of the Battle of Endor, an Elegance drone arrived at the Death Star debris and was retrieved by Wedge Antilles and Luke Skywalker. Its timely data alerted the Rebel Alliance to the impending invasion of Bakura by the Ssi-ruuk.

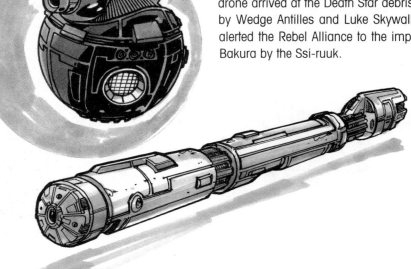

Message Droid-Front View

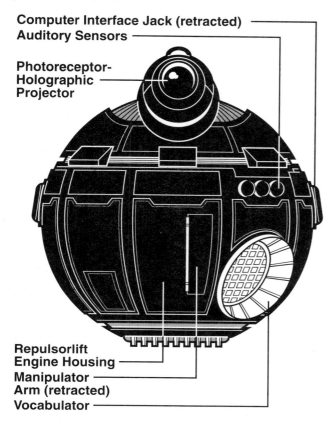

Computer Interface Jack (retracted)
Auditory Sensors

Photoreceptor-
Holographic
Projector

Repulsorlift
Engine Housing
Manipulator
Arm (retracted)
Vocabulator

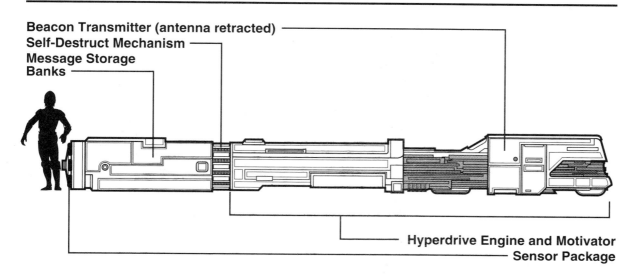

Beacon Transmitter (antenna retracted)
Self-Destruct Mechanism
Message Storage
Banks

Hyperdrive Engine and Motivator
Sensor Package

Message Drone-Side View

COURIER/TRANSPORT
DRONE BARGE

In most cases, droids lack the intuition, quick thinking, and situational awareness to make truly great star pilots. But when the pace is predictable, the route well-traveled, and the cargo of little value, drone barges are substantially more cost-effective than hiring a captain and crew.

Drone barges are voluminous cargo tankers steered by simple droid brains. Literally thousands of configurations exist, varying by manufacturer and the type of payload being hauled. Drone barges ship grain from Orron III, ferry ice blocks from Ohann, and dispose of industrial waste from the stardocks at Kuat, Corellia, and Fondor.

Drones possess only the intelligence needed to calculate elementary hyperspace jumps, home in on directional guidance beacons when in port, and run self-diagnostic checks on their cargo and propulsion systems. Personality programming for these droids is nonexistent. Due to their simplicity, many are produced by starship transport manufacturers instead of by automata specialists such as Cybot Galactica. Gallofree Yards marketed a modestly successful drone carrier before the company went bankrupt, and a few of these are still in use among smaller shipping companies. But the heavy-freight market is dominated by Corellian Engineering Corporation, which currently sells more than two dozen stock versions of the gigantic StarHauler drone barge.

On a planet like Fondor, StarHaulers remain docked at surface landing pads when not making actual runs. Over a period of days, the external tanks and interior cargo holds are loaded with scrap metal, worthless ore, and toxic by-products generated by shipyard construction and resource mining. When several StarHaulers have reached capacity, they lift off *en masse*, using their repulsors and sublight engines to progress to the automated beacon marking their hyperspace jump point.

Since organic beings never serve aboard drones, the vessels lack crew quarters, comfort amenities, and life-support systems. Their cramped hallways carry only the few gulps of planetary atmosphere that happen to find their way inside during freight loading, which aren't nearly enough to sustain stowaways during weeks-long voyages. Only the suicidally desperate hitch rides on drone barges.

Inevitably, some StarHaulers don't make it back from their missions due to navigational error, hyperdrive failure, and even piracy. A certain number of these losses are anticipated by large shippers as the cost of doing business, a fact that has been exploited by shipjackers who know their thefts are unlikely to be fully investigated. Tanith Shire, a shuttle pilot at the Fondor yards, regularly reprogrammed the control systems on the local drone barges, causing the vessels to prematurely drop out of hyperspace and crash on the desolate planet of the Serpent Masters, where their cargo and shipboard electronics could be ransacked at leisure.

Star Hauler 131-T3 (Side View)

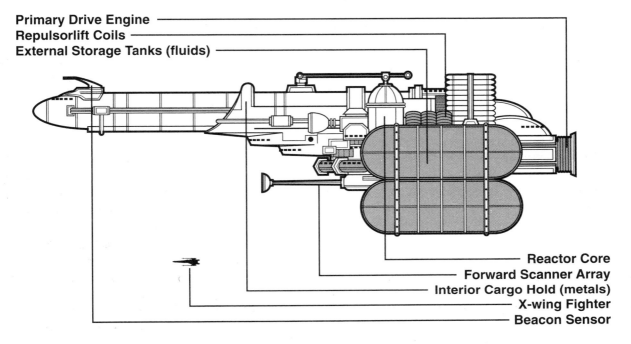

Primary Drive Engine
Repulsorlift Coils
External Storage Tanks (fluids)

Reactor Core
Forward Scanner Array
Interior Cargo Hold (metals)
X-wing Fighter
Beacon Sensor

Star Hauler 131-SX2 (Side View)

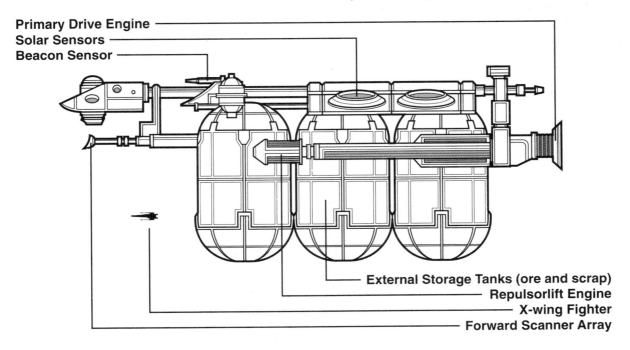

Primary Drive Engine
Solar Sensors
Beacon Sensor

External Storage Tanks (ore and scrap)
Repulsorlift Engine
X-wing Fighter
Forward Scanner Array

For most galactic citizens, hardly a day goes by when they don't cross paths with an Asp droid. From repair to maintenance to sanitation to delivery, the Asp can do it all—provided the tasks are kept nice and easy.

Industrial Automaton conceived of the Asp as a versatile, entry-level droid to attract young, lower-income, and first-time buyers, with the long-term purpose of establishing brand relationships. A typical Asp retails for one thousand credits, a remarkably low sum for a new automaton. This fact, combined with the durable droid's long operational life, accounts for the Asp's ubiquity on every world from Coruscant to Tatooine.

IA manufactures more than two dozen variants on the Asp design, identifiable by their numerical designations. These models don't differ greatly in price or intelligence, but some are taller, stronger, more maneuverable, or have greater range. The ASP-7 is a solid middle-of-the-road unit and has been the top-selling Asp variant for the last decade.

The droids have skeletal humanoid frames cast from a metallic-gray alloy. Joints and pivot points are simple and left in plain sight—with an Asp, what you see is usually what you get. The limbs are hydraulically powered and quite strong, mak-

ing Asps capable cargo handlers for small loads.

The head contains an elementary cognitive module, a single photoreceptor in human range, and two auditory sensors. An Asp's vocabulator is particularly primitive, capable of producing only two words: "affirmative" and "negative." As many owners can attest, trying to get information out of an Asp can be a slow, tedious, and frustrating process.

Reliable, but none too bright, Asps are usually assigned to basic jobs where little supervision is needed. Owners are happy so long as their Asps start up in the morning, do what they're supposed to do, and return intact at the end of the day. But even then, when unexpected situations arise, the droids often abandon their half-finished tasks and shuffle back to their masters for further instructions.

Because of this irritating trait, many buyers modify their Asps far beyond their original specs. It is not uncommon to encounter an Asp with a more versatile vocabulator, an array of fine manipulators, or a state-of-the-art AA-1 Verbobrain. Darth Vader was known to use an army of ASP-19s—outfitted with armor plating, hyperfast reflexes, and exhaustive logs of fencing techniques—as lethal lightsaber training opponents.

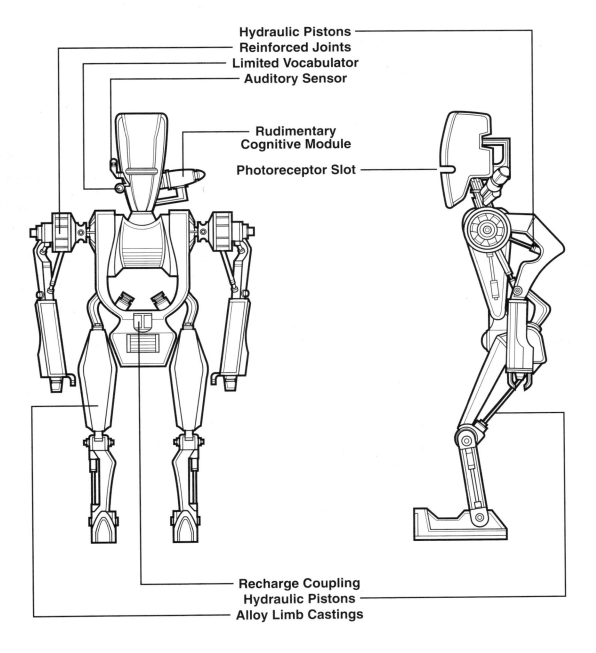

Front View

Side View

Hydraulic Pistons
Reinforced Joints
Limited Vocabulator
Auditory Sensor

Rudimentary
Cognitive Module

Photoreceptor Slot

Recharge Coupling
Hydraulic Pistons
Alloy Limb Castings

LABOR

CLL-8 BINARY LOAD LIFTER

So slow-witted they can scarcely be called droids at all, binary load lifters heft and stack cargo in industrial warehouses throughout the galaxy. Only a primitive cognitive module and a rudimentary level of self-awareness prevent them from being classified as nonthinking machines.

Load lifters were among the first droids ever developed, being autonomous alternatives to hauler vehicles and power suits. They have changed very little in the last several thousand years. Dozens of makes and models flood the market, but Cybot Galactica's CLL-8 is one of the better units for low cost and reliability.

The three-meter-tall CLL-8 looks vaguely like an undersized Imperial scout walker, stomping around determinedly on two jointed legs. Each leg is reinforced with industrial-grade durasteel and powered by hydraulics to support the droid's considerable bulk and the weight of its load. The drive system is not particularly fast, but is extremely well-balanced. Thanks to a gyro-stabilization mechanism, incidents where a CLL-8 overturns or spills its cargo are rare.

Each lifting arm contains hydraulics and three pivot joints. The metallic hands are flat enough to slide under cargo skids and wide enough to distribute the weight evenly. Protrusions at the rear of each hand prevent taller stacks from tipping off the back end.

An armored housing protects the droid's internal workings from damage and houses the cognitive module. All CLL-8s are well-protected against shocks, dents, and impacts. The exterior of the housing supports a binary vocabulator, an auditory sensor, and a single photoreceptor featuring a merchandise code scanner.

The CLL-8, like almost all load lifters, can only communicate in binary. This elementary language—also used by moisture vaporators and other machines—cannot be understood by humans without a video display screen or interpreting device. Though the CLL-8 can respond to simple verbal commands, most owners prefer to have other droids program their load lifters. Protocol units, with their wide language databases, can perform this task with ease—in fact, See-Threepio spent some time as a binary programmer.

If a lifter's greatest asset is its brute strength, its greatest drawback is its grievous stupidity. The droids never stray from their orders, but they lack the smarts to modify those orders when the situation demands it. In a ridiculous incident on Stassia, a CLL-8 continued stacking heavy crates in a depot corner despite obvious signs that the floor was under severe stress. The droid ignored the creaking, overlooked the sagging, and was utterly oblivious to the screeches of wrenching metal and splintering wood as the entire story collapsed onto the one beneath it. Whereupon the load lifter, shaken but not damaged, obediently whirred to its feet and clomped back to get more boxes.

Front View

Side View

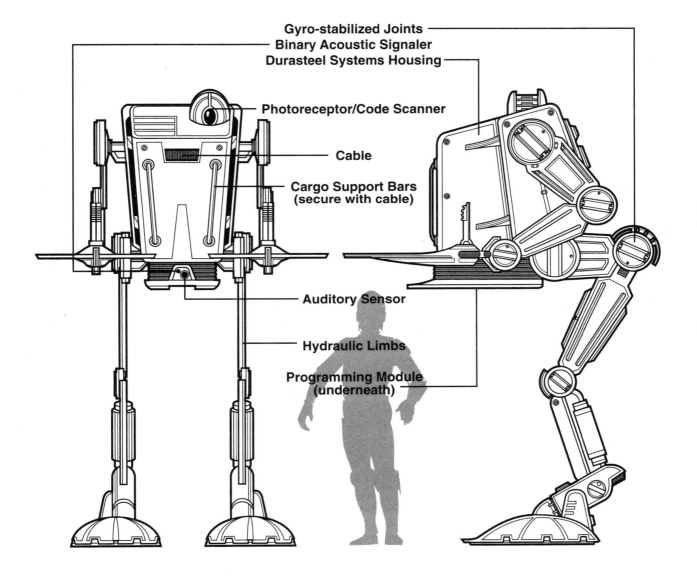

Gyro-stabilized Joints
Binary Acoustic Signaler
Durasteel Systems Housing

Photoreceptor/Code Scanner

Cable

Cargo Support Bars
(secure with cable)

Auditory Sensor

Hydraulic Limbs

Programming Module
(underneath)

LABOR
X10-D DRAFT DROID

Trandoshans have scaly hides, pointed teeth, bloodshot eyes, and a disturbing proclivity for killing and skinning Wookiees. One thing they *don't* have is dexterous hands with nimble fingers. Ever since their first contact with the outside galaxy, the claw-fisted Trandoshans have imported advanced technologies to make manipulating their environments easier.

The X10-D draft droid is a unique specialty product tailored specifically for the lanky reptilian species. The autocratic government of Trandosha is the exclusive manufacturer of the model line, and few units are encountered away from the lizards' arid homeworld.

Trandosha's planetary regime keeps close tabs on its X10-Ds. Most are assigned to government offices, public storage dens, and interstellar spaceports where freight loading is common. A few are allowed to be purchased by individual citizens, but only those subjects deemed "worthy" by the regime. Worthiness is achieved by scoring sufficient jagannath points—typically earned through bounty-hunting kills—to bring honor to the Scorekeeper, the Trandoshan deity. It can also be achieved much easier and faster with a hefty bribe.

At three meters plus, the X10-D is an imposing construct. Its head, arms, and massive conical torso are painted in vibrant hues of red and bronze. Each loader arm contains an extendible limb that can reach a maximum

length of three meters. The droid moves about on a broad pair of treaded roller feet.

The most unusual aspect of the X10-D is its utter lack of internal programming. Without a cognitive module or behavioral matrix, the droid relies exclusively on orders transmitted to it from a remote site. In essence, the X10-D is a mobile extension of a city's central computer.

The bounty hunter Bossk, perhaps the galaxy's most famous Trandoshan, kept an X10-D in the cargo hold of his state-of-the-art pursuit vessel *Hound's Tooth*. Exten-dee was operated by the *Hound*'s shipboard computer brain and performed simple tasks such as securing loose equipment for flight. The draft droid was Bossk's sole crew.

Soon after the Battle of Hoth, Bossk took on two accomplices—Tinian I'att and her Wookiee partner Chenlambec—in the search for Han Solo. The new arrivals managed to smuggle in a positronic processor named Flirt, who then subverted the *Hound*'s computer and used Exten-dee to trap Bossk in the ship's rear security locker.

Following Bossk's arrest by Imperial officials, Chenlambec plugged Flirt into the much larger draft droid's torso power point. With her new body, Flirt possessed a tough armored housing and staggering physical strength. "Now," she complained, "if I could just get a blue detail job…"

Front View

Rear View

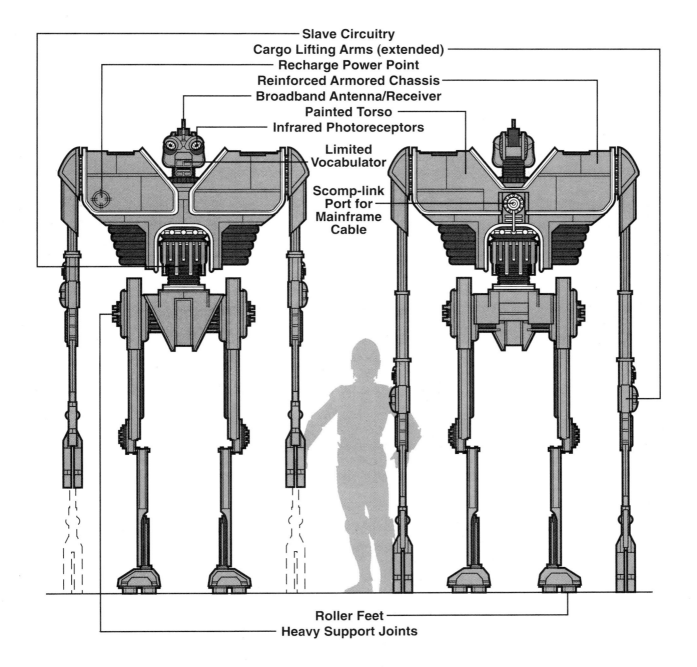

Slave Circuitry
Cargo Lifting Arms (extended)
Recharge Power Point
Reinforced Armored Chassis
Broadband Antenna/Receiver
Painted Torso
Infrared Photoreceptors
Limited Vocabulator
Scomp-link Port for Mainframe Cable
Roller Feet
Heavy Support Joints

LABOR
J9 WORKER DRONE

What looks like a giant, two-legged mantis is actually a Roche Worker Drone, a basic laboring unit that the insectoid Verpine species initially designed as a protocol droid.

Over the years, the Roche hive has produced many superior automatons—Verpines are innate geniuses at assembling and repairing mechanical devices. But their shared insect culture makes it difficult for them to read other aliens' motivations, particularly humans. The J9 Worker Drone was a crash-and-burn disaster for three reasons: its personality was flat, its name was unappealing and misleading, and its buglike appearance was a turn-off to countless mammalian species throughout the galaxy.

Simply put, the Verpine had no idea how to market a protocol droid. Buyers avoided the J9s like the luf virus, and Roche was forced to slash prices to offset their mounting losses. When consumers finally purchased these bargain-basement remainders, they often took the appellation "Worker Drone" literally, placing the droids in factories and starports where their advanced cognitive functions were wasted. Roche has tried to advertise J9s to fellow arthropods such as the Sic-Six and the Flakax, but this tactic has only caught on, to a very limited degree, with the Xi'Dec.

Though most J9s toil away in menial drudgery, they are the most *intelligent* labor droids you'll ever see. Each one possesses an Arjan II logic computer that has a processing capacity to rival SyntheTech's AA-1 Verbobrain. This, combined with a TranLang II communications module featuring over one million languages, easily makes the droid sophisticated enough to interact with organics—in theory. In practice, their vacant, emotionless natures and occasional fidgety tics often leave them banished to the stockroom.

J9s are tall, with stretched-out arms and legs. The hips are joined by awkward joint mechanisms that are the droid's most vulnerable feature. The large streamlined head seems out of proportion to the rest of the body, with features that resemble compound eyes and mouth pincers.

The huge photoreceptors are keyed to the Verpine optical range, much of it in the ultraviolet spectrum. An excellent olfactory sensor and a Torplex microwave sensor allow the droid to perceive details far beyond visual wavelengths. The Arjan vocabulator can vocalize any of the TranLang II's dialects, though the J9's normal speaking voice has a slightly buzzy undertone.

One Worker Drone designated BG-J38 was purchased by Jabba the Hutt as a laborer, but Jabba's courtiers discovered he made an excellent hologame opponent. Following the Hutt's death at the Great Pit of Carkoon, Beegee vanished for parts unknown.

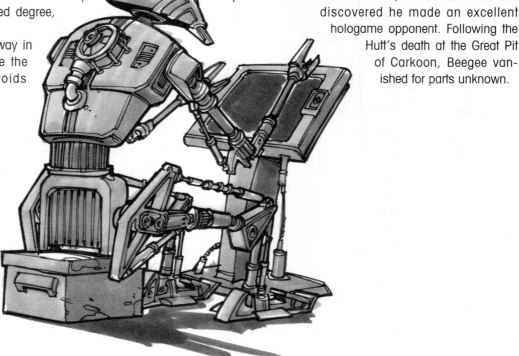

Front View

Side View

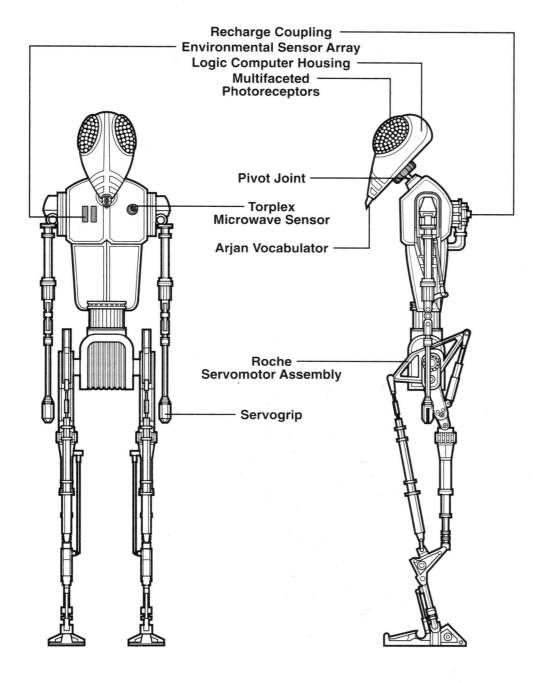

Recharge Coupling

Environmental Sensor Array

Logic Computer Housing

Multifaceted
Photoreceptors

Pivot Joint

Torplex
Microwave Sensor

Arjan Vocabulator

Roche
Servomotor Assembly

Servogrip

MAINTENANCE

IMPERIAL CITY MAINTENANCE DROID

Imperial City, sprawling across the galactic capital world of Coruscant, is a miniature world in itself. Millions of pocket ecosystems thrive between the dense multilayered skyscrapers. Thousands of ferrocrete city-sections have their own distinct weather patterns. And hundreds of local animal species—mutated offshoots of their long-ago ancestors—are found nowhere else in the galaxy. Cybot Galactica's decision to manufacture a droid specifically for this eclectic labyrinth was a clever and profitable one.

The Imperial City Maintenance droid, or IC-M, was officially launched over a century ago under the name RC-M—the "Imperial" classification was not applied until the rise of Palpatine. All ten thousand units in the test batch were sold to the Public Works department of the Old Republic government. The simple automatons had a wide variety of uses, from general upkeep to elementary repairs, and were soon seen on nearly every major thoroughfare and public sidewalk. Before dispatching each droid, Public Works painted its logo on the gray chassis and affixed a combination restraining bolt/locational transponder, greatly reducing the likelihood of the unit being lost or stolen.

There were several succeeding generations of the RC-M/IC-M, but all bore some resemblance to the WED Treadwell. Seven manipulator arms spread out from a central pod, each tipped with a variety of sweeping, tighten-

ing, and weeding tools. Extendible accordion joints at the base of the torso allowed the droid to reach high places. Two wide treads provided locomotion, while a rear storage bay held tools, spare parts, supplementary limb attachments, and jars of cleaning fluids.

Standard IC-Ms had two heads, each facing the other. One glowed with optical sensors, the other displayed a constantly scrolling list of orders, situational data, and Imperial Building Code specs. The earliest RC-Ms often had single heads, cruder joints, and auxiliary powerbus cables running down the outside of their chassis.

The droids were originally assigned to beautify the higher, more visible levels of the city by pruning bushes and fixing public comm-booths. As time and age took their toll, however, the increasingly outdated IC-Ms were relegated to the shadowy urban underbelly, where they resheathed ancient power conduits and exterminated colonies of granite slugs. About a decade after Emperor Palpatine's accession, Cybot Galactica finally retired the line, due to flagging government sales.

Jacen and Jaina Solo, the twin children of Han Solo and Leia Organa Solo, encountered one of the antiquated droids while lost in the dark bowels of Coruscant. The forgotten maintenance unit, overgrown with moss, was still carrying out its decades-old programming by trying—and failing—to replace a string of burnt-out glowcrystals.

Front View

Side View

Extendible Accordion Base
Quad-tread Locomotion
Tool Assembly Arm
Laser Beamcleaner Arm
Visual Scanner Head
Heavy Pincer Arm
Visual Display Head

Spray Nozzle Arm
Internal Storage Bay
Soil Aeration Arm
Fine Manipulator Arm

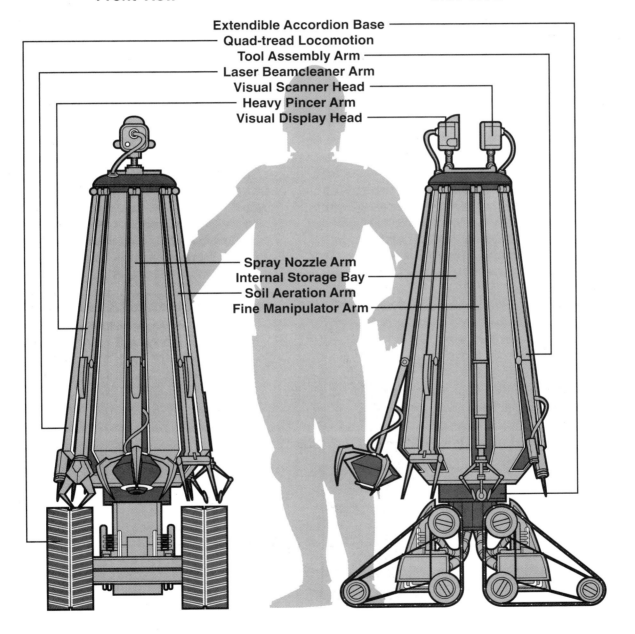

MN-2E GENERAL MAINTENANCE DROID

The Grand Corridor in Coruscant's Imperial Palace is an architectural marvel. Stretching from the Council chamber to the Assemblage auditorium, the awe-inspiring colonnade is decorated with sparkling cut-glass windows and spectacular observation balconies. When Emperor Palpatine rose to power he commissioned a sweeping beautification of the Grand Corridor, redesigning many elements and installing a breathtaking double row of *ch'hala* trees. The care and preservation of such a galactic treasure couldn't be left to just *any* maintenance droid.

The facilities director of the Imperial Palace contacted Industrial Automaton with a precise set of design specs for a new automaton. Because of the Grand Corridor's sheer vastness, the proposed unit would require a powerful repulsorlift engine in order to reach the lofty ceiling. Various manipulative and cleaning appendages would be needed for diverse tasks such as pruning the *ch'hala* boughs and dusting the buttressed roof supports. IA considered the detailed request list and soon produced the MN-2E.

This unsophisticated, but highly effective, droid possesses a central pod, four jointed limbs, and a repulsorlift engine with a flight ceiling of 500 meters. The arms fold against the metal chassis when not in use and sport different specialized attachments including a buffer, a cleanser, a fingered manipulator, and a pair of vibro-shears. Additional attachments, stored behind hinged body panels, can be added at will.

At the base of the droid lies its mouth, a circular portal that leads directly to an internal Wastestream Systems refuse recycling unit. The recycler can convert twenty kilograms of garbage to a useful cellular pulp three times per day. Photoreceptors arrayed around the mouth and a refuse collection scanning computer help the MN-2E identify and dispose of litter moments after it hits the ground.

A limited vocabulator produces random squawks of binary code while the droid scrubs and polishes. For sensitive or unfamiliar tasks, instructional programming modules can easily be plugged into the droid's dorsal circuit slots.

With an "Imperial goodwill" cost of only six hundred credits each, the MN-2E units were a bargain for the Palace staff. Several hundred were purchased and set to work. Within a year, Industrial Automaton began marketing the droids to the general public at a slightly higher price.

A near-disaster occurred when the repulsorlift engine of one MN-2E failed in the middle of a routine Grand Corridor ceiling sweep. The helpless droid plummeted to the burnished floor, impacting like a miniature bomb and missing the Garosian ambassador's head by a half meter. Industrial Automaton survived the debacle by installing backup repulsors in all existing droids and making a generous restitution donation to Emperor Palpatine's "charity fund."

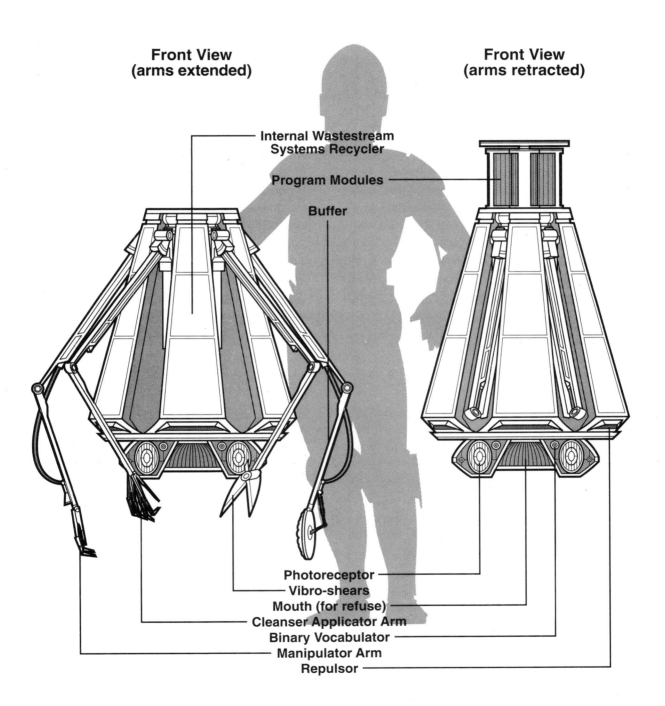

Front View
(arms extended)

Front View
(arms retracted)

Internal Wastestream
Systems Recycler

Program Modules

Buffer

Photoreceptor
Vibro-shears
Mouth (for refuse)
Cleanser Applicator Arm
Binary Vocabulator
Manipulator Arm
Repulsor

MAINTENANCE
EG-6 POWER DROID

If there ever was a sillier-looking automaton than the EG-6 Power Droid, it has yet to show its face. Featureless dark boxes shuffling around on stumpy legs, devoid of external manipulators of any kind, the droids baffle those who aren't familiar with their function. But without them, starships would sputter, instruments would falter, and modern society would generally grind to a halt.

Power droids are ambulatory fusion generators—"walking batteries," some say. Their job is to provide systems energy to mechanical devices in situations where a permanent power grid is unavailable or inconvenient. The droids are common sights in ship hangars, repulsor pools, and tech domes.

Their single-function purpose accounts for their rather bland appearance. A large part of an EG-6's innards consists of its fusion generator, which is protected from shocks by a heavy armored exterior. The droid is built to survive a variety of disasters, up to and including a radiation conduit breach. In emergencies involving extreme temperatures, small relief valves on the outer casing and the bases of both feet bleed off vaporizing coolant fluid as steam.

The few adornments on the EG-6's unremarkable "face" consist of a plug-in port; a visual sensor; an acoustic signaler, capable of droid and computer languages only; and a sophisticated systems diagnostic package incor-

porating a spectrometer and three scanners—infrared, sonar, and X-ray. The droid uses these sensors to run detailed safety checks on the equipment it is servicing. If the number and severity of flaws fall outside the droid's preprogrammed tolerance ranges, it refuses to fuel the item. This dramatically decreases the number of accidental explosions, but gives the EG-6 a justified reputation for stubbornness.

Even people who work around power droids every day rarely see one use its manipulator arm. This delicate appendage is normally stored behind a tiny portal and is built for ultrafine electronics work. Since important repairs are best entrusted to an LE unit or a Treadwell, the arm usually remains hidden.

Apart from their highly advanced diagnostic programming, power droids are notoriously stupid. If ordered to walk a straight line, the automaton will determinedly keep its feet pumping even after it has marched straight off the edge of a cliff. Fortunately, its durability often allows it to survive such witless mishaps.

Veril Line Systems, manufacturer of the EG-6, clearly dominates the energy-supply market, but their massive lead has been nibbled down a bit since Industrial Automaton's rollout of the near-identical GNK unit. In response, Veril has introduced the S9 Heavy Power Droid, a larger and more expensive variation on the EG-6.

Side View

Front View

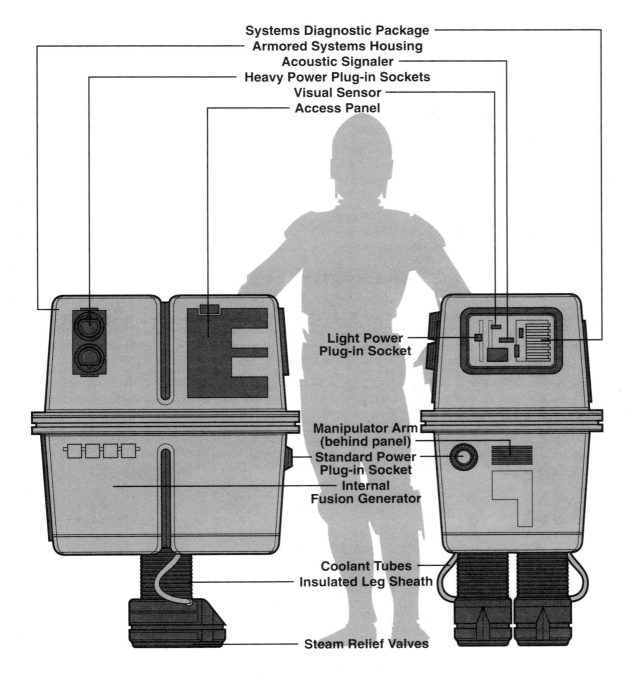

Systems Diagnostic Package
Armored Systems Housing
Acoustic Signaler
Heavy Power Plug-in Sockets
Visual Sensor
Access Panel

Light Power
Plug-in Socket

Manipulator Arm
(behind panel)
Standard Power
Plug-in Socket
Internal
Fusion Generator

Coolant Tubes
Insulated Leg Sheath

Steam Relief Valves

850.AA PUBLIC SERVICE HEADQUARTERS

A massive mobile command base, the 850.AA Public Service Headquarters is a formidable weapon in the war against urban blight. Wherever cracked roadways loom or trash heaps lurk, the 850.AA disgorges armies of worker robos armed for battle with vacuum hoses, laser welders, and buffing rags.

Built by Publictechnic, the 850.AA is an imposing thirteen meters tall. Its sheer size—and considerable cost—make it suitable primarily for large industrialized centers in the Core Worlds, Colonies, and Corporate Sector, where it performs its duties with reliable competence.

The mammoth droid has three separate stories, housing automata, vehicles, and equipment. The lowest level contains up to thirty smaller droids—a typical complement includes ten general-maintenance robos, five worker drones, five EG-6 Power Droids, and ten WED Treadwells. The units enter and exit the 850.AA through two retractable ramps on either side of the durable chassis.

The second level is a parking garage for ground vehicles, such as landspeeders, used by the human crew members and overseers often stationed aboard 850.AA base droids. It can comfortably accommodate two vehicles up to ten meters in length. The droid allows the speeders to leave by opening an upper-story rear hatch and extending its aft ramp.

The uppermost level is an open-air

landing pad for airspeeders and flitters. A protective guardrail encircles the area to prevent workers from falling while the droid is in motion. Mounted in the fore section is a large sensorlink network system, used to scan streets and public facilities for anything dirty, broken, or not up to code.

The 850.AA hovers above the ground on potent repulsorlifts, giving it a flight ceiling of 20 meters. If an avenue below needs cleaning, it lowers itself to a height of 1.5 meters and engages three abrasive scrubber brushes. Fourteen beamcleaners supplement the scrubbers with precise scouring power. In the unlikely event that passing citizens fail to notice the metal behemoth, it is outfitted with flashing lights, hazard labels, and a piercing warning siren.

For more detailed tasks, the 850.AA Public Service Headquarters stops in its tracks and dispatches one or more of its specialized droids. It issues orders to its troops via a tight-beam antenna, and has facilities aboard for recharging the units once they return "home." The 850.AA boasts a remarkably efficient energy-conservation system, allowing it to operate autonomously for weeks at a time.

On a few planets, older 850.AA units have been modified to serve as firefighters and construction units. A street gang on the anarchic world of Carratos has even hijacked one and turned it into an armored hideout and a frighteningly effective battering ram.

Front View

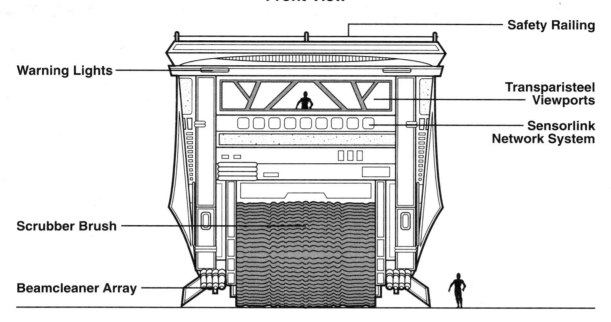

Safety Railing

Warning Lights

Transparisteel Viewports

Sensorlink Network System

Scrubber Brush

Beamcleaner Array

Side View

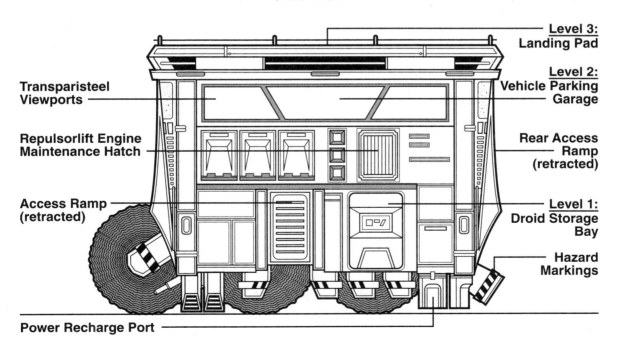

Transparisteel Viewports

Repulsorlift Engine Maintenance Hatch

Access Ramp (retracted)

Power Recharge Port

Level 3: Landing Pad

Level 2: Vehicle Parking Garage

Rear Access Ramp (retracted)

Level 1: Droid Storage Bay

Hazard Markings

REPAIR

WED TREADWELL

Treadwells have been around for decades. They last. They're cheap. And they are manufactured by one of the biggest names in the business. Simple and commonplace, the little droids are quite possibly the most popular repair units in history.

Cybot Galactica's WED Treadwell was named for its method of locomotion—two wide treads driven by a sequence of ten wheels. This drive system, combined with a low center of gravity, makes the droid difficult to topple and allows it to safely cross irregular surfaces.

But the Treadwell's most familiar feature is its array of jointed manipulator arms. These delicate appendages are normally folded up close to the body like the limbs of a desiccated spider. WEDs are shipped from the factory with only five arms—and sometimes four—though they possess sockets for six or more. Each appendage is designed for a particular job-specific task, such as arc welding, fine manipulation, electric rewiring, and even paint spraying. Cybot Galactica encourages buyers to mix and match arms to make their droids more efficient performers—the limbs are easy to install and can be found in any droid-parts store. Resourceful scroungers can often find a slew of salvageable Treadwell components buried in the local scrapheap.

Each WED Treadwell unit comes equipped with a visual sensor and an acoustic

signaler capable of communicating only in binary. Mounted atop the telescoping central stalk is a pair of video microbinoculars that allows the droid to pick out hairline fractures in a hyperdrive coupling or a loose weld on a microchip.

Repairing a Treadwell is an easy step-by-step process, which is one reason why the droids are so widely accepted. But some users complain that Cybot should have concentrated instead on making the units less likely to *need* repairs in the first place. They argue that WEDs are frustratingly flighty and needlessly glitch-prone.

Part of the problem is the fragility of the manipulator arms. The limbs are intentionally lightweight for precise work, but they often become jammed by grit or snagged on protuberances as the droids roll down narrow passageways. In the latter case, there's a better-than-average chance the appendage will snap off before the Treadwell realizes it should stop. The simplistic intelligence modules also cause headaches—at times, the droids make rookie mistakes like grasping electrified leads without using their insulated arms.

Despite its drawbacks, the WED Treadwell is a perennial bestseller. The droids can be found almost everywhere, from the halls of the New Republic to backwater Tatooine moisture farms to the crowded military hangars on Coruscant.

Microbinoculars - Side View

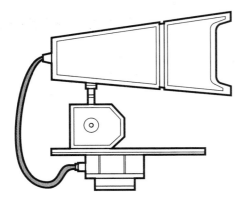

Microbinoculars - Front View

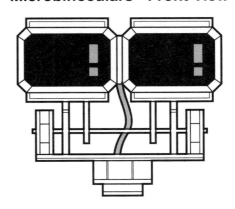

Side View　　　　　　　　**Front View**

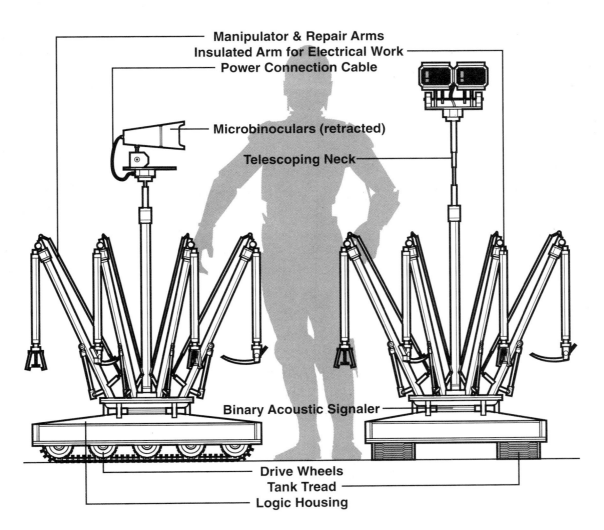

Manipulator & Repair Arms
Insulated Arm for Electrical Work
Power Connection Cable

Microbinoculars (retracted)

Telescoping Neck

Binary Acoustic Signaler

Drive Wheels
Tank Tread
Logic Housing

REPAIR

LE REPAIR DROID

The LE series was an ambitious attempt by Cybot Galactica to, as the promotional brochure put it, "combine the personality of a protocol unit with the utility of an astromech." While the droids weren't the spectacular profit leaders that Cybot's execs had hoped for, they did at least manage to carve out a modest market niche.

The first LEs were produced generations ago for use in starports. Though you could buy four Treadwells for the cost of a single LE, Cybot gambled that ship captains would be willing to pay a premium for droids intelligent enough to interact with port officials and customs inspectors. They were right.

Each LE stood 1.7 meters tall and sported a skeletal bipedal frame of silver-gray durasteel. Though the two-armed design couldn't match the versatility of the spiderlike Treadwell, the droid's humanoid shape made it easier to communicate with its biological masters.

Common equipment on the LE included visual and auditory pickups attuned to human sensory ranges, a vocabulator, and a holographic projector/recorder system. A broadband transmission antenna allowed the droid to receive data while working in a sealed repair conduit or on the far side of a crowded hangar bay. Working in con-

cert with the holographic recorder was a series of focusing lenses, permitting the LE to zoom in on distant objects or bring microscopic details into sharp clarity.

The primary function of the LE series was starship repair, and they came factory-installed with extensive databases on hyperdrives, acceleration compensators, artificial gravity, alluvial dampers, and all the other equipment needed to travel between worlds. Since Cybot Galactica assumed most buyers would be for-hire captains and independent traders, the LEs specialized in fixing bulk haulers and stock light freighters. With additional programming and sufficient on-the-job experience, LEs can competently manage starfighters, airspeeders, and even Capital ships.

The droids' secondary function was to deal with starport personnel and free their owners from annoying red tape. They are quite crafty at obtaining departure permits and cargo waivers, even when it means "bending" the rules just a bit. Some port offices keep LE units on their staffs full-time, using their talents to ensure that all arriving craft meet lift/mass guidelines and safety regulations.

The best-known member of the LE production run is LE-BO2D9, known to his friends as Leebo. The loyal droid and his master, Dash Rendar, helped the Rebel Alliance bring down Xizor, the dark prince of Black Sun. Though Leebo and Dash were believed killed in a ship explosion near Coruscant, there are rumors that the pair survived and have been lying low in the Outer Rim Territories.

Front View

Rear View

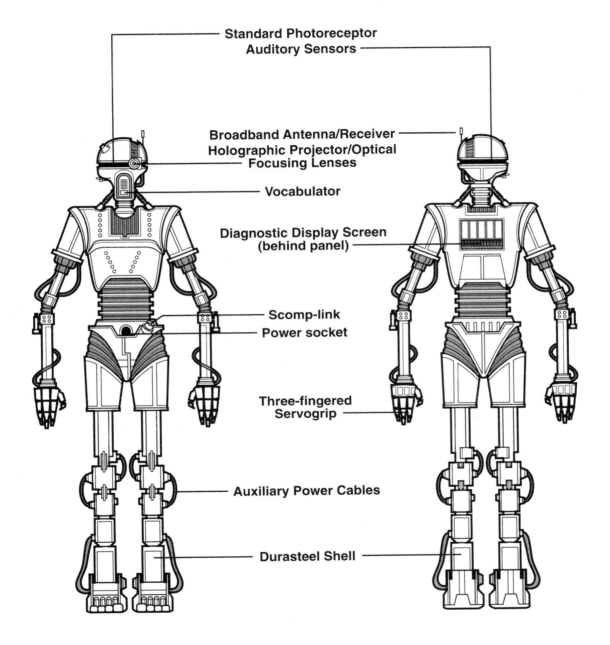

Standard Photoreceptor
Auditory Sensors

Broadband Antenna/Receiver
Holographic Projector/Optical
Focusing Lenses

Vocabulator

Diagnostic Display Screen
(behind panel)

Scomp-link
Power socket

Three-fingered
Servogrip

Auxiliary Power Cables

Durasteel Shell

GYROWHEEL 1.42.08 RECYCLING DROID

A massive spacegoing vessel such as an Imperial Star Destroyer employs more than 36,000 workers, pilots, technicians, and engineers—hardworking crew members who consume vast quantities of food on every mission. Since active warships rarely go more than a few weeks without resupply, a Star Destroyer's standard stock of foodstuffs and consumables is generally sufficient. Other vessels, however, aren't able to carry adequate edibles to survive a long-term deep space voyage. These ships rely heavily on recycling droids.

Most people wouldn't recognize a recycling droid if they saw one, since the units spend their entire operational lives aboard specialized starships—typically research and exploration vessels that venture into the Unknown Regions for months or years at a time. Occasionally the droids are installed aboard more conventional craft as an emergency backup system, but this is rare, due to the cost of maintaining the recycling network. To those who use them, their advantages are clear: recycling droids can produce a veritable mountain of bland, but perfectly edible, ration bars and protein wafers.

The model series, officially known as the Gyrowheel 1.42.08, is manufactured by Veril Line Systems. Unlike the clunky two-legged design that Veril used for its popular EG-6 Power Droid, the company instead adopted a radical one-wheeled configuration that provided superior speed and maneuverability on a smooth starship deck. The metallic body remains stabilized atop the wheel,

thanks to a gyroscopic balance system.

A cluster of sensors makes up the recycling droid's face. Whiplike, multijointed metal extensors function as amazingly flexible limbs, and each "hand" sports an optical sensor and removable gripping pincers. The Gyrowheel droids possess negligible individual intelligence, instead relying on the remote guidance of the ship's master computer. Extendible antennae allow the units to receive orders and transmit their own positioning data.

A vessel with a full recycling system will allocate most of its pantry space for technical equipment and miscellaneous cargo. In this case, full enzymatic breakdown of waste products will begin as early as the second week. During the process, the Gyrowheel droids flit through the ship locating discarded organic refuse and emptying the contents of the waste pipes. All the material is then brought to the ship's recycling chamber and dumped into one of three steaming biotic vats. Within these vats, bubbling enzymatic acid breaks down the cellular nutrients into a rich organic soup.

Plastics, metals, and other nonusable substances are ejected from a hatch in the side of each vat.

A number of recycling droids were stationed aboard the *Eye of Palpatine*, an armored battle-moon that was lost in a nebula nearly two decades before the Battle of Yavin. When Luke Skywalker discovered the ship, the *Eye*'s sinister computer brain ordered its Gyrowheel units to subdue the Jedi Master and fling his body into the recycling acid.

Side View

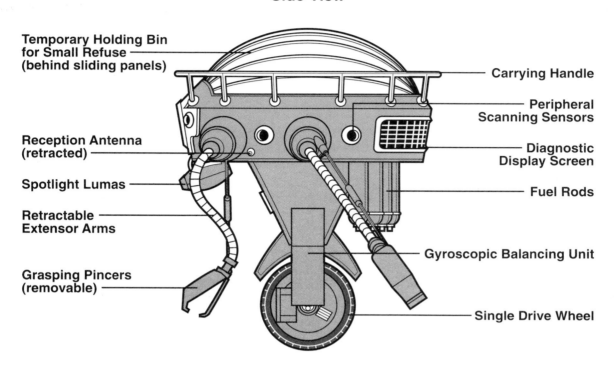

Temporary Holding Bin for Small Refuse (behind sliding panels)

Carrying Handle

Peripheral Scanning Sensors

Reception Antenna (retracted)

Diagnostic Display Screen

Spotlight Lumas

Fuel Rods

Retractable Extensor Arms

Gyroscopic Balancing Unit

Grasping Pincers (removable)

Single Drive Wheel

Front View

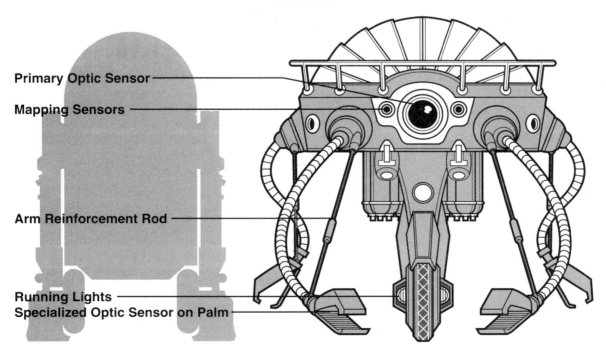

Primary Optic Sensor

Mapping Sensors

Arm Reinforcement Rod

Running Lights
Specialized Optic Sensor on Palm

STAR WARS

STARSHIP BASED

M38 EXPLORER

During the boom years of the Old Republic, adventurers and fortune-seekers blazed the uncharted expanses of hyperspace in search of lost civilizations, alien technology, and untapped mineral wealth. But in their eagerness to explore, many of these individuals set off across wild planets that hadn't been soil tested or chemically analyzed. As a result, many never returned, and soon, no one in his right mind would even *think* of selling a galactic scout life insurance.

Explorer droids were developed as safe, accurate, and expendable tools for reconnoitering hazardous worlds and, hopefully, giving their masters the "all clear." The M38 Explorer, manufactured by Les Tech, is one of the best.

Everything about the M38, from its size, a compact 1.3 meters, to its hull plating, blaster-resistant durasteel, was designed for maximum toughness and utility. It can withstand rockslides, lightning strikes, and acid rain without missing a beat and has environment scanners so sophisticated they'd make an Arakyd probe droid insane with envy. But Arakyd's probot still has the M38 beat in other areas—Les Tech's units are slow, maintenance-intensive, and lack weapons of any kind.

A concave durasteel plate sits atop the M38's head and serves as a sturdy hard-hat, protecting the sensitive detection equipment clustered beneath it. Each

droid has electromagnetic, movement, and radiation sensors, plus a seismic monitor for predicting geologic tremors. Twin photoreceptors can see in normal and infrared visual ranges, and a holocam records all proceedings for later playback.

The body contains an internal specimen hopper with a holding capacity of five kilograms. An adjacent chemical tester scrutinizes new samples for trace toxins and unknown microorganisms. Its three-fingered arms look identical, but the left is lighter and better suited for fine detail work than its weightier counterpart. The M38 moves about on twin tank treads that require realignment each time the droid is sent out into the field.

An M38 Explorer is typically sent to a planet's surface in a tiny, automated shuttlecraft while the main ship waits in orbit. Its antenna is short-range only—if some catastrophe befalls either the droid or the shuttlecraft, all data gathered will be irrevocably lost. Because of this, some scouts have tried arming their M38s with defensive stun blasters, but the droids don't respond well to nonspec modifications.

A great number of M38 Explorers were used by the fugitive Rebel Alliance to investigate possible safe worlds and base locations. The droids proved surprisingly adept at studying the local terrain and compiling lists of the most strategically defensible battle sites.

116

Side View

Front View

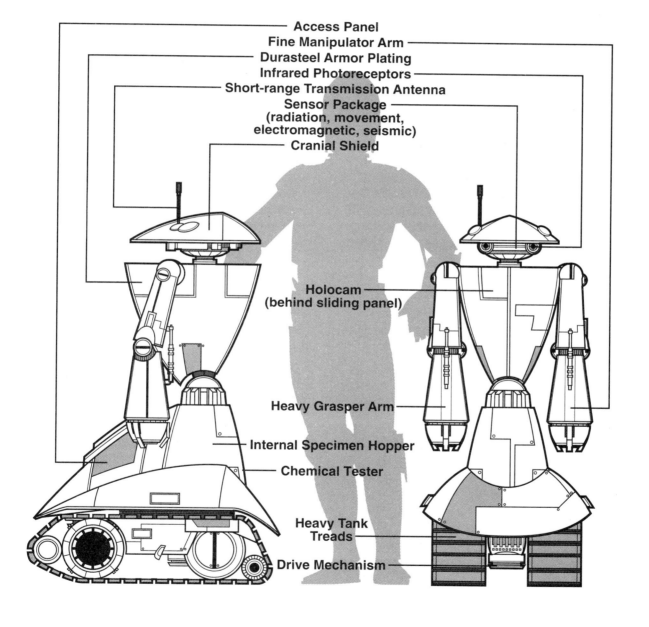

Access Panel
Fine Manipulator Arm
Durasteel Armor Plating
Infrared Photoreceptors
Short-range Transmission Antenna
Sensor Package
(radiation, movement,
electromagnetic, seismic)
Cranial Shield

Holocam
(behind sliding panel)

Heavy Grasper Arm

Internal Specimen Hopper

Chemical Tester

Heavy Tank
Treads

Drive Mechanism

SCOUT COLLECTOR & SURVEYOR PACKAGE

The 87-RM Scout Collector is a valuable tool for frontier biologists and botanists who wish to preserve organic samples for transport. Thanks to an advanced flash-freezing system, captured specimens remain in perfect stasis until they can be dissected under proper laboratory conditions.

Both the 87-RM and its companion unit, the Wanderer Scout Surveyor, were built by the SoroSuub Corporation from blueprints originally penned by an extinct alien race. Serv-O-Droid was the original manufacturer of the 87-RM, but sold the line after an embarrassing accident near the Minos Cluster. Both droids have proven to be effective and profitable products, though the market for them is admittedly small.

The 87-RM Scout Collector unit stands 2.5 meters high and moves about on antigravity repulsorlifts. Its boxy form is dictated by function, for in its guts is a cubical storage chamber large enough to hold a Tatooine dewback. The remainder of the interior is tightly packed with cooling circuitry and cryogenic flow pipes. This delicate equipment is protected from accidental damage by a durable hull and a moderate energy shield.

The 87-RM identifies its preprogrammed targets with an array of blinking sensors on its lower front face. It grasps the stunned animal with two heavy manipulator arms—doing its best not to damage the specimen— and gingerly lifts it. With a hiss of equalized pressure and a puff of escap-

ing vapor, the upper hatch splits, and the helpless creature is dumped inside.

The flash-freezing process takes less than three minutes. The temperature inside the chamber swiftly plunges, inducing cryogenic hypothermia, then a bank of sprayer nozzles releases a numbing chemical solution known colloquially as a "frost bath." The process concluded, the ponderous droid heads for its next victim, leaving a misty condensation trail in its wake.

In sales catalogs, the 87-RM Scout Collector is typically bundled with one or more Wanderer Scout Surveyors. These metallic arachnids use their sensors to track down biological specimens; if the target creatures prove dangerous, antagonistic, or particularly fleet-footed, the droids knock them unconscious for later pickup by the 87-RM.

Each Wanderer has eight jointed legs, a central detection package, and a cluster of tiny manipulator appendages. They can move with great speed and surprising agility. An unblinking photoreceptor and a powerful stun blaster are mounted atop a 360-degree swivel mount—whatever the droid can see, it can shoot. Wanderers communicate with one another on hypersonic frequencies and effortlessly coordinate their actions. Often, one droid will rush into the underbrush, flushing its target animal from cover and straight into the other's field of fire.

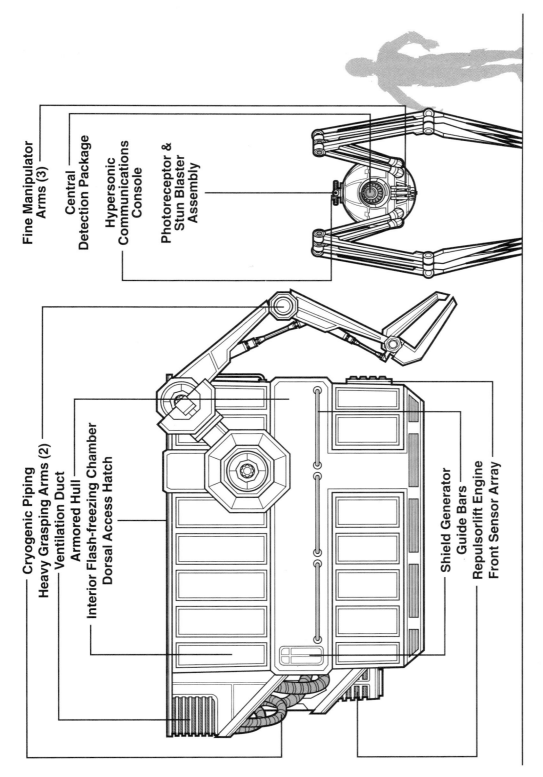

Fine Manipulator Arms (3)

Central Detection Package

Hypersonic Communications Console

Photoreceptor & Stun Blaster Assembly

Wanderer Front View

Cryogenic Piping

Heavy Grasping Arms (2)

Ventilation Duct

Armored Hull

Interior Flash-freezing Chamber

Dorsal Access Hatch

Shield Generator

Guide Bars

Repulsorlift Engine

Front Sensor Array

Collector Unit Side View

STAR WARS

Galactic scouts are frequently required to leave their recon crafts for weeks at a time, scouring the planetary terrain for rich mineral deposits or settlements of intelligent aliens. Most of these explorers won't set one foot outside the hatch without their tried-and-true Mechanical Universal Labor Eliminating Droid, or MULE.

The Les Tech MULE droid, technically known as the PackTrack 41LT-R, is a high-tech spin on an age-old concept. Beasts of burden have existed since the first animals were domesticated and are still used on many planets— banthas and rontos are common examples. But frontier scouts need a pack animal that is strong, tireless, obedient, and unlikely to fall dead after ingesting a strange virus from some uncharted planet's stagnant watering hole.

The quadrupedal design of the MULE is reminiscent of more traditional beasts, but the similarity to its organic forebears ends there. Instead of a furry hide, the droid is coated in a thick, ribbed plating of solid durasteel. All servos and gears are either covered by the plates or by a double layer of black flexiplast, making the MULE immune to driving rain and blowing sand.

A thick, powerful neck supports an impervious head, which sports an optical port,

auditory sensors, a terrain scanner, and a long-range antenna for relaying data back to base camp. The droid does not possess a vocabulator and is thus incapable of verbal communication.

Each one of the four legs ends in a row of three treaded wheels that are the droid's fastest and most energy-efficient mode of transportation. If the topography is particularly uneven or hazardous, the legs fold up against the MULE's belly as its low-power repulsor unit comes on-line. The repulsor allows the droid to hover one meter above the ground, but its forward speed is frustratingly slow.

Most of the body is empty space for the storing of provisions, equipment, rock samples, and drinking water. This internal compartment can hold up to two cubic meters of cargo, and most explorers fill it to overflowing, lashing down their bedrolls and excavation tools on top of everything else. A rugged lifting claw loads the heaviest items and folds away when not in use.

The MULE droid is built for reliability, not intelligence. Fortunately, its simple brain is less prone to breakdown, and if something *should* go wrong, there are fewer cognitive circuits to fix. Most of the programming in the MULE's databanks is of a self-diagnostic nature, allowing it to assist its owner in making on-the-spot field repairs.

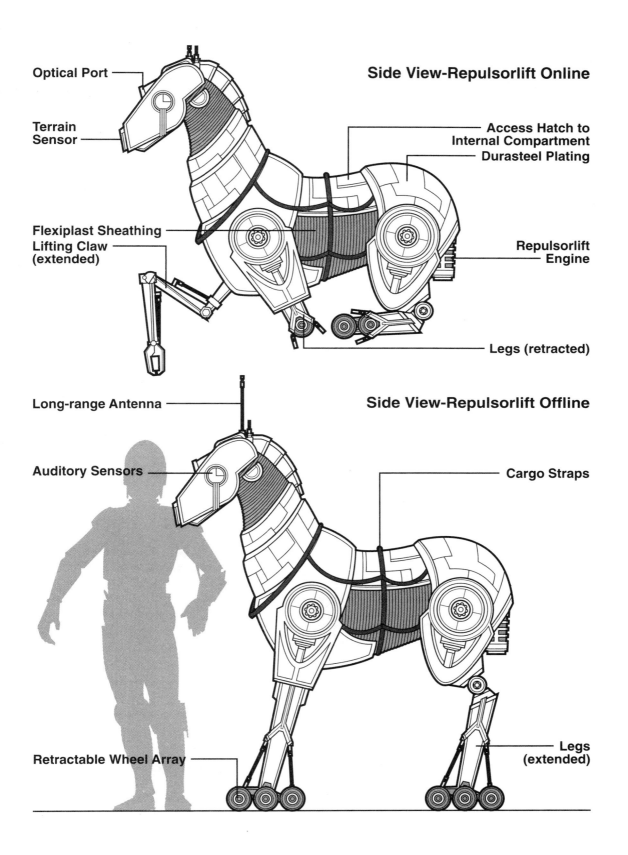

Optical Port

Terrain Sensor

Side View-Repulsorlift Online

Access Hatch to Internal Compartment
Durasteel Plating

Flexiplast Sheathing
Lifting Claw (extended)

Repulsorlift Engine

Legs (retracted)

Long-range Antenna

Side View-Repulsorlift Offline

Auditory Sensors

Cargo Straps

Retractable Wheel Array

Legs (extended)

STARSHIP BASED

SCAVENGER DROID

When scavenged equipment from old Imperial wrecks started appearing in black markets throughout the galaxy, the New Republic Senate quickly passed the Historic Battle Site Preservation Act. The measure, ostensibly designed to protect innocent citizens from unlicensed and dangerous devices, also gave the Republic a free hand in locating drifting debris and hoarding all the goodies for itself. Operation Flotsam, the muscle behind the Preservation Act, ensured that "friendly" scavenger crews would beat the outlaw plunderers at their own game.

Standard equipment on New Republic wreckage-retrieval vessels, the SM series of scanning and monitoring droids are similar to those that have been used on scavenger ships for centuries. Designed to operate best under zero-gravity conditions, the compact units float through the empty corridors of burnt-out starship hulks, searching for booby traps, dead bodies, or weak points in the superstructure; everything is recorded with a detailed holocamera and spectrometer.

Each droid features a set of zero-gee maneuvering jets and—in case a ship's atmosphere and artificial gravity are still intact—a repulsorlift engine and dual stabilizer fins. Its sensor eyes provide a panoramic view of the area ahead, while its dorsal holocam can zoom in on tiny details such as door locks and bulkhead lettering.

Two retractable manipulator arms allow the droid to operate simple controls and carry small objects.

SM units always operate in pairs grouped by numerical designation—for example, SM-1 with SM-2, SM-3 with SM-4. The reason for this is simple—if one droid accidentally triggers a dormant laser trap, the other can record its partner's untimely demise and determine a way to circumvent the deadly obstacle.

The droids' live visual data feed is continually broadcast back to the scavenger ship where it is monitored by a human operator and a data-analysis droid. The operator can take remote guidance of an SM unit at any time, but most droids follow simple preset search patterns according to the type of vessel they are investigating. Key search targets include hangars, control bridges, gun batteries, and power generators. Only after a wreck has been thoroughly scouted for hazards will a ransacking team head aboard with fusion cutters and power prybars in their hands.

Particularly notable among New Republic scavenger vessels is the fleet hauler *Steadfast*, which located the derelict Star Destroyer *Gnisnal* approximately twelve years after the Battle of Endor. The *Steadfast*'s successful deployment of an SM squad allowed her crew to uncover an intact memory core containing an Imperial Order of Battle, which proved instrumental in resolving the Black Fleet crisis.

Side View

Front View

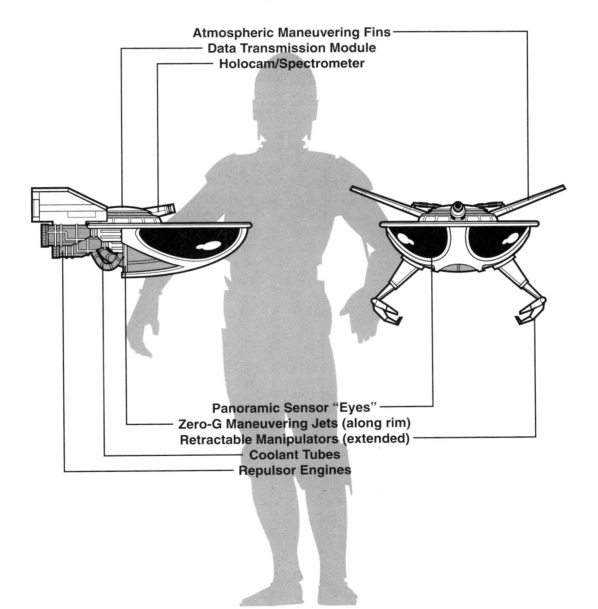

Atmospheric Maneuvering Fins
Data Transmission Module
Holocam/Spectrometer

Panoramic Sensor "Eyes"
Zero-G Maneuvering Jets (along rim)
Retractable Manipulators (extended)
Coolant Tubes
Repulsor Engines

MSE-6 ("MOUSE DROID")

Tiny, ubiquitous, and annoying, MSE-6 droids scurry through the corridors of Star Destroyers like scrounging rodents on the primitive sailing ships of yore. Even though most officers hate the sight of them, "mouse droids" are simple, reliable, and cheap, and are unlikely to disappear from the military any time soon.

The MSE-6 General Purpose Droid was introduced decades ago by a now-defunct Chadra-Fan company called Rebaxan Columni. Hoping to create a model that consumers would consider "cute," Rebaxan engineers patterned the MSE after a diminutive pet animal from their homeworld. Their disastrous next move is still taught in universities as how *not* to launch a product.

Without bothering to perform market research, Rebaxan produced billions of MSE-6s, counting on an expensive, four-hundred-sector advertising blitz to do their work for them. And it worked—until buyers realized the chirping robots reminded them of disease-carrying vermin. Sales plummeted, and billions of MSE-6s were returned for refunds. Rebaxan Columni was finished.

To help cushion the blow of bankruptcy, the company offered the Empire a cut-rate deal on the entire production run. The Navy, critically short on droids due to Emperor Palpatine's sweeping military expansions, accepted. Mouse droids are now found on nearly every Imperial starship and ground installation throughout the galaxy.

Each MSE-6 is equipped with a single modular circuit matrix that can only hold one skill at a time. The matrices are cheap and easy to install—so easy, in fact, that they are often reprogrammed by other mouse droids. Common MSE-6 skill matrices include elementary repair, security, janitorial cleanup, and basic computer programming.

The unassuming, "black box" outer casing conceals two retractable manipulator arms, one powerful and one delicate. A sensitive auditory sensor is located on either side of the body, while an electro-photoreceptor and miniature holocam are found on the front. The MSE-6 can move forward and backward quite rapidly with a maneuverable set of treaded wheels.

A small compartment in the top of the droid holds sealed orders and sensitive documents for the times when it is used as a courier. Once locked, the compartment cannot be opened without an authorized voice-code. In at least one documented case, this small cubbyhole was packed with explosive detonite in an unsuccessful attempt to assassinate High Inquisitor Tremayne.

Used MSE-6s can be purchased almost anywhere for as little as three hundred credits each. Despite the droids' inflexible programming and propensity to flee at the slightest racket, many cash-strapped smugglers use mouse droid armies for simple repairs and maintenance. The Empire also employed MSE-6s to guide troops through the labyrinthine corridors of the Death Star.

Front View-Unsealed

Fine Manipulator (extended)

Command/Order Tray (extended)

Rank Command Cylinder

Heavy Manipulator (extended)

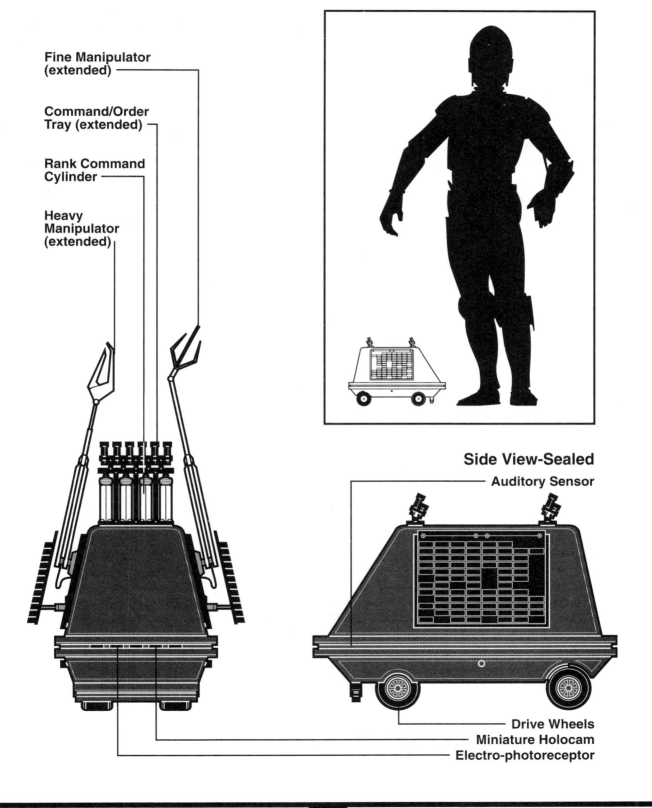

Side View-Sealed

Auditory Sensor

Drive Wheels

Miniature Holocam

Electro-photoreceptor

S T A R S H I P   B A S E D

RA-7 DEATH STAR DROID

Arakyd Industries' sole entry in the personal-assistant market was the RA-7, a substandard Imperial model with a disappointing processor and a drab personality. But the Empire praised Arakyd, snapped up the entire production run, and distributed the droids like party favors to its highest-ranking officers and planetary governors. Most recipients of this dubious honor chalked it up to bureaucratic excess, and never suspected the real reason behind their unexpected "gift"—the RA-7 units were remote spies for the Imperial Security Bureau.

This explained the low intelligence and cheap construction of the black-lacquered servant droid. While industry rivals crowed over Arakyd's apparent misstep— Julynn Kentas, Industrial Automaton's CEO, said in a *MechTech Illustrated* interview that her militaristic rival had "a lot to learn about pleasing the public"—Arakyd churned out thousands of second-rate droids that nonetheless matched the Empire's design specs perfectly. The RA-7s were rarely assigned complex tasks because of their general incompetence, but Imperial recipients didn't dare return them for fear of offending their superiors. Forgotten and ignored, the servant units lurked in the background, patiently awaiting orders while recording their masters' every move.

A clandestine documentation/surveillance system lay tucked away in the droid's insectoid skull, surrounded by multiple layers of benign cognitive circuitry. Sensor bafflers disguised as soldering welds prevented the surveillance unit from showing up on routine scans. Audio pickups recorded whispered conversations; photoreceptors operated under low-light conditions, captured panoramic images, and extrapolated dialogue through lip-reading.

The RA-7 droids made periodic dumps of their incriminating data to Imperial Security Bureau agents using encrypted frequencies on standard comm units. If the recordings revealed corruption, profiteering, or insufficient loyalty to Emperor Palpatine, the droids' masters often left abruptly on "business trips" to Imperial Center on Coruscant. Few ever returned.

After a time, rumors began to circulate among naval admirals that their bug-eyed servants might be concealing a sinister secret. Simply dismantling the units would be an admission of guilt, so many officers attempted to "lose" their droids while on shore leave. Repaired and remodeled RA-7s, stolen by petty thieves during these intentional incidents, are occasionally encountered in swap meets and droid auctions.

So many high-level officials were assigned to the first Death Star that the battle station's corridors seethed with RA-7s, prompting someone to invent the enduring nickname "Death Star Droid." When the prodigious superweapon exploded at Yavin, most of the RA-7 series went up with it.

Front View

Rear View

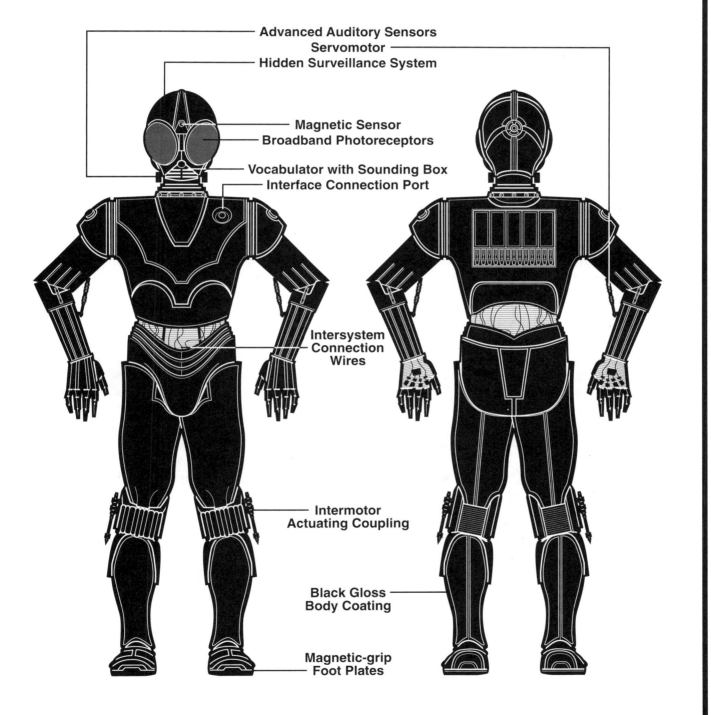

Advanced Auditory Sensors

Servomotor

Hidden Surveillance System

Magnetic Sensor
Broadband Photoreceptors

Vocabulator with Sounding Box
Interface Connection Port

Intersystem
Connection
Wires

Intermotor
Actuating Coupling

Black Gloss
Body Coating

Magnetic-grip
Foot Plates

BASILISK WAR DROID

Mandalorians! Once the mere mention of the fierce warrior clans struck terror into the hearts of galactic citizens. Now their legacy survives in the uniquely styled armor worn by the bounty hunter Boba Fett. Four millennia before the rise of the Empire, the proud nomads conquered the space lanes astride a deadly armada of Basilisk war droids.

Massive mobile weapons platforms, the Basilisk droids were much more than steeds to the Mandalorian soldiers who rode them. The war machines functioned as counterparts, comrades, fearless combatants, and loyal allies. Though they were only slightly more intelligent than domesticated beasts, the droids were so attuned to their masters' emotions that, in combat, they functioned as direct extensions of their riders' bodies.

Even in those ancient times, the Basilisk droids—incongruous, semiorganic alien constructs—looked peculiar. They bore some resemblance to gigantic beetles, but sported lasers instead of mandibles and intake jets where antennae should be. When entering a combat zone, the Basilisk lifted its rear "wings" to expose a set of high-boost rocket engines.

The Mandalorians employed a number of specialized Basilisks for different classes of warfare. Two-seater bomber models accommodated a pilot and a gunner; stealth models had light armament and supplementary engines. The most common variant was the open-combat model, a one-crew rig with an

efficient balance of weaponry, shielding, and speed.

The war droids could operate both in atmosphere and deep space, and their riders' flight armor could withstand long periods of hard vacuum. Two heavy, dangling front claws were used to batter down obstacles and slash through opponents, and also doubled as landing gear struts. With its fore and aft sensor clusters the Basilisk could identify an imminent attack from nearly any direction.

Weapons on the open-combat model included a nose cluster of shockwave generator rods. When fired, the rods combined their charges to release a devastating plasma burst that could puncture a starship's hull. Other firearms included pulse-wave cannons and shatter-missile launch tubes. The Mandalorian riders also secreted their personal weapons, such as axes, swords, and flashpistols, among the droids' hull plates. When assailing a large garrison or orbital station, two Basilisks often towed an atomic compression bomb between them and catapulted the mine into their target.

Basilisk war droids posed a grave threat to the Old Republic during the infamous Sith War. Led by their chieftain Mandalore, the Mandalorian clans conquered the Kuar system and assaulted the Empress Teta carbonite factories. After Ulic Qel-Droma defeated Mandalore in single combat, the ferocious nomads pledged fealty to the victor and unleashed their Basilisks on Coruscant, Ossus, and Onderon.

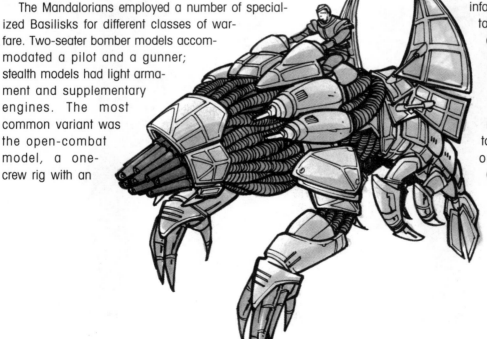

Front View

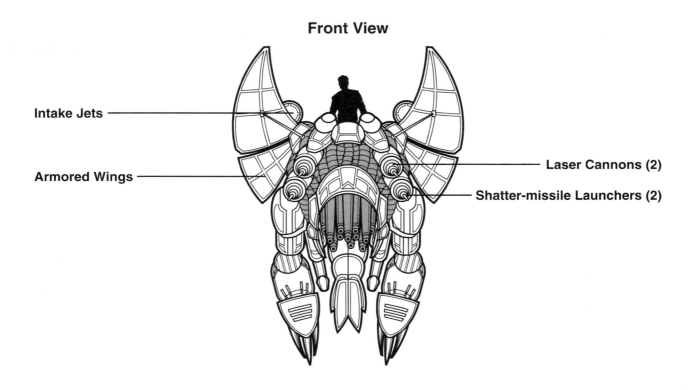

Intake Jets

Armored Wings

Laser Cannons (2)

Shatter-missile Launchers (2)

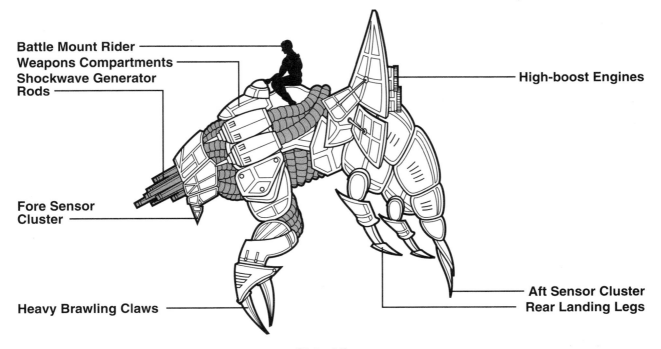

Battle Mount Rider
Weapons Compartments
Shockwave Generator
Rods

High-boost Engines

Fore Sensor
Cluster

Heavy Brawling Claws

Aft Sensor Cluster
Rear Landing Legs

Side View

XIM'S WAR-ROBOT

History is written by the victors, and those who doubt it need only look at the Third Battle of Vontor. The details of this ancient pre-Republic clash between Xim the Despot and Kossak the Hutt have been muddied over the past thousand generations, largely due to the Hutts' insistence on telling only their side of the story. Despite the obfuscation, Vontor is justifiably famous as the site of Xim's final defeat and the last time his infamous war-robots saw full-scale battlefield combat.

Xim's droids were nearly unstoppable in their day. The warlord was one of the first individuals to perfect mechanized combat, and entire star systems surrendered in the face of his ruthless automated armies. Even by modern standards, the robots are remarkably resilient and impressively lethal.

Built in a bipedal configuration, the droids nevertheless towered over normal human soldiers. Their bulky frames were covered with thick armor plating and reinforced stress points, making it extremely difficult for an enemy to hit a vital control system. Furthermore, the armor was coated with a mirrored reflective surface for parrying laser shots.

Shielded apertures built into the arms and hands housed various chemical and energy weapons, including archaic heatbeams and particle dischargers. Each robot's heavy cranial turret contained optical lenses and a speaker grille, and was adorned with tiny unit insignia markings.

The robots had limited reasoning power and took their orders from whoever controlled the transmission horn installed on Xim's various mil-itary command podiums. Certain droids were given slightly more autonomy than the rest—these were designated Corps Commanders and could be identified by the golden death's-head emblem on their breastplates, as opposed to the white death's-head worn by the rank-and-file robots.

Xim the Despot's overwhelming ambition got the better of him at Vontor. The tyrant committed nearly all of his military forces to a single engagement, hoping to wipe out the Hutts and become the undisputed leader of the Si'klaata Cluster. Unfortunately for Xim, the Hutts had recently made a pact with the Nikto, Vodran, and Klatooinian species. The fierce aliens decimated Xim's war-robot army and vaporized his orbital platforms, ending the dictator's legendary reign in a single bloodstained day.

One thousand of the war-robots survived the debacle as guardians aboard the treasure ship *Queen of Ranroon*. When the vessel arrived at Dellalt, the droids were off-loaded and kept in perfect working order by a cult called the Survivors. Not long before the Battle of Yavin, Han Solo and Chewbacca landed on Dellalt and became the first outsiders to see the war-robots in thousands of years.

Nearly all the droids were destroyed after an attack on a nearby mining camp, but a number of archaeologists and researchers, including Skynx of Ruuria, have put every effort into uncovering their secrets and reconstructing their distinguished histories.

Front View

Rear View

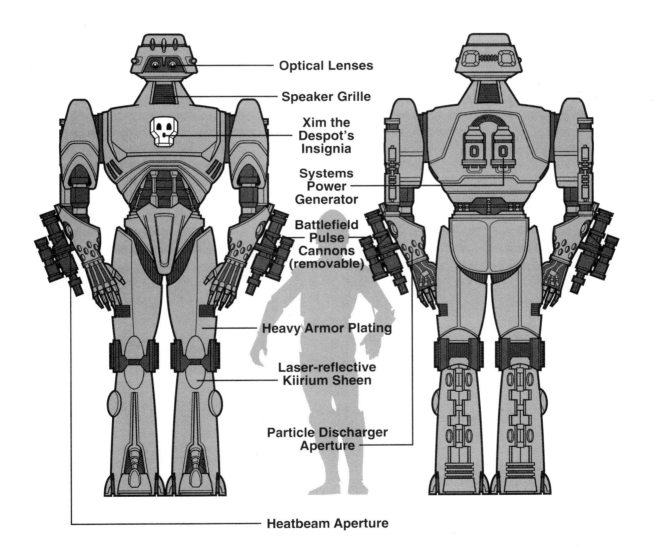

Optical Lenses

Speaker Grille

Xim the
Despot's
Insignia

Systems
Power
Generator

Battlefield
Pulse
Cannons
(removable)

Heavy Armor Plating

Laser-reflective
Kiirium Sheen

Particle Discharger
Aperture

Heatbeam Aperture

MILITARY

KRATH WAR DROID

The Krath was a secret society founded four thousand years before the Galactic Civil War by the spoiled nobles of the Empress Teta system. The Krath members, dabbling recklessly in dark side magic and the secrets of the ancient Sith, grew so corrupt that they instigated a bloody military takeover of the seven Tetan worlds. When the Old Republic's Jedi Knights dared oppose them in the battle of Koros Major, the Krath knew it was time to strike back.

The evil instrument of their revenge was a lithe and lethal war droid. Constructed in the black foundries of Cinnagar, the sleek machines were designed to surprise and overwhelm their enemies in devastating shock assaults. The droids had limited cognitive matrices—they knew only to hit hard, hit fast, and eliminate the greatest threat first. This kept expenses to a minimum and allowed the Krath to produce great numbers of the monsters.

In one fist, each Krath unit clutched a short sword for gutting its enemies at close quarters. The other fist incorporated an antique pulse-wave firing assembly. The attenuated induction spines on this unique weapon generated the pulse-wave charge and could also be used as a spearlike skewering tool in a pinch. The droids traveled hunched over like animals, sprinting forward on two powerful legs.

When the Krath learned of a great meeting of ten thousand Jedi Knights and Masters to be held on the planet Deneba, they saw the perfect opportunity to field test their combat unit and humiliate their enemies. First, their spies altered the programming of many of the servant droids that would be present at the event. Second, their soldiers loaded a Tetan corsair with over a hundred modified life pods, each one carrying a new war droid.

Moments after the peaceful meeting began, the Krath struck. The reprogrammed servant units turned on their Jedi owners, sowing fear and confusion. Simultaneously, the orbiting Tetan corsair shot its pods toward Deneba's red surface and a legion of supple war droids emerged from the impact craters.

Surprise proved to be a deadly enemy as dozens of heroic Jedi fell to the Krath's ruthless swordsmen. Jedi Master Arca Jeth tore apart many of the attacking automatons with subtle Force tugs on their internal circuitry, but he soon succumbed to a fatal plasma barrage. Though the Jedi eventually prevailed, the death toll was shocking and horrific. The Old Republic was roused to action by this insidious incident, and ultimately defeated the Krath and their allies in the Sith War.

Front View

Rear View

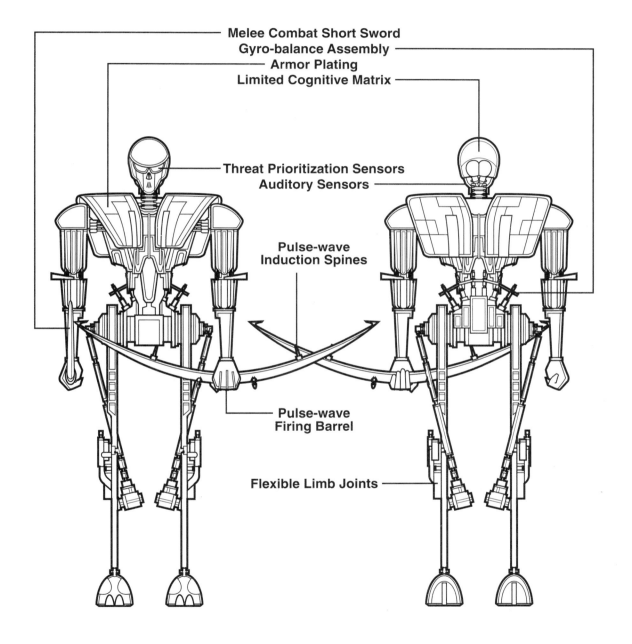

Melee Combat Short Sword
Gyro-balance Assembly
Armor Plating
Limited Cognitive Matrix

Threat Prioritization Sensors
Auditory Sensors

Pulse-wave
Induction Spines

Pulse-wave
Firing Barrel

Flexible Limb Joints

DARK TROOPER

Few know the details of the infamous Dark Trooper project. The files were heavily encrypted. The Imperial engineers were sworn to secrecy. And the Rebels who faced the machines in combat never lived long enough to pass on any information.

All except one—Kyle Katarn, commando and Jedi Knight. Katarn's briefings to Alliance Command, coupled with classified data sliced by Bothan spies, have revealed critical facts about the Empire's ambitious attempt to create "super stormtroopers." Though Katarn downplays his accomplishments, it appears he nearly single-handedly derailed the entire undertaking.

The Dark Troopers were the brainchildren of General Rom Mohc, a decorated Imperial officer obsessed with personal combat. He vociferously protested the construction of the Death Star, arguing that all soldiers deserved the chance to face their enemy one-on-one. When the Death Star detonated above Yavin, Mohc was given the perfect opportunity to advance his cause.

Several dozen of Mohc's mechanical men swiftly went from prototype to finished version aboard the *Arc Hammer*—a titanic spacegoing construction facility completed at the starship yards of Kuat. The droids' first combat test, a brutal, one-sided massacre, utterly decimated a Rebel base on Talay. An impressed Darth Vader ordered Mohc to continue with production.

The battle droids had three distinct stages, each one suitable for armed conflict. The Phase One Dark Trooper, little more than a metal skeleton, was primitive but relentless. Its structural frame, forearm shield, and razor-edged carving blade were cast from phrik, an exceptionally durable alloy found primarily on the moons of the Gromas system.

The Phase Two was the standard combat unit. Its additional phrik body shell made it tougher than the Phase One, while its repulsorlift engine and flight jets gave it superior maneuverability in the air. Each Phase Two carried a devastating assault cannon that fired plasma shells and long-range explosive rockets.

The Phase Three was conceived as the ultimate Dark Trooper, and Katarn claims he faced only one. It appears likely that this unit, stationed aboard the *Arc Hammer*, was the only finished prototype for a planned, but uncompleted, line. Even more massive than the Phase Two, this unstoppable behemoth sported a nasty cluster of firing tubes connected to a seemingly endless supply of seeker missiles. These rockets, while slow, homed in on a target's heat signature and packed enough detonite to obliterate the strongest personal shielding. The Phase Three prototype was designed to operate independently but could also be worn by a human operator as an exosuit.

Katarn's destruction of the *Arc Hammer* cost the Empire billions of credits and marked the death of the Dark Trooper project. Emperor Palpatine, still smarting from the loss of the Death Star, was so infuriated by the newest setback that he refused to approve funding for a new construction facility.

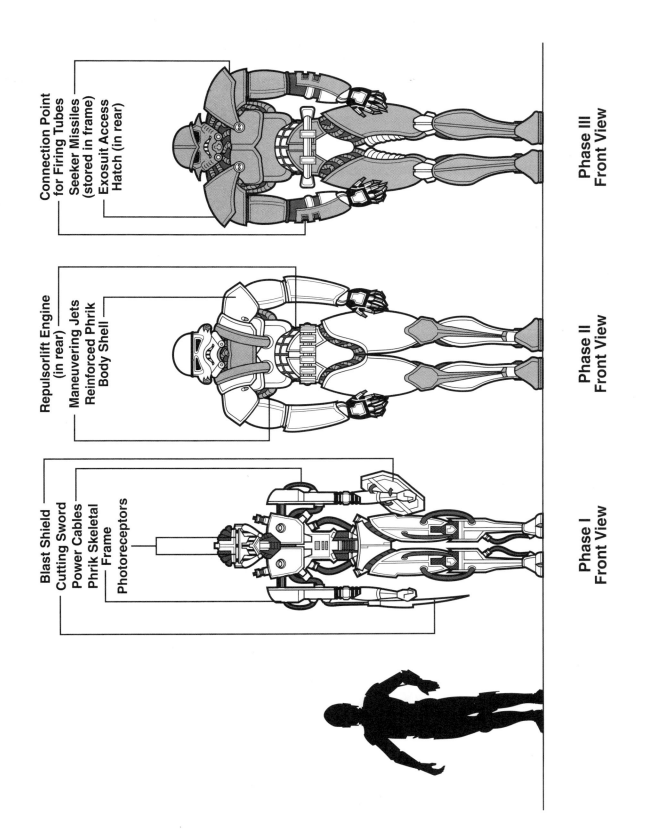

Connection Point for Firing Tubes
Seeker Missiles (stored in frame)
Exosuit Access Hatch (in rear)

Phase III
Front View

Repulsorlift Engine (in rear)
Maneuvering Jets
Reinforced Phrik Body Shell

Phase II
Front View

Blast Shield
Cutting Sword
Power Cables
Phrik Skeletal Frame
Photoreceptors

Phase I
Front View

SD-9 AND SD-10

Robotic infantry soldiers have been an elusive dream since before the dawn of the Old Republic. Xim the Despot, the Krath, and other violent groups developed armies of mechanized killers, but all were rendered obsolete on the modern battlefield by advanced signal jammers and electronic scramblers. It took the futuristic factories of Balmorra and the malignant intellect of Umak Leth to produce the SD series, the deadliest foot soldiers in history.

Governor Beltane, ruler of Balmorra, green-lighted the Empire's SD project during the waning days of Imperial rule. The first three prototype models packed an impressive offensive punch, but lacked the tactical insight to prioritize and eliminate multiple threats. Balmorran Arms solved this problem with the SD-4 and SD-5, after illegally slicing top-secret programming data from General Mohc's Dark Trooper program. Three successive models incorporated the stolen programming and, with the fall of the Empire, were given limited release throughout the fledgling New Republic, culminating with the SD-9's rollout for use as offensive weapons during Grand Admiral Thrawn's campaign.

The immense SD-9 incorporated laser-reflective armor, ionization shielding, tireless servomotors, and pinpoint targeting sensors. In lieu of hands, the droid's forearms brandished a heavy repeating blaster and an explosive plasma cannon. Governor Beltane boasted to potential investors that a single SD-9 was the equivalent of one hundred fully outfitted infantrymen. This was true, but Beltane failed to mention the droids had a cost to match.

Within months, however, the resurgent Empire subjugated Balmorra once again. All SD-9s were sold to the ground forces of the cloned Emperor Palpatine, and a new designer was assigned to work with the engineers of Balmorran Arms—Umak Leth, creator of the World Devastator. Leth added his brilliance and considerable armament experience to the development of the SD-10.

This latest SD was stronger, tougher, and more intelligent than its predecessor; it also came equipped with a miniature concussion missile launcher and an improved sensor package. But Governor Beltane shrewdly saw the SD-10 as an opportunity for his world to squeeze out from beneath Palpatine's heel. Unknown to Leth or his dark side master, Beltane's crews beefed up the new battle droids with fast-reaction servos, point-of-impact shielding, and experimental self-healing metals. Furthermore, their databanks contained all the warfare tactics programmed into the SD-9s, along with foolproof methods for frustrating and defeating those tactics.

The governor's duplicity paid off when Palpatine's military executor tried to seize direct control of the Balmorran factories. In open combat outside the capital city, Beltane's fresh-from-the-assembly-line SD-10s made bantha hash out of the Empire's outmatched SD-9s. Unfortunately, the grounded automatons fared poorly against aerial attack, as Palpatine's Shadow Droids soon proved.

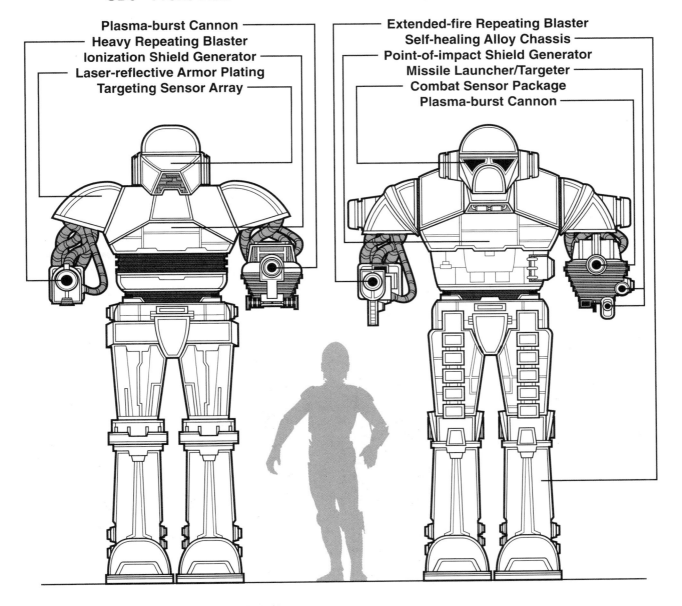

SD9 - Front View

Plasma-burst Cannon
Heavy Repeating Blaster
Ionization Shield Generator
Laser-reflective Armor Plating
Targeting Sensor Array

SD10 - Front View

Extended-fire Repeating Blaster
Self-healing Alloy Chassis
Point-of-impact Shield Generator
Missile Launcher/Targeter
Combat Sensor Package
Plasma-burst Cannon

MILITARY

SHADOW DROID

Malevolent machines piloted by surgically implanted organic brains, Shadow Droids are actually cyborgs rather than true droids. Their biotic nature gives them an additional advantage that automatons can't match—the sleek fighters are armed with the power of the dark side of the Force.

Shadow Droids would never have existed had it not been for Emperor Palpatine's sick experimentations. Following the debacle at Endor, Palpatine's anima inhabited a fresh clone body and set in motion new plans of military conquest. Research into the Shadow Droid project began on the Emperor's throneworld of Byss and soon spread to several think-tanks and manufacturing centers sequestered on hidden worlds throughout the Deep Core.

It is possible that the Shadow Droid concept came about from Palpatine's interest in the life-enslaving technology of the Ssi-ruuk; his offer to buy a shipment of Ssi-ruuvi battle droids is a matter of record. Regardless, chief engineer Umak Leth could not duplicate the reptilian aliens' complicated "entechment" process and instead fell back on the proven success of a direct circuit-to-cerebrum neural link.

To do this, he removed the still-living gray matter from scores of grievously wounded or incapacitated TIE fighter aces. Sustained in a protected cocoon awash with nutrient fluids, the brains were hardwired to external sensors, flight-control and weapons-control systems, and sophisticated tactical computers. The cybernetic hardware stripped the pilots of every remain-

ing shred of humanity, but augmented their reflexes and abilities far beyond anything they would otherwise have known. As a final twisted "gift," Palpatine's clone bestowed upon his creations the limited ability to touch the dark side, making them essentially remote extensions of his own will.

Shadow Droids are distinctive, streamlined constructs capable of keeping pace with an X-wing in space. In atmosphere, they utilize a maneuverable repulsorlift system, but can easily reach supersonic speeds with a short blast from their ion engines. The droids are covered with a glossy black alloy difficult to pinpoint on sensor scans.

Twin wings extend from the sides of the control pod, supporting repeating blasters, ion cannons, and electromagnetic pulse guns. Two additional weapons pylons serve as racks and launchers for proton torpedoes and concussion missiles. Two small dorsal lasers cover the rear field of fire, and a long-range antenna allows the fighters to transmit their dense binary code stream between each other and their command ship. It is unclear how the machines manipulate the Force, but it is likely they use it as a "sixth sense" for identifying potential threats.

Shadow Droids were used by the Empire during the Battle of Balmorra, and in defense of Palpatine's flagship *Eclipse II* near Onderon. The subsequent collapse of Imperial authority means that the knowledge to build such monstrosities has likely been lost forever.

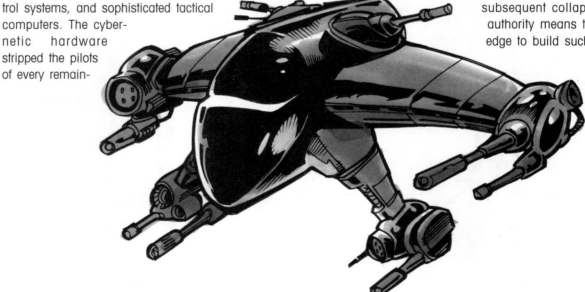

Front View

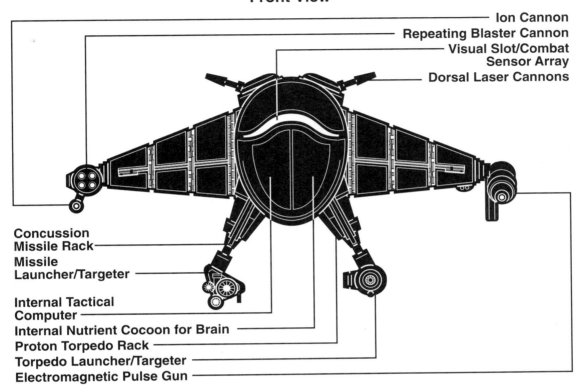

Ion Cannon

Repeating Blaster Cannon

Visual Slot/Combat
Sensor Array

Dorsal Laser Cannons

Concussion
Missile Rack

Missile
Launcher/Targeter

Internal Tactical
Computer

Internal Nutrient Cocoon for Brain

Proton Torpedo Rack

Torpedo Launcher/Targeter

Electromagnetic Pulse Gun

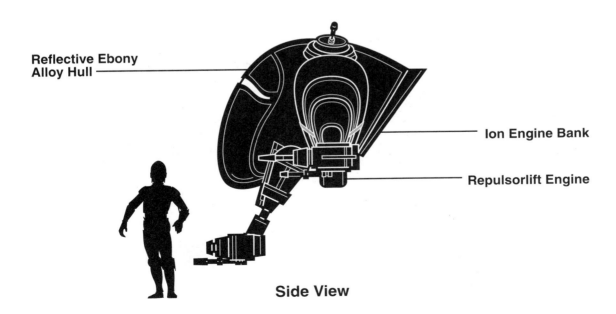

Reflective Ebony
Alloy Hull

Ion Engine Bank

Repulsorlift Engine

Side View

X-1 VIPER ("AUTOMADON")

The X-1 Viper is the size and general shape of a giant Kubindi sun-beetle. All similarities, however, end there. The Viper trades sloth for speed, passivity for belligerence, and feebleness for a lethal arsenal of weaponry.

Unaccountably nicknamed "Automadon" by members of the design team, the Viper was one of the first products Balmorran Arms developed, manufactured, and marketed entirely on its own, without any outside influence from the Empire. Governor Beltane intended to sell the new battle droid to the New Republic army, but the rise of the cloned Emperor Palpatine put a major crimp in his plans.

With his world once again forced to serve the Imperial war machine, Beltane secretly put the finishing touches on the X-1 Viper while his main assembly lines churned out SD-10s for the public eye. When Palpatine's military executor attempted a forcible takeover of all Balmorran operations, Beltane decided the time for a Viper field test had finally arrived.

The Imperials were stunned. Lumbering onto the battlefield, the strange, stocky machines proved more than a match for the Empire's best SD-9s, AT-STs, and Shadow Droids. The Vipers' six-limbed construction allowed them to stand bipedally on their rear legs while hosing down the immediate vicinity with a withering spray of fire. The middle

set of appendages ended with advanced blaster cannons, each packing the knockout punch of a Capital ship turbo-laser; two smaller laser cannons were concealed beneath the chin. The heavy front pincers had the lightning reflexes to snare a low-flying airspeeder, and the tensile strength to maintain their grip while steering the unfortunate craft straight into the ground.

The Vipers' most formidable tool, however, was full-body molecular shielding, an experimental technology that absorbed the energy of a laser blast and shunted it into the power cells of the droids' own weapons systems.

The Balmorran skirmish ended with a negotiated peace, but Beltane secretly allowed the New Republic to hijack a new shipment of X-1 Vipers. Since the droids were designed for supervised combat—and thus had manual override controls in their heads—a strike team headed by Lando Calrissian and Wedge Antilles stowed away inside their cramped innards during their transport to Byss.

Once there, the commandos commandeered their rides and steered the unstoppable Vipers right up to the gates of the Imperial Citadel. But when confronted by Palpatine's grotesque chrysalis beasts, General Calrissian came to a sobering realization—fancy molecular shields were useless against primitive claws, fangs, and muscle.

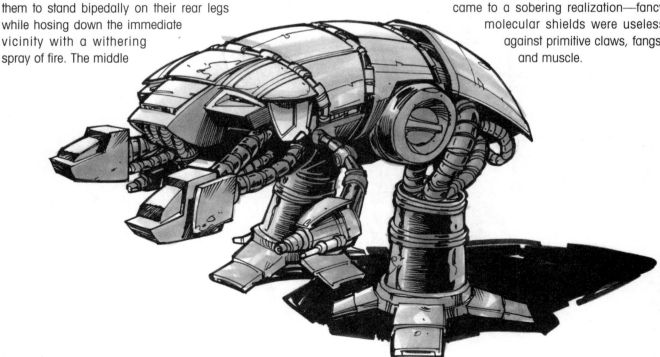

Front View

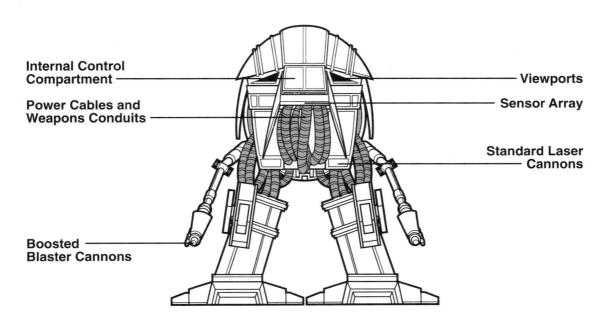

Internal Control
Compartment

Viewports

Power Cables and
Weapons Conduits

Sensor Array

Standard Laser
Cannons

Boosted
Blaster Cannons

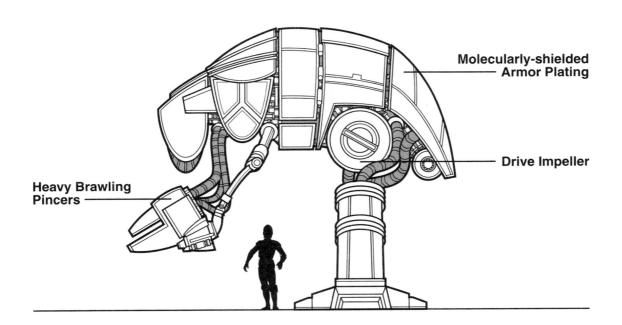

Molecularly-shielded
Armor Plating

Drive Impeller

Heavy Brawling
Pincers

Side View

ARAKYD PROBOT SERIES

War is good for business. That old aphorism could very well be Arakyd Industries' corporate slogan, for the company grew fat and happy off a string of lucrative Imperial contracts. The evolution of their successful probot series is a perfect example of how to tailor a product to suit changing political climates.

The earliest probe droids, during the days of the Old Republic, were designed to chart new hyperlanes and map undiscovered planets. But after the rise of Emperor Palpatine, benign exploration was an unneeded luxury. Arakyd swiftly beefed up their probots' sensors and stealth programming, and marketed the units—as Arakyd Vipers—to the Imperial Navy as mechanical spies for ferreting out Rebel bases.

The redesign was a hit, and Lord Darth Vader personally commissioned an enhanced version of the Viper to be built on the factory world Mechis III. It is rumored that the rogue assassin droid IG-88 was involved in their programming, but this remains unconfirmed.

As the Rebellion intensified, the Empire's needs shifted from espionage to security and pacification. The Hunter-Killer probot was an ambitious corporate gamble that paid off handsomely.

H-K probots are true behemoths. At 150 meters, they are among the largest combat droids in existence. Primarily used for customs inspections, blockade enforcement, and pursuit and detainment opera-

tions, they have been known to make smuggling ships break and run by their mere presence.

The H-K operates best in deep space, though it can still function in atmosphere with slightly reduced speed and maneuverability. Like its smaller cousins, it possesses a bulbous insectile head and an array of dangling manipulator arms. Its internal program banks are loaded with over 11,000 planetary and national registries so it can quickly identify transponder forgeries. It also boasts powerful scanners that can penetrate thick hulls and energy shields, and has several high-beam searchlights.

If a ship fails the initial scan, it is pulled into the H-K's belly with a powerful tractor beam. This internal security chamber measures thirty meters square by ten meters tall and can accommodate a stock light freighter. If the vessel foolishly decides to flee, the H-K can deliver a withering barrage from two quad blasters and a pair of ion cannons.

A large number of Hunter-Killer probots were stationed on and around the planet Byss, site of the cloned Emperor Palpatine's triumphant return. A potentially devastating flaw in the design was revealed when a smuggler, dragged inside an H-K's holding compartment, broke into the primary circuitry and hijacked the droid to cover his own escape.

Front View

Side View

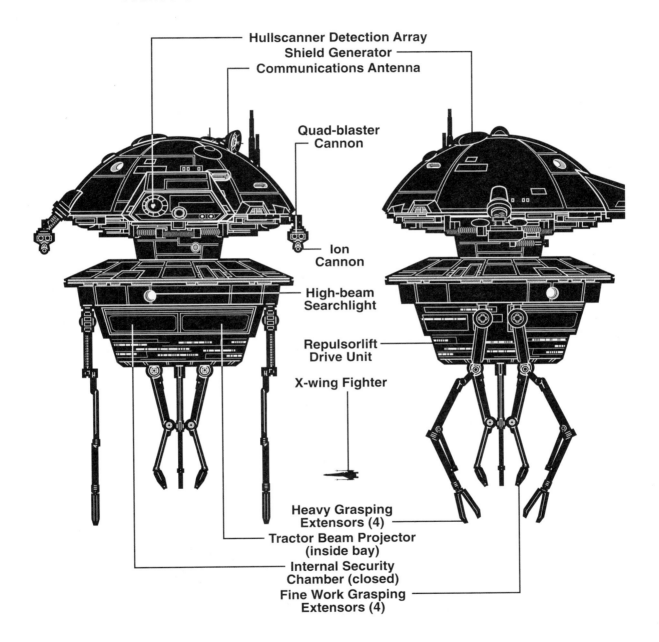

Hullscanner Detection Array

Shield Generator

Communications Antenna

Quad-blaster
Cannon

Ion
Cannon

High-beam
Searchlight

Repulsorlift
Drive Unit

X-wing Fighter

Heavy Grasping
Extensors (4)

Tractor Beam Projector
(inside bay)

Internal Security
Chamber (closed)

Fine Work Grasping
Extensors (4)

FROMM TOWER DROID

The Tower Droid was a product of Tig Fromm's genius, created by the youthful designer years before the Battle of Yavin. They were churned out by the hundreds at his secret base on the stark planet of Ingo.

Tig Fromm, son of the notorious gangster Sise Fromm, believed droids and other mechanicals were superior to organic beings because of their greater loyalty, durability, and firepower. His most ambitious creation was the mammoth weapons satellite *Trigon One,* but the Tower Droid was an early success on a much smaller scale.

The droid is symmetrical fore and aft. Standing four meters tall, it moves about on six oversized pneumatic wheels. The tires are puncture resistant, with a self-sealing mechanism, and allow the droid to easily cross most types of open terrain. On a flat stretch, the Tower Droid can reach a maximum speed of one hundred kilometers per hour.

A squat, armor-plated chassis houses the vulnerable engine and drivetrain, and provides a foundation for the tower assembly. The cylindrical tower is capped by a saucer-shaped head, which is able to rotate 360 degrees. The rim of the head is dotted with a variety of detection devices, including visual, auditory, infrared, electromagnetic, and seismic sensors. A broadband antenna relays

guidance data to its seeker drones and receives orders from a central command post.

The primary cognitive module is stashed inside the red-and-gray tower cylinder, between twin firing racks of repulsor balls. The droids' intelligence is unremarkable and their personality programming nonexistent, but they perform admirably as perimeter sentries.

When a Tower Droid identifies a hostile target, it releases an obsidian repulsor ball from beneath one of two sliding chest panels. The antigravity spheres are small, maneuverable, and much faster than their "parent"—they can outrace a fleeing vehicle at speeds exceeding two hundred fifty kilometers per hour. When they close to within one meter of their target, they explode with devastating force. Up to five spheres can be remote piloted by a Tower Droid at one time.

After a large number of his Tower Droids were destroyed during a prisoner rescue—in which the famous droid duo R2-D2 and C-3PO participated— Tig Fromm briefly stepped up production to cover the losses. There were 431 operational Tower Droids on Ingo when Tig and Sise Fromm were captured by the bounty hunter Boba Fett. Rival gangsters seized the operation, and the Tower Droids have since found their way into the hands of revolutionaries, arms dealers, and private collectors.

Front View

Visual Sensor

Radionic Sensor

Infrared Sensor

Seismic Sensor

Repulsor Ball Release Hatches

Self-sealing Pneumatic Tires

Side View

Auditory Sensor

Broadband Antenna/Receiver

Electromagnetic Sensor

Tower Assembly

Laser Cannons

Armored Chassis

Drivetrain

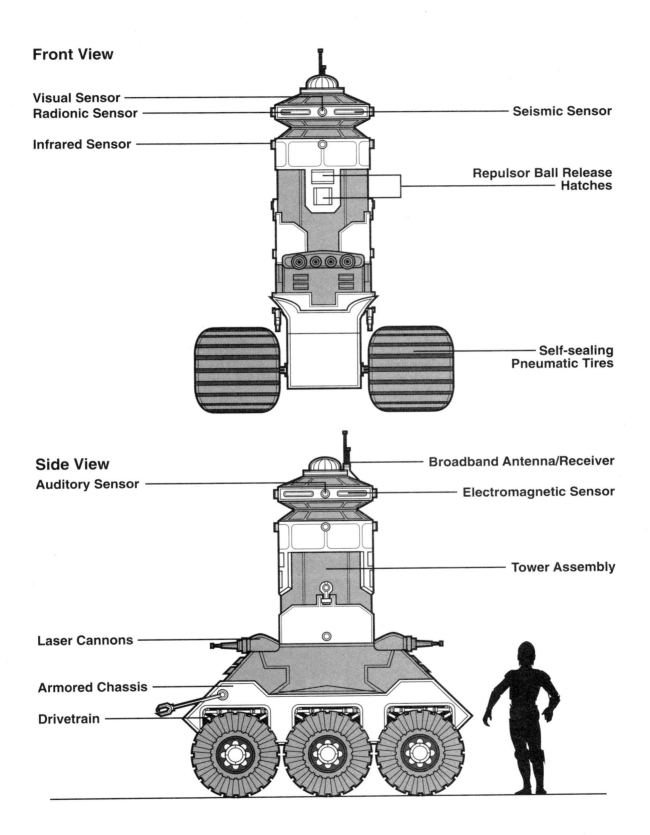

MILITARY
ROBOT RAMSHIP

Ramships are a deceptive, dishonorable, and flagrantly destructive innovation in the annals of space warfare. But they are still used by outlaw armadas for one simple reason—when they work, they are spectacular weapons.

No droid manufacturer produces robot ramships, and you won't find them advertised in the business section of the newsnets. Rather, the automated vessels are assembled by the Outer Rim's shadiest outlaw-techs with the shell of a junked warship—often a Corellian Engineering Corporation design—and the brain of a suicidal pilot droid. The resulting gestalt is smart enough to put up a convincing fight and crazed enough to ram its opponent at the first opportunity—predictably destroying itself, as well.

The droid brains are quite similar to those installed in drone barges. The two key differences are the ramship's extensive database of military tactics and its complete lack of self-preservation safeties. Due to the sobering nature of ramship missions, the vessels are never staffed by an organic crew.

The outer hull conceals a dense interior packed from stem to stern with solid durasteel. This gives the ramship an incredible mass and makes it difficult to maneuver. But when the ship impacts against an enemy hull, the released kinetic energy vaporizes all but the largest vessels in a rippling multimegaton blast.

Arrayed along the exterior are dozens of painted-on portholes and underpowered lasers, giving the ramship the deceitful appearance of a typical "ship of the line." When the droid decides it is in attack position, it fires its high-boost engine and accelerates to ramming speed. Since the vessel's thick hull can absorb even the most sustained blaster volleys, all a targeted ship can do is initiate evasive maneuvers and hope for the best.

Robot ramships were used to great effect during the Battle of Centerpoint Station, the final conflict of the Corellian crisis. The Sacorrian Triad deployed a fleet that included four bulbous-nosed frigates guided by unstable droid intellects. When battle with the New Republic was joined, the quartet of ramships zeroed in on the Bakuran flagship *Intruder* from disparate vectors.

The *Intruder* opened fire on its attackers and attempted to shake them without success. It wasn't until Admiral Ossilege realized the enemy laser barrage was merely a diversionary light show that the aggressors' true nature became known. By then, it was too late.

The lead ramship punctured the *Intruder* just forward of her bridge; the second and third followed suit. The fourth ramship missed its target and, engines spent, could not swing around for another pass.

The *Intruder*, however, was already dead. While her crew evacuated, Ossilege and Gaeriel Captison triggered the cruiser's self-destruct, consuming the final ramship and ripping a devastating hole through the heart of the Triad armada.

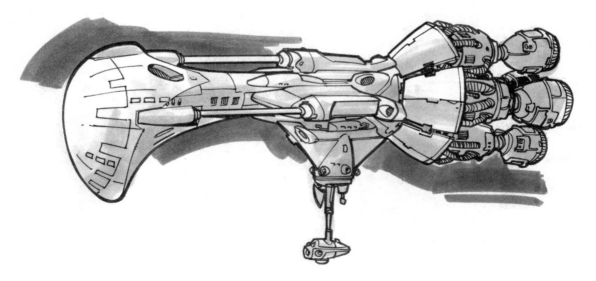

Top View

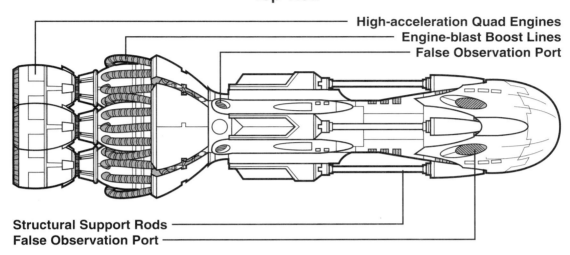

High-acceleration Quad Engines
Engine-blast Boost Lines
False Observation Port

Structural Support Rods
False Observation Port

Solid Durasteel in Nose
Droid Brain in Vessel's Computer Core
Diversionary Laser Cannons
Durasteel Ballast Beneath Hull

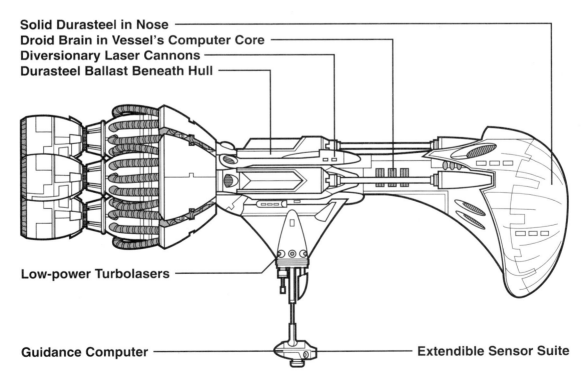

Low-power Turbolasers

Guidance Computer

Extendible Sensor Suite

Side View

ASSASSINS
IG ASSASSIN DROID

The IG assassin droid is the most coldly efficient killing machine ever invented. Its programmers, smugly assuming they could control their creation, gave it unprecedented creativity and intelligence. They paid for their arrogance with their lives.

Project Phlutdroid was a top-secret undertaking financed by Imperial Supervisor Gurdun in the laboratories of Holowan Mechanicals. Chief Technician Loruss developed a team of mechanical annihilators, the IG series, with the intention of squashing the rising Rebellion. She also approved the use of experimental, autonomous combat programming. Five prototypes were completed.

Roughly humanoid in shape, each IG's blaster-resistant armored frame stood two meters tall. A cylindrical head, studded with glowing red sensors, allowed the unit to see in all directions at once. The droid lacked olfactory detectors, but compensated with advanced auditory, radionic, movement, and temperature sensors. Its multiple optic lenses could access a wide variety of spectral filters under hazy or low-light conditions.

The IG's weapons complement was astounding, especially when one realized that the entire arsenal was integrated directly, and unobtrusively, into the standard body structure. Each forearm contained a repeating blaster cannon. A concussion grenade launcher was built into the left hip. And behind various panels and ports lurked a flamethrower, a sonic stunner, a paralysis cord, an array of throwing flechettes, and a rack of poison gas canisters.

The fingers of the right hand doubled as miniature cutting lasers. The mirrored palm of the left hand was capable of intercepting blaster bolts and deflecting them back along their original path. The IG could also dramatically raise the temperature of its exterior plating, allowing it to burn through nets or melt a stream of immobilizing Stokhli spray.

When Loruss's experimental sentience programming was downloaded into one of the finished automatons, the code unexpectedly self-replicated at blinding speed. Within seconds, the droid came on-line, identified the technicians in the room as threats, and eliminated every one of them in novel and bloody ways. This unit, IG-88A, then copied his consciousness into three duplicates designated B, C, and D. The final IG prototype, IG-72, struck off on his own.

The four IG-88s participated in a number of bounty-hunting assignments, including run-ins with Artoo-Detoo and See-Threepio on Hosk and Tammuz-an. They also systematically exterminated every surviving planner of the IG series to ensure no one could exploit their design flaws. Most of the droids were believed destroyed prior to the Battle of Endor, but at least one of their body shells was discovered on Mechis III years later and reprogrammed as a bodyguard by the wealthy Thul family. It is unknown whether Holowan Mechanicals produced any other IG assassins or if a rival company has managed to duplicate the blueprints.

Front View

Rear View

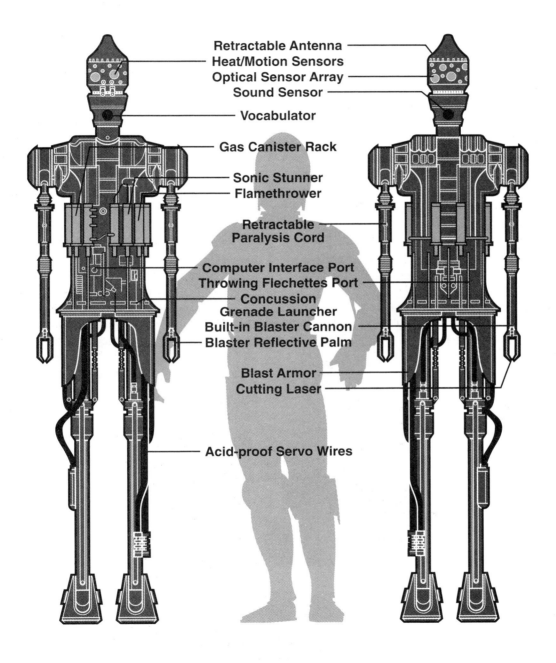

Retractable Antenna
Heat/Motion Sensors
Optical Sensor Array
Sound Sensor

Vocabulator

Gas Canister Rack

Sonic Stunner
Flamethrower

Retractable
Paralysis Cord

Computer Interface Port
Throwing Flechettes Port
Concussion
Grenade Launcher
Built-in Blaster Cannon
Blaster Reflective Palm

Blast Armor
Cutting Laser

Acid-proof Servo Wires

ASSASSINS

E522 ASSASSIN DROID

The Empire outlawed assassin droids after a notorious incident in which a rogue robot on Caprioril massacred over twenty thousand swoop-racing spectators to ensure the death of just *one* of the onlookers, Governor Amel Bakli. This official decree, however, did nothing to prevent the Empire from constructing their own top-secret assassins. In fact, it merely eliminated all the competing manufacturers.

Sienar Intelligence Systems accepted an Imperial commission to design and build the E522, a weapons-laden executioner intended to permanently silence the Emperor's earliest and most vocal critics. During the formative years of Palpatine's New Order a classified number of E522s lurked in the galaxy's shadows, furtively tracking their targets for weeks or months before finally dispatching them in bright bursts of blaster fire.

The E522 isn't particularly tall, but its hulking upper body makes it look like a cyber-augmented weightlifter. Within the core, protected by heavy armor, lies an internal power plant that provides firm strength to the limbs and limber quickness to the joints. The narrow waist supports the entire bulk of the massive torso and is under tremendous stress. It is thus the most vulnerable part of the body—nevertheless, the chance of disabling the droid with a hit in this area is negligible.

The droid's flat head provides a minimal target profile; it also contains a sensor

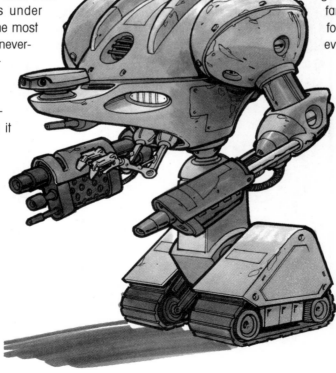

package that excels at picking up residual heat signatures. Two spotlights are located on either side of the head—these lights are used to blind and disorient targets, preventing them from mounting last-ditch defensive attacks. Manipulator arms fold up within a small belly cavity. Thick tank treads provide mobility and are capable of a top speed of thirty kilometers per hour.

Weapons on the E522 are formidable. The right arm consists of a multifunction apparatus that incorporates a heavy repeating blaster, a neurological needler, and an ion device for disabling personal shielding fields. The left arm ends in a cannon that fires explosive hunter-seeker projectiles. External power cells are necessary to keep the powerful weapons charged at all times.

Jabba the Hutt once owned an E522, though he seldom assigned the droid hit jobs. Instead, he grew bored one afternoon and ordered Eefive-Tootoo to be slathered with dripping meat juice and thrown to the rancor. The bloodthirsty beast eventually spat out the indigestible lump of metal, but the fang-chewed Eefive was fit only for the scrap heap. There, however, the droid was repaired by Jawas and sold to Jabba's crosstown rival Lady Valarian. The female crime boss put the reprogrammed assassin to work as a courier and delivery boy.

Front View

Side View

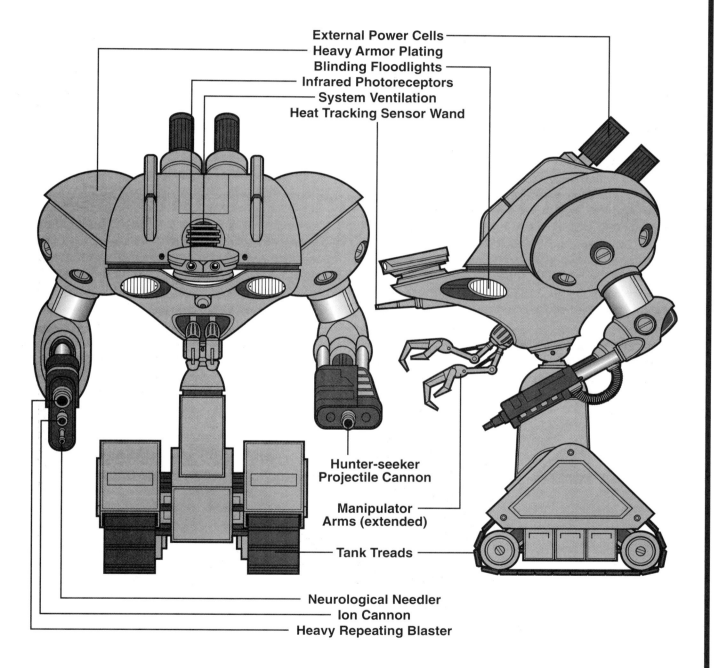

External Power Cells
Heavy Armor Plating
Blinding Floodlights
Infrared Photoreceptors
System Ventilation
Heat Tracking Sensor Wand

Hunter-seeker
Projectile Cannon

Manipulator
Arms (extended)

Tank Treads

Neurological Needler
Ion Cannon
Heavy Repeating Blaster

ASSASSINS
SCARAB DROID

Professional assassins know that stealth can be just as potent a weapon as a dart shooter or a sniper rifle. This was the simple principle behind scarab droids.

Tiny, quiet, and unobtrusive, the insectile destroyers can locate and terminate a slumbering target without the victim ever stirring from a peaceful afternoon nap. Most household security systems aren't focused enough to detect the minuscule killers, and when they do, they are often misidentified as harmless garden beetles.

Only in the last few decades has electronic miniaturization progressed to levels where scarab droids were practical. Since the covert assassins were also highly *illegal*, Sienar Intelligence Systems furtively developed them in their top-secret Black Ops laboratories. When perfected, the entire line was sold under-the-table to the assassination branch of Imperial Intelligence. Many "enemies of the Empire" soon felt the sharp sting of their needle fangs . . . and very little after that.

All scarab droids can fit comfortably in the palm of one hand. Collectively, there were eighteen varieties of scarab, each with a different configuration of weapons and appendages. The later generations, in particular, tended to be gruesomely nasty, sporting spines, claws, and flesh-eating shredders. The simpler Scarab Mark VI posted the best kill ratio and was the most widely produced of the various models.

Each Mark VI possesses a

compact body, six jointed legs, and a hard head tipped with poison injectors. These piercing fangs connect to a small internal reservoir filled with fast-acting nerve toxins or hallucinogenic stimulants. In a notorious incident on Coruscant, one of Emperor Palpatine's senatorial critics abruptly appeared on the roof of the Imperial Bank and shrieked that he was being chased by a flame-eyed, snake-tongued Rodian batwing. He then plunged two hundred and seventy stories to his death. The newsnets called it stress; those in the know recognized scarab-induced dementia.

Scarabs have specialized sensors to aid in locating their quarry. High-gain photoreceptors are keyed to work efficiently under dim lighting conditions. Heat detectors, pheromone sniffers, and biorhythm analyzers ensure that the droids make a positive ID on their quarry before beginning their evil work. In human subjects, the prime target area is the soft neck skin just above the carotid artery.

For maximum secrecy, a single scarab works best. But a swarm of scarabs has its advantages in case something goes wrong—even a fully alert subject will find it difficult to exterminate a dozen or more of the skittering beetles without suffering a fatal bite. The cloned Emperor sent a horde of scarab droids to murder Luke Skywalker in his quarters on New Alderaan; only Luke's strength in the Force and the healing powers of Vima-Da-Boda saved the Jedi Master from certain death.

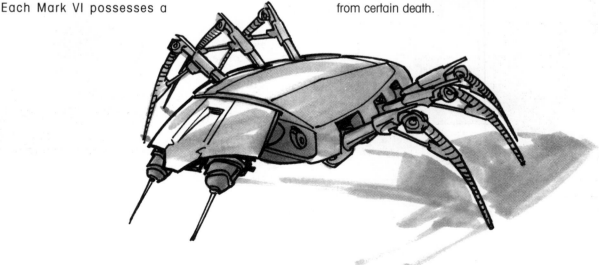

Front View

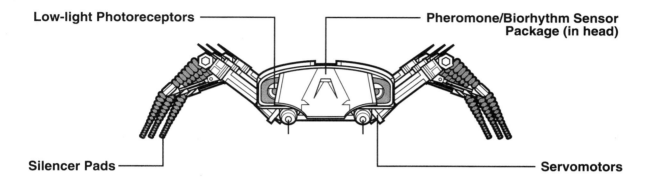

Low-light Photoreceptors

Pheromone/Biorhythm Sensor Package (in head)

Silencer Pads

Servomotors

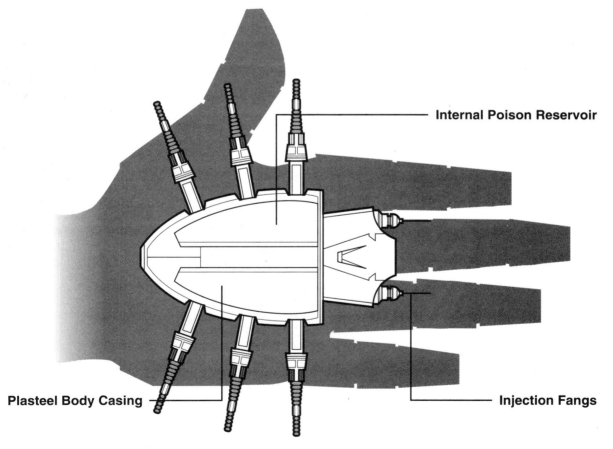

Internal Poison Reservoir

Plasteel Body Casing

Injection Fangs

Top View

ASSASSINS
DZ-70 FUGITIVE TRACKER DROID

"DO NOT ATTEMPT ESCAPE. MUTINEERS AND EVADERS WILL BE CONSIDERED IN VIOLATION OF THE CAPITAL POWERS ACT." That chilling pronouncement, delivered in a flat, metallic monotone, accosted those who rejected mandatory service on the Imperial battlemoon *Eye of Palpatine*. Reluctant recruits could be stunned and hauled away with electronic ease, for the speakers were Arakyd Industries' DZ-70 Fugitive Tracker Droids.

Trackers aren't limited to the Imperial military by any means. Corporations love a great concept and consumers love a great design. Hundreds of different tracker droid types are available on the industrial exchange and the black market, from top-notch DZ-70s to outlaw-tech chop jobs.

All of them, however, have one thing in common: a single-minded droid brain that will not rest until it has hunted down its designated target. Trackers are superior to the smaller seeker balls in nearly every way except price. Their programming is more complex, their range is greater, and their accessories are more lethal.

The DZ-70 is an outstanding model that has stood the test of time. Swollen spheres, with a glossy, blaster-reflective silver finish, the droids hover above the ground on maneuverable repulsorlifts. High-gain photoreceptors are located near the sphere's equator, evenly spaced around the body so the droid can look in all directions at once. Custom irised apertures allow the eyes to widen and contract.

Beneath the droid, dangling like the tentacles of an Arkanian jellyfish, hang a number of pincers, sensor wands, and weapons emplacements. Thanks to the powerful repulsor engine, the DZ-70 can haul an unconscious—or dead—human several kilometers to a pickup area with its largest grasper arm. It takes several DZ-70s working in concert to budge heavier quarries such as Wookiees.

The DZ-70's stun blaster and laser cannon protrude from its underbelly and can track and fire in any direction. Under Imperial law, it is a felony for civilians to own a lethally modified tracker, but this fact is routinely ignored in frontier territories like the Outer Rim.

The primary circuit matrix of the DZ-70 is sophisticated, but not at all versatile—it does one thing only, and it does it well. The droid can be programmed with its target's appearance, mass, body temperature, heart rate, and movement patterns, and its sensors can detect these parameters even in a public stadium or crowded commutube.

Unfortunately, the DZ-70 is maintenance-intensive. Its delicate detection equipment requires constant cleaning and realignment, with a complete diagnostic overhaul every twelve to fifteen months. The trackers stored aboard the *Eye of Palpatine* had gone nearly thirty *years* without repair checks and were no longer capable of making metabolic distinctions. Consequently, while searching for brigades of long-vanished stormtroopers, the droids hauled aboard everything from furious Gamorreans to timorous Jawas to befuddled Talz.

Arms (folded)
Front View

Arms (extended)
Side View

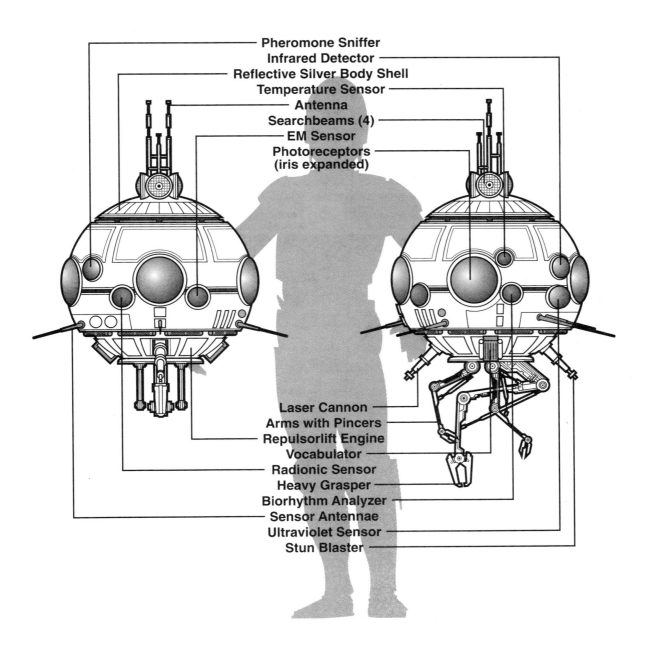

Pheromone Sniffer
Infrared Detector
Reflective Silver Body Shell
Temperature Sensor
Antenna
Searchbeams (4)
EM Sensor
Photoreceptors
(iris expanded)

Laser Cannon
Arms with Pincers
Repulsorlift Engine
Vocabulator
Radionic Sensor
Heavy Grasper
Biorhythm Analyzer
Sensor Antennae
Ultraviolet Sensor
Stun Blaster

TRAINING/GLADIATORIAL

RHTC-560 HUNTER TRAINER

Rodians are the best bounty hunters in the galaxy—the ill-fated Greedo being a notable exception—and they didn't become so by remaining idle. Their D-Tec RHTC-560 is the culmination of years of research, providing the perfect target for turning callow hopefuls into tough, seasoned trackers.

The RHTC-560 system consists of one master control unit and several hunter trainer drones. The controller is sometimes used as a target itself, but more frequently it remains stationary while remote piloting its drones through the thick jungle undergrowth. It can command up to ten HT drones in this fashion and is programmed with the most advanced stealth and evasion techniques available.

Humanoid in shape, the master control unit looks like a bizarre cross between a Rodian and an armor-plated arachnid. Wicked claws protrude from the hands and feet. Its speed and agility make the droid difficult to subdue, as many surprised Rodians will attest after their first encounter with one.

Standard equipment on the controller unit includes a vocabulator, a wideband transceiver, and a sophisticated sensor array. A scomp-link access port allows the droid to download visual recordings from its drones and replay the data at post-hunt debriefings. A popular add-on package includes twin forearm-mounted stun blasters.

The HT drones are small and compact, moving about on either legs or an antigravity repulsor unit, depending on the difficulty of the hunt program. The drones do not possess independent brains and are incapable of making decisions without the guidance of the control unit. Their effective range is approximately fifty kilometers.

Each drone is equipped with two retractable manipulator arms, a high-intensity searchlight, and a stun blaster. The Rodian Grand Protector Navik the Red is rumored to have an RHTC-560 system whose drones are fitted with lethal disruptor cannons. Navik purportedly unleashes the system on captured prisoners for his own sadistic amusement.

What sets the system apart from previous hunter trainers is the versatility and adaptability of its programming. It responds to threats in novel ways, from taking cover beneath the surface of a river—the controller is fully submersible—to using its drones to flush wild game as a startling distraction. This creativity subroutine is disabled during low-difficulty simulations.

The RHTC-560 is just beginning to be sold widely off of Rodia. A new controller unit will cost around 5,500 credits, with an additional 2,000 credits per HT drone. Bounty-hunting guilds have been snapping them up, and a handful of sales have even been made to planetary militias and police academies.

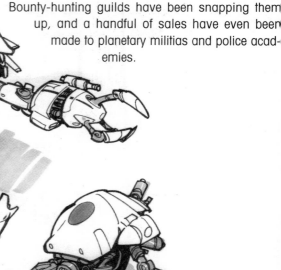

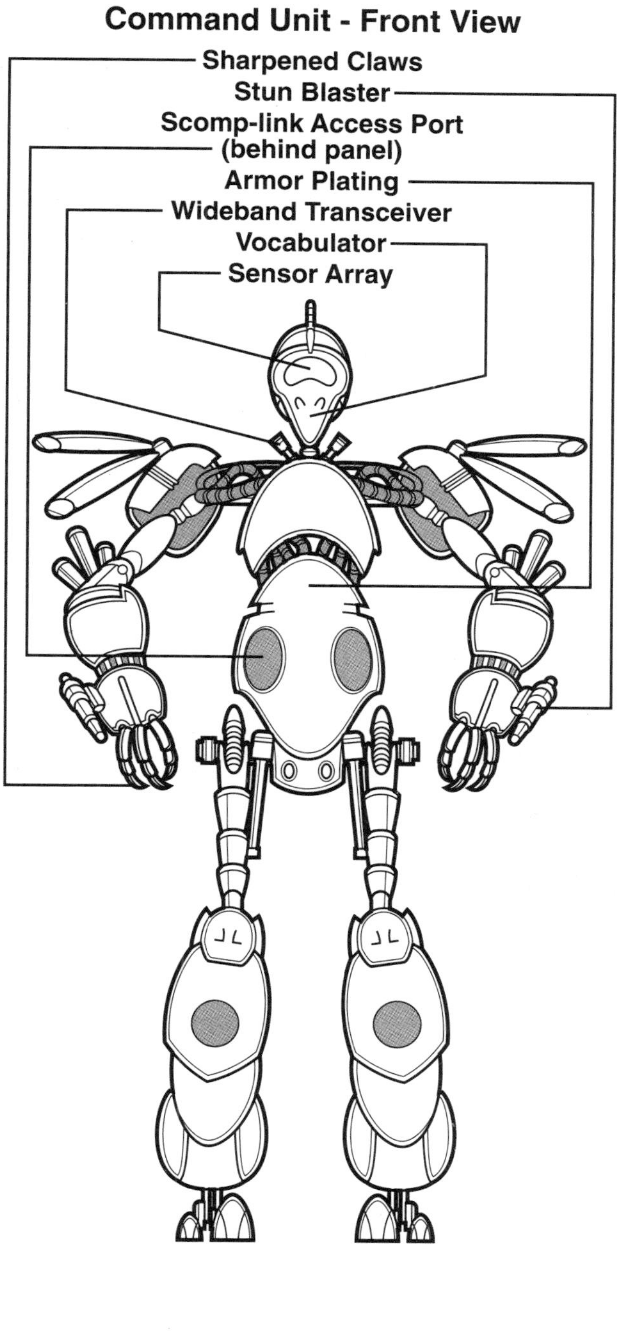

Command Unit - Front View

Sharpened Claws
Stun Blaster
Scomp-link Access Port
(behind panel)
Armor Plating
Wideband Transceiver
Vocabulator
Sensor Array

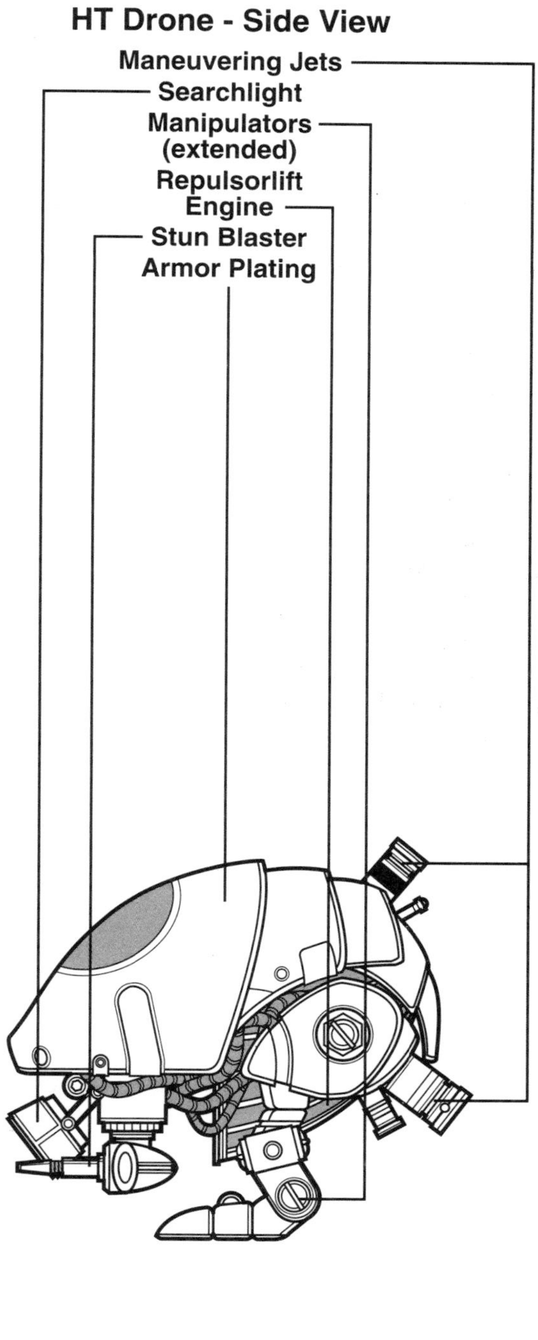

HT Drone - Side View

Maneuvering Jets
Searchlight
Manipulators
(extended)
Repulsorlift
Engine
Stun Blaster
Armor Plating

DUELIST ELITE

Droids make excellent trainers. They can reproduce a technique precisely, perform it endlessly, and slow their speed and reaction time to suit even the most inept beginner. A dueling droid can be a great asset for a practicing warrior. It can also be quite deadly. Let the buyer beware—literally.

Trang Robotics is the largest player in an exclusive and patrician market. The company's Duelist Elite has served as the preeminent trainer for a generation of promising fencers, and few competitors have come close to duplicating its limber grace, lightning parry, and unerring lunge.

The torso resembles the body shell of a Too-Onebee surgical unit, but the Duelist's limbs are longer and more durable. Swiveling socket joints allow for a wide range of movement, and a sensitive internal gyroscope gives the droid a superior sense of balance. A red scoring circle on the torso triggers a loud beep when touched by the tip of a blade; in low-difficulty scenarios, a hit in this area causes the droid to switch off.

Each hand consists of several gripper fingers curled around a small connection port. Sword hilts are fitted directly into this socket. Every Duelist comes packaged with three flexisteel rapiers—saber, foil, and epée—to suit the classic fighting styles. With a little work, the unit can be modified to wield a vibro-shiv, a force pike, or even a lightsaber.

The Duelist's head contains a high-speed optic visor. Wires sprouting from each auditory pickup extend behind the droid in twin arcs and plug into an induction spur protruding from the lower back. These filaments allow the automaton to generate a low-level electromagnetic field within a two-meter radius, greatly boosting its sensory abilities at close quarters. A backpack of voltage generators powers the induction spur and the Duelist's own internal systems—an archaic method, but it is part of the droid's singular charm.

A highly advanced cognitive matrix permits the droid to learn idiosyncrasies in its adversaries' fighting styles and exploit them. A Duelist equipped with an edged blade and set on "expert level" is quite capable of lethally skewering its opponent. Master fencers such as the space pirate Raskar relish the thrill offered by this no-holds-barred swordplay.

Trang's Duelist Elites are exclusive and expensive—no more than four thousand are hand-crafted each year at a cost of 275,000 credits apiece. Aristocrats consider them to be works of art and family heirlooms. Darth Vader owned several of the droids, but since his hack-and-slash lightsaber drills would have reduced them to neat metal chunks, his standard challengers were modified Asps.

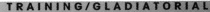

Front View

Rear View

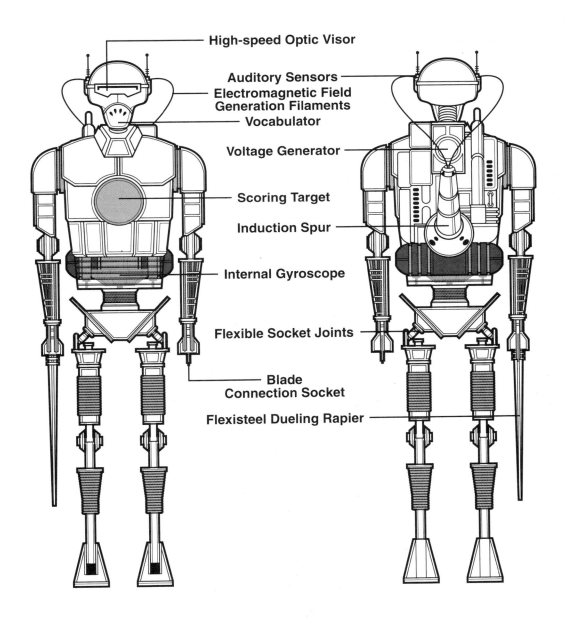

High-speed Optic Visor

Auditory Sensors

Electromagnetic Field
Generation Filaments

Vocabulator

Voltage Generator

Scoring Target

Induction Spur

Internal Gyroscope

Flexible Socket Joints

Blade
Connection Socket

Flexisteel Dueling Rapier

TRAINING/GLADIATORIAL

MARK X EXECUTIONER

The favorite spectator sport of bored dictators and their decadent subjects, gladiatorial combat is the oldest and bloodiest of games. Just one thing spoiled the enjoyment of the fans who packed those ancient arenas—their favorite champions had the unfortunate habit of *dying*.

Robotic combatants changed all that. Although gore hounds and self-professed purists hated them, gladiator droids could wield nastier weapons and take substantially more damage than their organic counterparts. Even a droid that had been sawed in half with a vibro-ax could often be repaired and ready for more action within a few days.

Gladiatorial technology was largely an offshoot of military science. But while army droids were straightforward and practical, arena droids had to be *entertaining* victors. Consequently, nearly every small-scale weapon—particularly those that required physical contact of the slashing, burning, or pummeling kind—was packed into a durable armored chassis. Adding to the spectacle, the droids' programming required them to switch between their varied instruments of death as the combat situation dictated.

Arakyd Industries' Mark X Executioner is not the largest, cheapest, or most common gladiator droid. It is, however, the best. Thirty-five thousand credits buys a reinforced durasteel destroyer with enough arms to shame an Aquaris demonsquid. Each retractable append-age is fitted with a lethal and often messy gadget. Standard weaponry includes a neuronic whip, vibro-ax, vibro-saw, blaster rifle, missile launcher, flame projector, force pike, sonic cannon, flechette canister, and a primitive, but effective, spiked club.

All that equipment, combined with the Mark X's heavy armor, dictates a wide dual-tread drive system for moving the massive unit around the playing field. The small underside patch lying between the treads is the only area on the droid's body that lacks armor—inventive opponents can sometimes exploit this vulnerability by diving between the rollers and tearing at the external cooling circuitry.

Most foes, however, never get the chance. In formal competitions, the Mark X's lethal skills are so respected that it is often barred from battling anything less than another Marx X. Some psychotic warrior fraternities use the droids as sparring partners, while crime bosses such as Bwahl the Hutt employ them as an offbeat way to execute employees who have disappointed them.

The late Mirkovig Hirken, former viceprex in the Corporate Sector Authority and ex-administrator of the Stars' End penal facility, was a noted connoisseur of gladiator droids. He kept one Marx X Executioner—his pride and joy—in a private dueling amphitheater on Mytus VII and frequently pitted it against outmatched mechanical opponents.

Front View

Right Arm - Side View

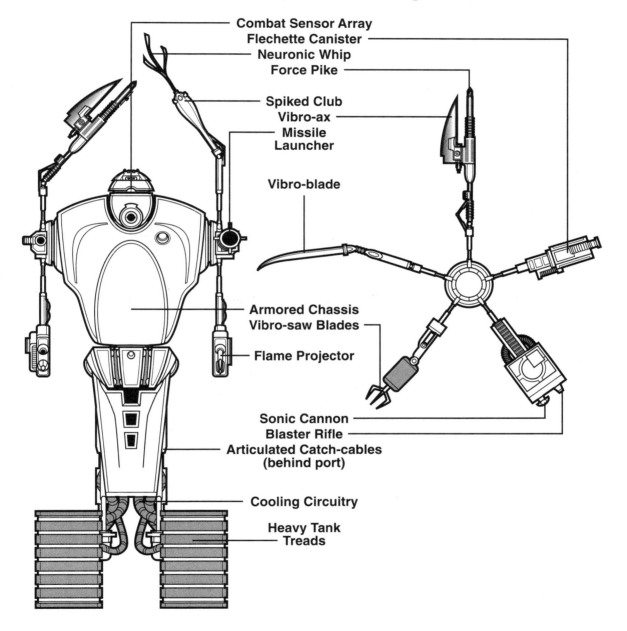

Combat Sensor Array
Flechette Canister
Neuronic Whip
Force Pike

Spiked Club
Vibro-ax
Missile
Launcher

Vibro-blade

Armored Chassis
Vibro-saw Blades

Flame Projector

Sonic Cannon
Blaster Rifle
Articulated Catch-cables
(behind port)

Cooling Circuitry

Heavy Tank
Treads

RED TERROR

Based on a gladiatorial design from Ulban Arms, the five hundred members of the Red Terror compose an intimidating automated police force patrolling the factory moon of Telti. Any droids that don't abide by the Red Terror's stringent behavioral bylaws are circuit-purged, ripped to pieces, and randomly scattered so they can never again be reassembled. As far as Telti's meek robotic population is concerned, the crimson-armored bullies have earned their frightful nickname several times over.

Beneath the scarlet paint each member of the Red Terror is recognizable as an Ulban Arms Warden 10-24, a droid model conceived while Ulban was still a division of LeisureMech Enterprises. Because of its parent company's entertainment focus, Ulban positioned the Warden 10-24 as a gladiator unit, but fully intended it to be used in a security and bodyguard capacity. Serious production difficulties delayed the release of the Warden until nearly six years after the Battle of Endor.

Ulban Arms utilized the assembly plants of Telti to produce their new droid. When the Force-sensitive human Brakiss assumed control of the factory moon, he was struck by the menacing lethality of the Warden 10-24 and requested five hundred of the units from Ulban for his own security needs.

The droids have thick, powerful limbs and a protected cranium; even at rest they exhibit a hunched, threat-

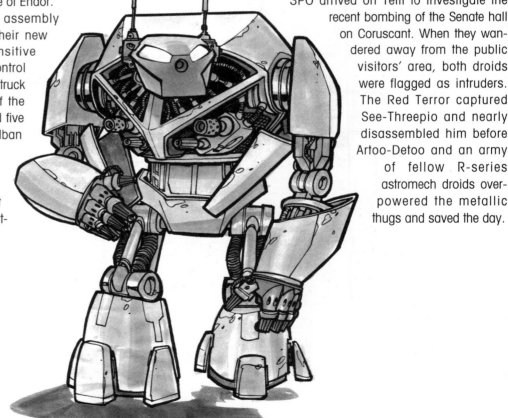

ening stance. The fingers on each bulky hand are thinly disguised blasters, while two double laser cannons are hidden beneath a set of swinging chest panels. A set of broadband antennae allow the droids to receive orders and transmit hypersonic signals to one another when working as a team.

Brakiss made several nonstandard modifications to his elite security force in addition to the bright cosmetic coating. He divided them into ten troops of fifty and gave each group the responsibility of maintaining order in a particular zone on Telti. One droid of each fifty was designated a "lieutenant," and the remaining forty-nine had portions of their cognitive circuitry removed to make them more willing to take orders. All five hundred units were issued handheld electronic scramblers for zapping wayward droids that ventured into unauthorized areas.

Thirteen years after Endor, R2-D2 and C-3PO arrived on Telti to investigate the recent bombing of the Senate hall on Coruscant. When they wandered away from the public visitors' area, both droids were flagged as intruders. The Red Terror captured See-Threepio and nearly disassembled him before Artoo-Detoo and an army of fellow R-series astromech droids overpowered the metallic thugs and saved the day.

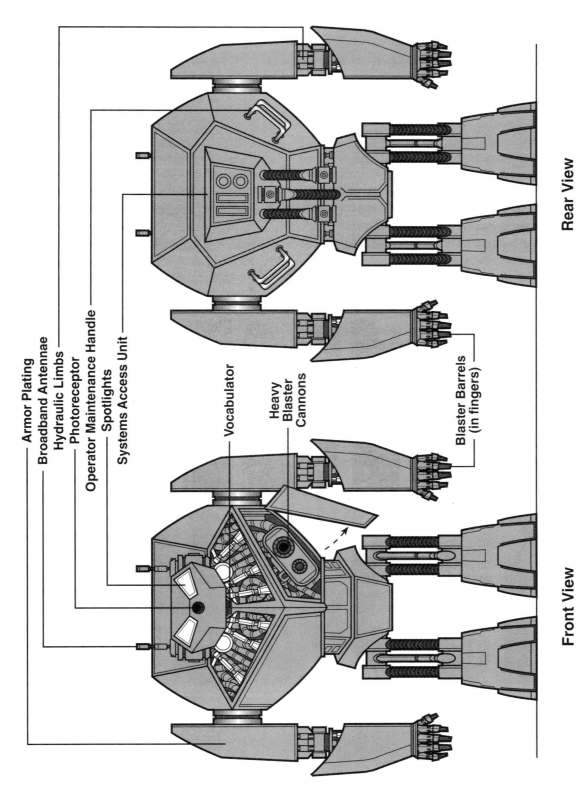

Armor Plating
Broadband Antennae
Hydraulic Limbs
Photoreceptor
Operator Maintenance Handle
Spotlights
Systems Access Unit

Vocabulator

Heavy
Blaster
Cannons

Blaster Barrels
(in fingers)

Rear View

Front View

SECURITY

G-2RD GUARD

Shudderingly familiar to anyone who has ever done hard time in a cell block, G-2RD droids have a well-deserved reputation for tenacity, stubbornness, and a fanatical devotion to order. As Han Solo once remarked, "You get a G-2RD droid going, and you'll have to take its head off to stop it."

Arakyd Industries' engineers seem fascinated by the repulsorlift engine—a great number of the company's products rely on antigravity buoys for locomotion. The G-2RD, like so many of its nameplate brethren, floats weightlessly through the air with admirable speed and maneuverability. It can reach a flight ceiling of over nine hundred meters, an eye-opening feature designed with the vertical prisons of Byblos in mind.

Optical sensors stud the exterior of the ebony droid, allowing panoramic scans in low-light conditions and in the infrared and ultraviolet ranges. Directionalized audio pickups augment the scanners, while a broadband antenna transmits and receives remote data. A tinny vocabulator delivers orders in a distinctively flat monotone and can also produce a shrieking alarm siren in case of jailbreak.

Three arms, spaced equidistant from each other, extend from the G-2RD's central sphere. The first is tipped with a stun prod, able to fire a short-range paralysis burst or deliver a nonlethal jolt via direct physical contact. The second sports an unerring blaster cannon—most G-2RDs are permitted to use deadly force when necessary. The third appendage is a heavy gripper arm for unlocking cell doors and dragging away unconscious subjects.

The G-2RD series is demanding, even abusive, but Arakyd considered these to be favorable qualities for units that worked with hardened criminals. The tactic has backfired slightly, since those who have bought the droids for industrial security or bodyguard duty report problems getting them to obey their orders. And more than one innocent guest to a prison ward has had visiting privileges revoked by an overly touchy G-2RD.

Not as tough as front-line combat units, the G-2RD series can still shrug off an ion blast or a limited volley of laser fire. Like all security droids, they are unaffected by standard restraining bolts. But a select number of freelance lawbenders have discovered a creative end-run around this latter feature and are sometimes able to deactivate G-2RDs with a homemade bolt and a quick, precise strike.

The Empire, the Corporate Sector, and countless planetary and local governments use the G-2RD. The New Republic "inherited" a number of the units by capturing the Imperial Palace on Coruscant, and quickly put them to work. These same G-2RD droids were used to guard both Admiral Ackbar and Mara Jade during their brief Palace incarcerations at the time of Grand Admiral Thrawn's military campaign and his siege of the capital planet.

Front View

Rear View

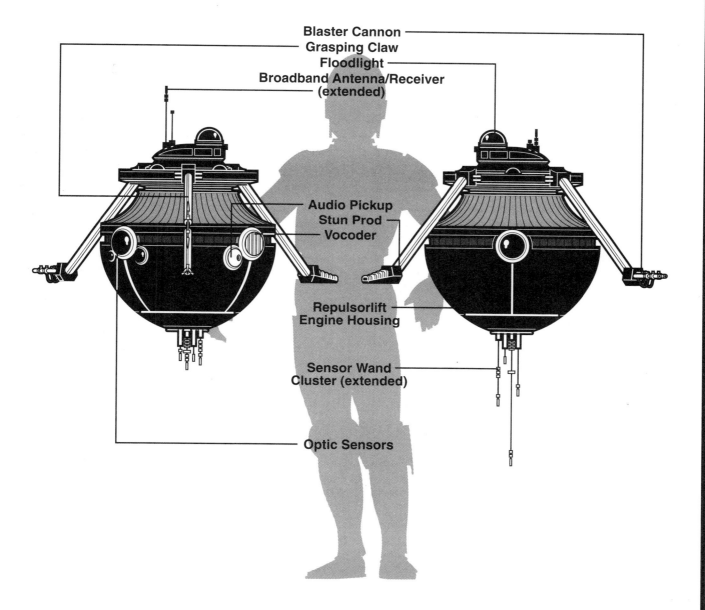

Blaster Cannon
Grasping Claw
Floodlight
Broadband Antenna/Receiver
(extended)

Audio Pickup
Stun Prod
Vocoder

Repulsorlift
Engine Housing

Sensor Wand
Cluster (extended)

Optic Sensors

S-EP1 SECURITY

Ulban Arms' S-EP1, more commonly known as "Sleepy," is a potent antiterrorist weapon despite its relatively eccentric appearance. Its usefulness as a security guard has endeared it to media figures and planetary potentates, who are unfazed by a cost of over two hundred thousand credits each.

Ulban's unique design was introduced to the marketplace only recently, following a decade of intensive research and development. Since the security field is crowded with dozens of models, including Ulban's own Warden 10-24, the company staked a claim to an undiscovered and unexploited market niche. By combining the best features of a robotic bodyguard with the best features of a law-enforcement scanner such as the Hound-W2 SPD, Ulban produced an antiterrorism superstar, equally proficient at disarming an assassin or deactivating a bomb.

A sophisticated cognitive module makes it all possible. The electronic brain is based on the Arjan IV logic computer and incorporates several innovative advances exclusive to Ulban Arms. The S-EP1's databanks are crammed with battle tactics, criminal profiles, ambush evasion techniques, emergency medical care, ground and air vehicle operation instructions, and the physical vulnerabilities of thousands of alien species. Though programmed for non-lethal combat, the S-EP1 will resort to deadly

force if there is no other way to save the life of its master.

This priceless cerebral circuitry is sheltered inside a spherical cranium that swivels vertically within a C-shaped durasteel neckpiece. The bulky collar controls horizontal rotation at the neck pivot joint and houses a floodlight, vocabulator, and thermal/radionic sensor package. Two photoreceptors incorporate spectral filters and a microscopic imaging system, and can produce blinding "flash" bursts to temporarily incapacitate foes.

The S-EP1's central torso is a thick, sturdy barrel that is resistant to energy weapons and minor explosions. Built into the upper body section is a high-imaging holocamera that is always on, recording every event in the vicinity for later playback and analysis. Heavy, piston-driven limbs pack vigorous strength, and each hand sports twin thumbs for greater manual dexterity. Each of the droids carries a stun staff and is a certified expert in its use.

Chief of State Leia Organa Solo's personal security staff purchased an S-EP1 unit soon after the line's rollout, just prior to the crisis in the Koornacht Cluster. Even though the Chief of State was typically accompanied by two human bodyguards—nicknamed the Sniffer and the Shooter—the S-EP1 was employed as a permanent guard at her personal residence. That Princess Leia trusted the S-EP1 with the lives of her three children is silent testament to the droid's dependability.

Front View

Side View

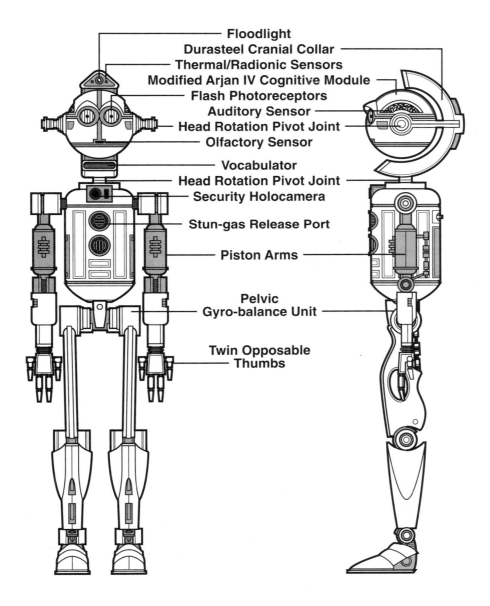

Floodlight

Durasteel Cranial Collar

Thermal/Radionic Sensors

Modified Arjan IV Cognitive Module

Flash Photoreceptors

Auditory Sensor

Head Rotation Pivot Joint

Olfactory Sensor

Vocabulator

Head Rotation Pivot Joint

Security Holocamera

Stun-gas Release Port

Piston Arms

Pelvic
Gyro-balance Unit

Twin Opposable
Thumbs

FOREIGN INTRUDER DEFENSE ORGANISM

Brainstormed by Admiral Ackbar and brought to life by a team of top Mon Calamari scientists, the Foreign Intruder Defense Organism is a uniquely menacing mechanical creation. In its first combat test, the FIDO droid successfully wiped out half of an MT-AT assault force at a secret New Republic base on Anoth.

The FIDO unit is designed to protect the entrance to a bunker, safe house, or military installation. Its chief weapon—aside from its claw-tipped tentacles—is surprise. If installed correctly, enemies won't detect the system until it is far too late to turn back. And, in that instant, they will be seized by dozens of unbreakable durasteel cables and immobilized, tossed around like rag dolls, or torn to tiny bits.

Ackbar, inspired by the sea creatures of his watery homeworld, patterned the devastating FIDO cables after the predatory krakana's mouth tentacles. Like the krakana, each serpentine twist is capped with a razor-toothed pincer. But unlike that fearsome fish, these pincers are cast from solid plasteel. They can saw through transparisteel, and when propelled by a whipcracking tentacle, they can punch straight through the armored hull of a Juggernaut assault vehicle.

There are twenty-six cables in all, each extendible to a maximum length of one hundred meters. They are the droid's only weapons. It possesses no shrapnel grenades, energy beams,

or projectile cannons, keeping "friendly fire" and collateral damage to a minimum.

If the attack tentacles seem to mimic a school of sharp-toothed krakana, the FIDO controller plainly resembles an overfed krabbex. The eight-meter pod is sheathed in a thick plasteel shell, and its four jointed legs complete the illusion of a massive crustacean. The legs do not provide mobility—they are designed only to anchor the unit firmly in place once a strategic site has been chosen.

The pod is equipped with a sensitive long-range sensor and a state-of-the-art motion detector. The cables, coiled within the body cavity, unspool through a central grid. If the controller is buried for camouflage purposes, the sensor and cable grid must be left partially uncovered.

The cognitive module is reasonably sophisticated, intelligent enough to distinguish friend from foe, and well-versed in conventional battle tactics. The controller "watches" the action through protected sensors at the end of each tentacle and, if the fight is going badly, can improvise a new strategy on the fly.

Although the original FIDO was destroyed in the skirmish on Anoth, a handful of new units have been manufactured since then. To prevent others from exploiting the design, the blueprints are categorized as Class Red classified information by New Republic Intelligence.

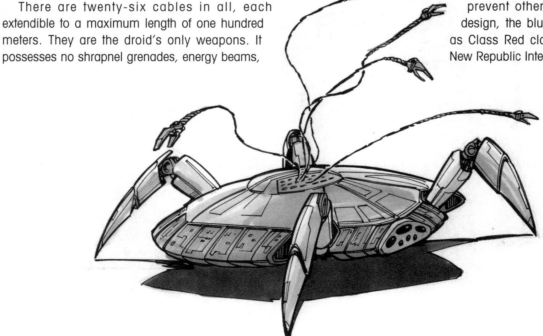

Tentacle/Pincer Closeup - Side View

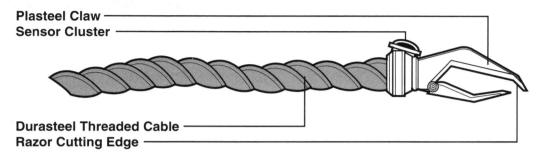

Plasteel Claw
Sensor Cluster

Durasteel Threaded Cable
Razor Cutting Edge

Top View

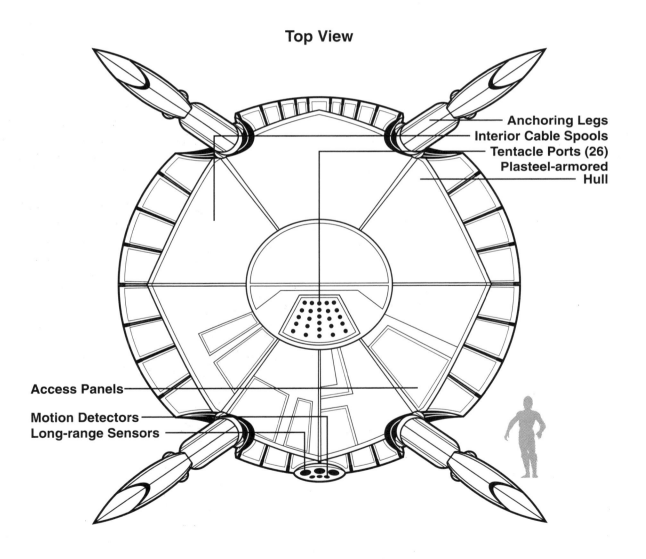

Anchoring Legs
Interior Cable Spools
Tentacle Ports (26)
Plasteel-armored Hull

Access Panels

Motion Detectors
Long-range Sensors

SECURITY
501-Z POLICE DROID (ZED)

One of the most autonomous police droids ever manufactured, the 501-Z marked SoroSuub Corporation's only foray into the law-enforcement market. The droid's bravery and tenacity were marred only by its penchant for getting in over its head.

The 501-Z, nicknamed "Zed," was designed to handle security and law enforcement on frontier outposts, or to supplement understaffed constabulary districts on high-traffic planets such as Teyr. Consequently, it was equipped with a complex cognitive matrix unprecedented for a simple security droid.

Unit Zed's personality module is as advanced as the most sophisticated protocol unit. It can easily interact with other officers, be they robotic or organic. Furthermore, Zed's intelligence allows it to "get into the mind" of a criminal suspect, resulting in remarkably accurate predictions of where a lawbreaker might be hiding or what his next target might be. 501-Zs make first-rate detectives.

They are also empowered to hunt down and arrest fugitives, even between far-flung planets and star systems. This occasionally creates problems, since many local governments do not recognize the authority of a robotic constable.

But Zed's programming contains a subroutine that allows it to improvise when confronted with a difficult challenge. 501-Zs will exhaust every legal resource to bring in a wanted felon. This determination is a great asset, though some find the droid's unflagging optimism more than a little irritating.

The Zed series is tough and powerful, standing nearly 1.9 meters tall. The crimson durasteel body is shock-resistant, but unable to withstand sustained blaster fire. Strong piston-driven arms allow the droid to haul objects many times its own weight. The droids can operate for extended periods without recharging.

All Zeds are programmed to respond to threats with nonlethal force only. If a scuffle develops, the droid typically subdues the assailant with an electrical stun stick. In addition, some Zeds carry low-power stun blasters. A portable lumin-rod can be used as a source of illumination in dim warehouses or alleyways.

The Unit Zed assigned to Kalarba's Hosk Station provides an insightful look at the strengths and weaknesses of the 501-Z design. This particular droid, chief of automated station security, bravely battled a rogue wrecker droid and continued to fight even after his right leg had been torn off. His efforts helped save Hosk from destruction. But when Zed decided to pursue a fleeing criminal into Hutt Space, he overconfidently assumed his authority would carry weight on a lawless world like Nar Shaddaa. Within an hour of his arrival, Unit Zed was nothing but smoking scrap.

Front View

Rear View

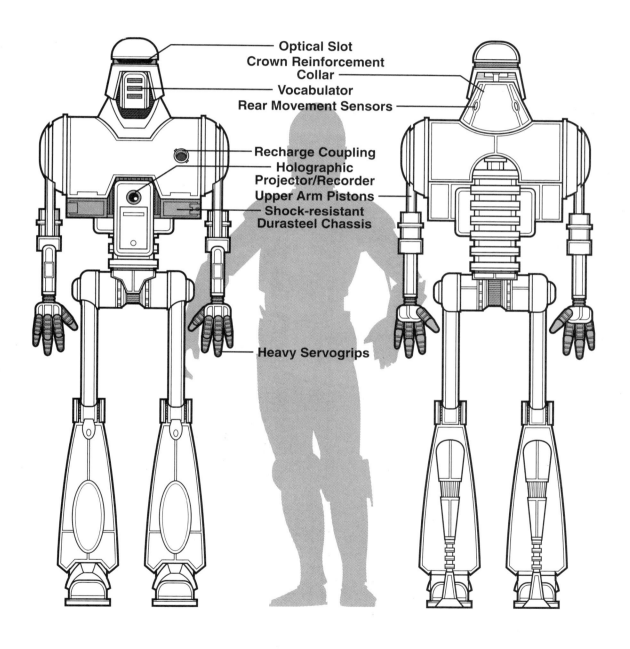

Optical Slot

Crown Reinforcement
Collar

Vocabulator

Rear Movement Sensors

Recharge Coupling

Holographic
Projector/Recorder

Upper Arm Pistons

Shock-resistant
Durasteel Chassis

Heavy Servogrips

SECURITY
HOUND-W2 SPD

The Scanning Patrol Detail (SPD) series of high-tech security droids is one of Industrial Automaton's proudest achievements, resulting in near-universal praise from the law-enforcement community. The W2 model, in particular, is so skilled at "sniffing out" sabotage devices and hidden contraband that it has been aptly nicknamed "Hound."

SPD droids are squat boxes less than a half-meter in height that move about on twin tank treads. Each comes armed with an extendible video sensor for telescopic and microscopic scans and a retractable grasping appendage for operating simple controls. A state-of-the-art Fabritech communications/sensor array, featuring keen olfactory, chemical, thermal, radionic, and electromagnetic receptors, forms the heart of the detection package.

A slight drawback to all SPDs is their lack of standard Basic-capable vocabulators. Like Industrial Automaton's R series of astromechs, SPDs communicate in the trilling electronic language known as Droidspeak. When working with biological police officers, which they often do, the units require a protocol interpreter or a scomp-linked datapad translation module.

The Hound-W2 is easily the most advanced of the SPDs. Packed into its modest shell are four extensor arms, each one capable of extending an incredible fifteen meters for poking into inaccessible crannies. At the tip of each limb is a different sensor module—standard equipment

includes a thermal imager, a directionalized audio receptor, a laser scan emitter, and a pulse scan emitter. An internal probability projection computer helps the W2 determine possible illicit origins for seemingly innocuous trace elements.

Hound-W2s are frequently seen at security checkpoints and customs desks scanning individuals and their belongings for a host of illegal items: narcotics such as glitterstim and sweetblossom, bomb-making ingredients such as detonite and baradium, undeclared plant and animal specimens, hazardous biological agents, and concealed personal weapons. They are also used by diplomatic envoys to ferret out hidden wiretaps and surveillance devices. Underworld gangsters occasionally employ them for similar purposes.

The New Republic kept a stable of Hound-W2 SPD units in the most important government buildings on Coruscant, including Senate Hall and the Imperial Palace. They were routinely put to use scanning sensitive areas such as the War Room and the Crypt, and employed during times of emergency to scrutinize arriving guests at diplomatic functions. When Leia Organa Solo suspected that a mysterious information leak code-named "Delta Source" was localized in the Palace's immense Grand Corridor, several Hound-W2s were fitted with repulsors and ordered to perform a meticulous centimeter-by-centimeter sensor sweep.

Front View

Side View

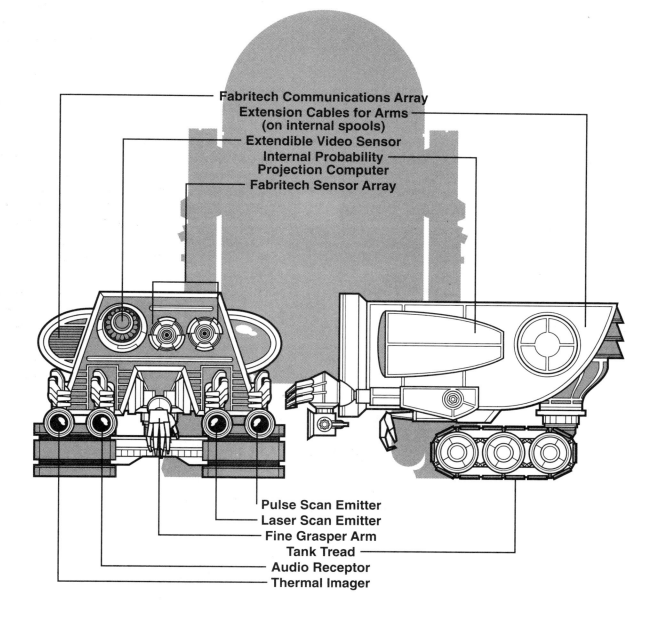

Fabritech Communications Array

Extension Cables for Arms —
(on internal spools)

Extendible Video Sensor

Internal Probability —
Projection Computer

Fabritech Sensor Array

Pulse Scan Emitter

Laser Scan Emitter

Fine Grasper Arm

Tank Tread —

Audio Receptor

Thermal Imager

SECURITY

SSI-RUUVI SECURITY DROID

The Ssi-ruuvi security droid is unremarkable on the outside, looking vaguely like a swollen R-series astromech. But the automaton was built on the distant planet Lwhekk by the odd and inscrutable Ssi-ruuk aliens. Beneath its bland exterior, it is utterly unlike any droid in the known galaxy.

Most mechanicals are powered by electricity, fusion, or some common fuel. Ssi-ruuk creations are powered by enslaved life-energy. Though the full details of the procedure remain a mystery, the aliens somehow transfer an organic being's consciousness and life essence into a waiting circuitry matrix via an "entechment" rig. Commander Luke Skywalker, who used the Force to touch several of these trapped minds during the historic truce at Bakura, reports that the process is painful, degrading, and utterly abominable.

Though the Ssi-ruuk prefer to use humans, most of their entechment victims are dull-witted servant P'w'ecks. It takes a single P'w'eck psyche to operate a security droid, but the life energy begins to fade after several weeks of continuous use. Eventually, the ebbing droid is revitalized by the installation of a fresh animate essence.

Ssi-ruuvi security droids are spherical and stand roughly 0.8 meters tall. They move about on three wheeled legs, and are quicker and more agile

than they appear at first glance. Their armored chasses are a dull metallic green with no distinguishing marks or imprints.

The central photoreceptor is keyed to a Ssi-ruuk's visual range, which includes a small portion of the ultraviolet spectrum. Additionally, since smell is one of the most important Ssi-ruuk senses, the droid has olfactory detectors that rival those on the Hound-W2 SPD. A small cluster of hexagonal power conduits is located in the rear of the upper hemisphere.

The droid's primary weapon is a short-range stun blaster, mounted on a rotating apparatus slightly offset from the main body. The beam is intense, modulated to bring down a stocky P'w'eck with a single shot. Humans struck by the beam run a higher-than-average risk of catastrophic heart failure and permanent synaptic damage.

The security droids are not well-insulated against power surges or ionization. If struck by another stun cannon, they invariably short-circuit. This flaw, however, is seldom exploited on caste-driven Lwhekk, since criminals seldom have access to personal weapons.

Several dozen of the Ssi-ruuvi security droids were seized by the New Republic following the capture of the flagship *Shriwirr* at Bakura. These units were immediately sent to various top-secret research installations in the hopes that the alien technology would provide some future strategic benefit.

Side View

Front View

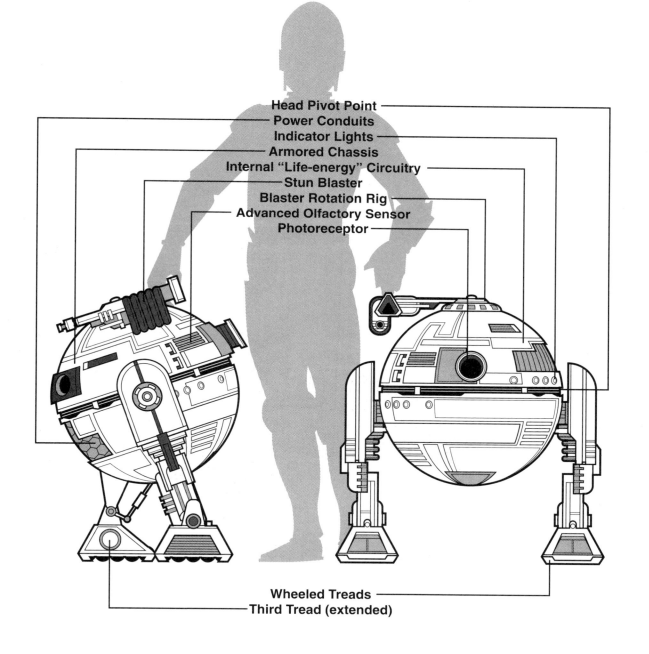

Head Pivot Point
Power Conduits
Indicator Lights
Armored Chassis
Internal "Life-energy" Circuitry
Stun Blaster
Blaster Rotation Rig
Advanced Olfactory Sensor
Photoreceptor

Wheeled Treads
Third Tread (extended)

SECURITY

IMPERIAL MARK IV SENTRY DROID

Pesky and intrusive, Imperial Sentry Droids are the classroom squealers of the robotic world. From grand larceny to gratuitous littering, from murders to misdemeanors, the speedy little units record the crime and whisk away to alert the nearest law officer.

The compact Imperial Mark IV Sentry Droid isn't much more than a repulsorlift engine and a double-fistful of optical scanners. Hovering above the ground at all times, it can reach an operational ceiling of ten meters and can generate impressive short-term bursts of speed. Steering nozzles at the rear of the droid control direction, while two stabilizer fins ensure a smooth flight.

Judiciously applied sensor clusters at the front, rear, and top of the Mark IV permit it to scan in nearly all directions at once. The forward array is by far the most sophisticated, incorporating electromagnetic and infrared detectors in addition to detailed visual scanners. Its miniature macrobinoculars have a built-in holorecording feature, allowing a fifty-meter line-of-sight recording radius and up to three hours of playback time. A broadband antenna/receiver communicates solely on coded Imperial alert frequencies.

The droids' databanks contain historical data on law enforcement and the full text of the mammoth Imperial Legal Code. When Mark IVs are assigned to a particular planet or city, the local constabulary uploads supplementary lists of regional statutes and topographical maps of the patrol area, and sometimes fits them with low-power blasters.

Often, the droids are used as intentional targets, scouting around corners and inside darkened warehouses so their stormtrooper owners won't walk into an ambush. Their personality programming is minimal, but they can develop loopy, unexpected quirks if not given regular memory wipes.

Manufactured exclusively for the Imperial military and pro-Imperial planetary governments, the Mark IV is not available for sale. Inevitably, however, a few have been nabbed by crooks and repackaged for the black market, despite the fact that tampering with an Imperial Sentry Droid is punishable by life at a hard-labor colony. The units constantly transmit low-frequency transponder signals back to their base of operations; if the signals are interrupted for any reason, it is certain to attract attention.

During the Empire's search for two escaped droids on Tatooine, a large number of Mark IVs assisted in the hunt. IM4-099, nicknamed "Face" by the Mos Eisley Militia, was assigned to patrol the stormtrooper checkpoint along one of the spaceport's main thoroughfares. A minor predicament arose when the city's Asp droids, ordered to set up additional communications repeaters, were repeatedly interrupted by Mark IVs who interpreted the boosted comm signals as illegal broadcasts. One Asp determined that a well-aimed swat was the most efficient way to deal with the problem.

STAR WARS

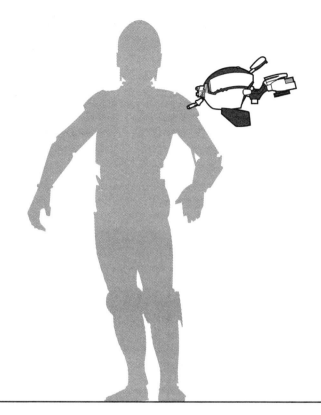

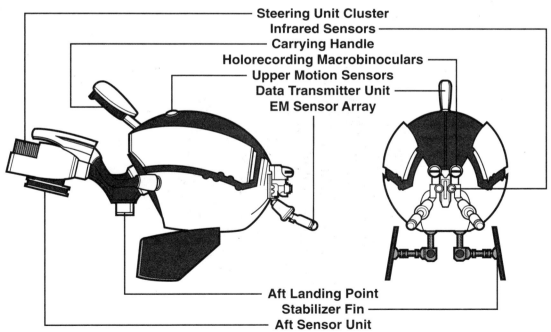

Steering Unit Cluster
Infrared Sensors
Carrying Handle
Holorecording Macrobinoculars
Upper Motion Sensors
Data Transmitter Unit
EM Sensor Array

Aft Landing Point
Stabilizer Fin
Aft Sensor Unit

Side View

Front View

STAR WARS

INTERROGATION

IT-O INTERROGATOR

Torture droids are an abomination, a crime against nature and society. But evil people are driven to create evil devices, and evil thrived inside Emperor Palpatine's New Order.

The IT-O Interrogator was no secret within the Empire. Rumors abounded of its horrifying techniques and brutal sadism, and those citizens unlucky enough to have been rounded up by the Imperial Security Bureau can personally attest to its cruelty...those who aren't too traumatized to speak, that is.

A glossy black sphere less than a meter tall, the IT-O hovers above the ground on low-power repulsors. Its shiny surface is studded with a hateful array of needles, probes, optic sensors, and audio receptors. A vocabulator is capable of producing speech, though this is seldom required. The droid's "tools" speak for themselves.

One of the most prominent devices is a hypodermic injector syringe, deliberately oversized to inspire anxiety and fear. The needle dispenses a number of liquid chemicals, including the truth serum Bavo Six, that are stored in internal reservoirs. These drugs can lower pain thresholds, stimulate cooperation, and trigger hallucinations.

In addition, the droid features a laser scalpel, a grasping claw, and power shears. Many of these items were originally designed for use on illegal assassin droids. Rebel agents have reported

seeing modified IT-Os that fire stun bursts patrolling sensitive Imperial installations. Since none have been captured intact, this information remains unconfirmed.

Twisted as their use might be, the medical diagnostic matrices of the IT-O are quite sophisticated. The droids have expert programming in medicine, psychology, surgery, and humanoid biology. Their vital-sign monitors make them capable of predicting and preventing the onset of catalepsy or unconsciousness. IT-Os are notorious for bringing their victims back from the brink of death so they can endure further questioning.

Thankfully, in many cases IT-Os aren't used at all—their mere presence is enough to frighten most subjects into an admission of guilt. The droid's sensors can then evaluate the confessor's truthfulness on the basis of heart rate, muscle tension, and voice patterns.

Despite the boasts of the ISB, it is possible to withstand the torments of an interrogation droid. While imprisoned on the Death Star, Leia Organa survived an IT-O *and* a psychic probe by Darth Vader without revealing the location of the main Rebel base.

Inevitably, the IT-O was succeeded by newer models with more refined pain-inducing equipment, but these later versions did not see widespread use. Allegedly, state-of-the-art IT-3s were stationed in Imperial Security Bureau headquarters on Coruscant.

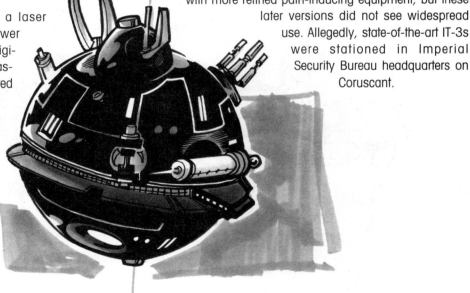

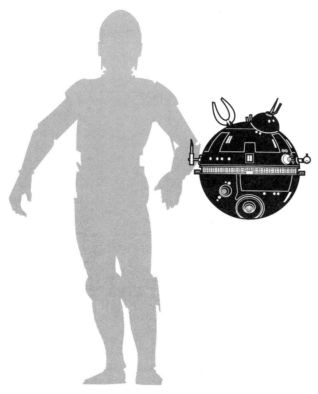

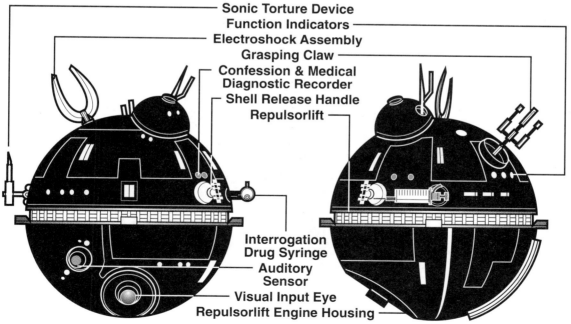

Sonic Torture Device
Function Indicators
Electroshock Assembly
Grasping Claw
Confession & Medical
Diagnostic Recorder
Shell Release Handle
Repulsorlift

Interrogation
Drug Syringe
Auditory
Sensor
Visual Input Eye
Repulsorlift Engine Housing

Front View

Side View

INTERROGATION

EV SUPERVISOR DROID

The MerenData EV series began as a benign industrial midmanagement product, but a bizarre factory foulup gave many of the droids the sick, sadistic personalities of professional torturers. The embarrassing details behind the disaster are known to almost no one outside the stuffy offices of the MerenData board of directors.

The frail-looking droids were built for a life in the factory, but not as brute laborers. Rather, the EV was designed to oversee other droid workers, report production problems, and maintain a safe and efficient working environment. MerenData hoped their new product, equipped with a high-frequency binary comlink, a broadband broadcast antenna/receiver system, and a sophisticated cognitive matrix, could replace organic shift bosses in assembly plants throughout the Core.

Unfortunately, disaster struck. Whether through negligence or sabotage, an employee substituted a case of MDF motivators, intended for use in torture droids, for the standard EV motivators. When the supervisors were finally released for sale, an uncomfortable number of them had temperaments variously described as "ruthless," "vicious," and "psychotic."

MerenData did not take immediate action. Torture droids were highly illegal, and the company wasn't even supposed to have access to MDF motivators. Besides, the affected droids seemed to make excellent

supervisors—their efficiency ratings were off the scale. Unfortunately, so was the attrition rate of their overworked droid underlings. Faced with a massive lawsuit, MerenData instituted a full recall, replaced the faulty motivators, and covered up the incident as best they could. But their replacement models (including an Imperial-issue "V series") were unimpressive performers. The EV series was a financial failure.

Not all of the tainted units were brought in during the recall. Chief among them was EV-9D9, head of automated security on Bespin's Cloud City. Eve possessed an odd third photoreceptor, which blinked out of sync with her scanning cycle, and a monstrous appetite for inflicting agony by manipulating other droids' pain-simulator buttons. She personally dismantled more than a quarter of Cloud City's droid population before being discovered and making a quick escape.

Later, a few of Jabba the Hutt's henchmen ran across EV-9D9 at a remote Go-Corp repulsor plant and brought her back to oversee the droid labor pool in their master's palace on Tatooine. Eve continued in her malicious ways, but met a well-deserved end when a mechanical survivor of her Bespin rampage executed a justifiable and gruesome revenge. There are, however, more EV droids still on the loose, including the outlaw EV-4D9 (owned by Ploovo Two-For-One), and EV-9D9.2, head of interrogation on the moon Telti.

Front View

Side View

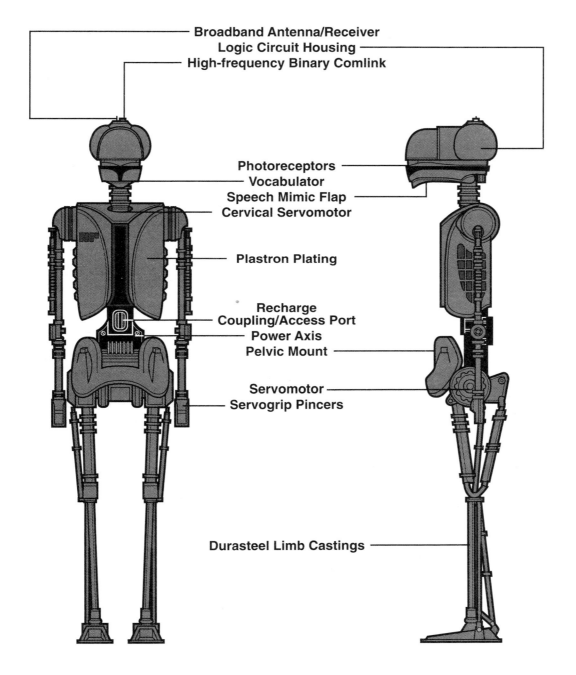

Broadband Antenna/Receiver
Logic Circuit Housing
High-frequency Binary Comlink

Photoreceptors
Vocabulator
Speech Mimic Flap
Cervical Servomotor

Plastron Plating

Recharge
Coupling/Access Port
Power Axis
Pelvic Mount

Servomotor
Servogrip Pincers

Durasteel Limb Castings

ESPIONAGE

MOON MOTH

Moon moth: A brainless blue-winged insect pest common to nearly every colonized planet in the galaxy.

Moon moth: A diabolically clever espionage gadget built by Arakyd Industries in the droid factories of Mechis III.

The mechanical cousin of the ubiquitous moon moth benefits from the same technological boom that spawned scarab droids. Extreme electronic miniaturization, in this case coupled with ultra-lightweight construction, makes the tiny moon moth droid a potent tool for spies and trackers. Even more impressive than its convincing camouflage is the fact that it actually flies on wing power alone, with no help from a repulsorlift engine.

Arakyd rejected dozens of larger, less-convincing organic prototypes when considering the Empire's order for a new espionage droid. When the company finally agreed on a disguise configuration—the moon moth—the programming team started a bitter feud with the engineering team over design specs that both groups considered utterly unworkable. The former lobbied for increased computing power; the latter wanted a stripped-down featherweight model that could flutter through the air as planned.

The end result was a compromise, though the engineers scored the moral victory. The moon moth perfectly reproduces the looping, erratic flight pattern of true lepidoptera and feels no heavier than expected when it alights on a subject's shoulder. Its finger-sized body contains sufficient circuitry to carry out its missions, but those missions have to be kept simple and straightforward to prevent overtaxing the droid's rudimentary brain.

A moon moth only understands a handful of verbal commands, including "pause," "launch," "return," and "acquire target." Its twin antennae act as visual sensors and electromagnetic field receptors, helping it home in on its quarry. Once it nears a target, it lands only long enough to affix its "egg"—a microdot homing beacon. The beacon's coded hyperwave signal can be detected from parsecs away.

To a trained eye, the moon moth has certain telltale physical characteristics that mark it as synthetic. Its body is a bit too angular, its legs contain machined hinge joints, and its antennae give off a metallic glint under certain lighting conditions. Most observers, however, never get the chance to make a close inspection. If the moth is in danger of discovery, a bean-sized wad of detonite hidden in the abdomen can be ignited with a remote trigger device. The flash-blast is more than sufficient to vaporize all evidence.

After the fall of the Empire, Arakyd began selling moon moths to New Republic Intelligence. One of the carefully crafted insects was used by General Crix Madine on an undercover mission to Nal Hutta. The moth's microscopic beacon egg exposed Durga the Hutt's secret base in the Hoth Asteroid Belt, which ultimately resulted in the collapse of the Darksaber project.

Top View

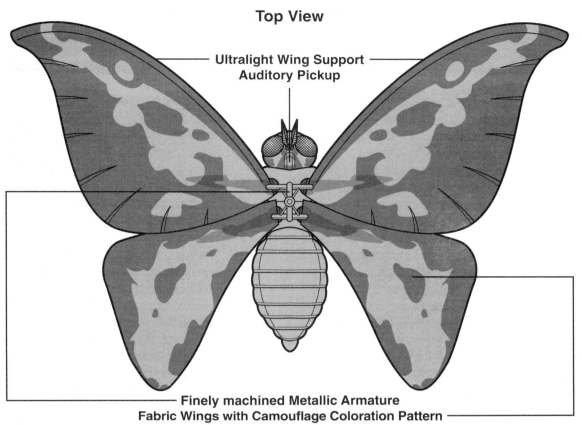

Ultralight Wing Support
Auditory Pickup

Finely machined Metallic Armature
Fabric Wings with Camouflage Coloration Pattern

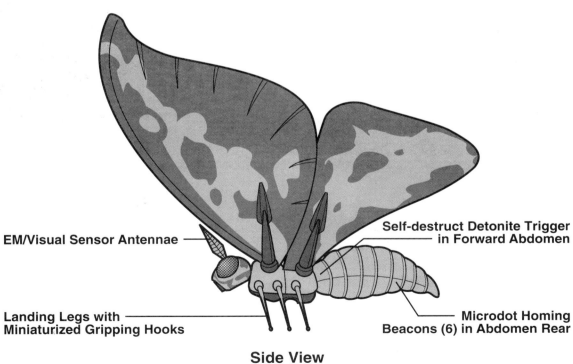

EM/Visual Sensor Antennae

Self-destruct Detonite Trigger
in Forward Abdomen

Landing Legs with
Miniaturized Gripping Hooks

Microdot Homing
Beacons (6) in Abdomen Rear

Side View

ESPIONAGE
FLY EYE

Observing the intimate details of someone else's life while remaining safely undetected is an irresistible attraction for most citizens, despite public protestations to the contrary. After Cybot Galactica developed the remote-controlled observation camera called the AC1 Surveillance "Spy-Eye," the Loronar Corporation trumped their rival with a smaller, lighter, and less obtrusive machine—the "fly eye."

Loronar's fly eye is another masterpiece of miniaturization, measuring no longer than three human finger-widths even with its legs fully extended. Its spherical body consists primarily of a tiny and remarkably quiet repulsorlift engine, able to provide a maximum forward speed of ten kilometers per hour and a flight ceiling of nine meters. The little engine gets quite hot after extended use, and four wide venting ports are necessary to keep the droid's delicate internal gears from frying under the extreme temperature.

Any scrap of space inside the body shell that isn't taken up by the repulsorlift is occupied by a high-imaging holographic lens and coded transmission circuitry. Visual data is sent in real time via a tightbeam signal to a remote receiving unit, usually a monitor screen a safe distance away. The droid is far too small to contain any sort of internal recording archive.

Fly eyes are usually directed from afar by operators with joystick control pads, though the droids possess sufficient intelli-

gence to follow rudimentary search-and-spy flight patterns. When a fly eye has reached a strategic observation vista, it secures itself to the wall or ceiling with its clawed limbs and shuts down its repulsorlift. This "passive mode" makes the droid difficult to detect on a security scan, though the tightbeam transmission signal is still vulnerable to sensor jamming. A fly eye's data feed is visual only—audio receptors would add too much body weight and overtax the small engine.

Immediately after their introduction, fly eyes became a hit with jealous lovers, fidgety paranoiacs, and scruple-free reporters of the sensationalistic media. Citing privacy concerns, respected news organizations such as Galaxy News Service refused to use the tiny droids, but soon found themselves scooped on the juiciest stories by the exploitative bottom feeders at NovaNetwork. Hundreds of planets have since passed local laws outlawing fly eyes, but most journalists are more than willing to pay a small fine in exchange for exclusive footage of a holo-celebrity's secluded wedding or an Imperial Moff's secret payoff.

TriNebulon News broke a major story four years after the Battle of Endor when one of its fly eyes, hidden inside the Imperial Palace, recorded Han Solo's shocking kidnapping of Princess Leia Organa. The silent but compelling footage was broadcast across the newsnets and touched off a firestorm of public interest until the princess and her abductor returned safely from the planet Dathomir.

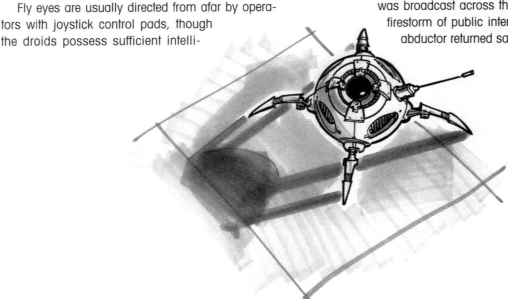

Top View

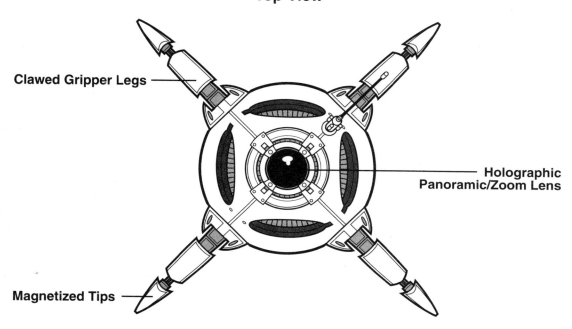

Clawed Gripper Legs

Holographic
Panoramic/Zoom Lens

Magnetized Tips

Tightbeam Transmission Antenna

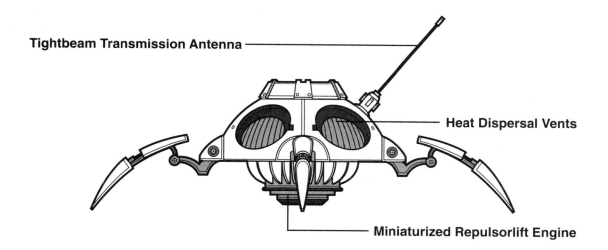

Heat Dispersal Vents

Miniaturized Repulsorlift Engine

Side View

ESPIONAGE DROID

With the installation of covert espionage programming, your droid is no longer just a mundane and overlooked household servant. It is now a mundane and overlooked household servant that can quickly get you arrested and sentenced to life at hard labor in the spice mines of Kessel.

A true espionage droid can look like almost anything on the outside, from a Model E to a binary load lifter. Their internal surveillance/recording modules, undetectable on standard scans, are what turn them into remote spies. Common units like 3POs and Asps make perfect espionage tools, since the average citizen's gaze just slides right past them. It's a simple truism that biological spies have known for generations: the less unusual, the better.

These types of espionage units are extremely difficult to build properly and, as a result, are typically manufactured by top-secret military think tanks deep within the Empire and the New Republic. After all, anyone can stick a data-recorder in a droid's chest cavity . . . but only a professional can sneak a robotic spy past security imagers, probe scanners, and spectrometer operators.

The Empire commissioned one type of these spy units in great numbers: the RA-7 "Death Star Droid," manufactured by Arakyd Industries. More often, however, the masquerading robots are produced on a

case-by-case basis to lessen the chance of a security leak. In one such instance, Grand Admiral Thrawn used a simple Industrial Automaton Decon III to infiltrate the Noghri homeworld of Honoghr and report any suspicious activity.

MerenData's RM-2020 is an entirely different type of espionage droid. It makes no attempt to hide its true purpose, for it is not designed to infiltrate polite society. Instead, the RM-2020 is used on the battlefield to gather intelligence data on troop movements and weak points in enemy lines.

The RM-2020 has a roughly humanoid torso and zooms high above the ground on a speedy repulsorlift engine. Its hardwired espionage module includes an information recording/broadcast system, while its visual/audio sensor package includes ultraviolet and infrared detectors. At 160,000 credits apiece the droid is quite expensive, but generally worth it, since its noncombat mission profile allows it to survive for years even in a frontline military environment.

Battlefield commanders who wish to risk their RM-2020s in something other than surveillance have been known to send the droids into enemy camps to engage in covert sabotage. In some cases this works—RM-2020s are experts at not being seen—but more often the droids are caught in the act and blasted to scrap.

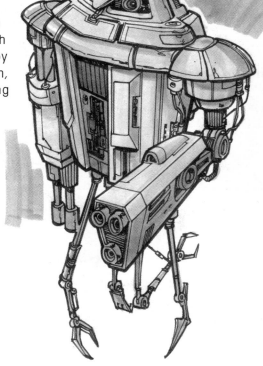

MerenData RM2020 - Front View

Vocabulator
Tightbeam Transmission
Antenna (retracted)
Visual/Audio Sensors
Information Storage Archive
Hardwired Espionage Module
Ultraviolet/Infrared Detectors

Specialized Manipulator Arms
Wide-dispersal Ionizer
Defensive Energy Cannon
Repulsorlift Engine

Modified Protocol Unit - Front View

Sensor Baffler
Removable Storage Module
Internal Scanning Buffers
3PO-Series Body Shell
High-gain Audio Sensors
Data Encryption Unit
Holorecording Photoreceptors

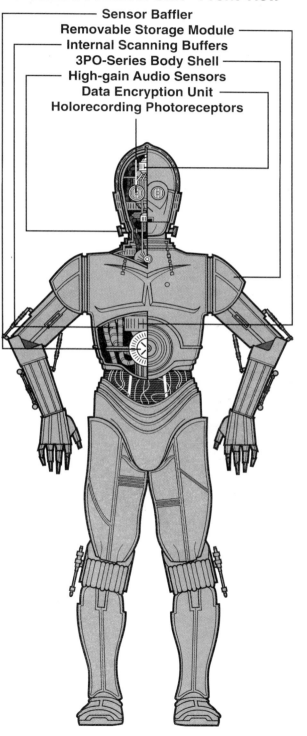

ESPIONAGE

SLICER DROID

In ancient times, primitive beings used their forefingers to extract sticky syrup from the soft centers of shellflowers. Eventually the flowers evolved thorns, and the primitives were forced to invent rudimentary tools to sidestep this new defense. Today, after hundreds of millennia, the essence of the struggle has changed very little—though syrup has been replaced by statistics and simple twigs by slicer droids.

The slicer droid is technology's inevitable answer to passwords, codes, and encryption algorithms. No matter what manner of defenses are installed to protect an information archive from prying eyes, a determined individual can always devise a method to circumvent them. Some observers insist that robots will never truly replace creative humans—and aliens—as master data-slicers, but most would agree that slicer droids make excellent tools.

Corporations and research firms have long used the mechanical infiltrators for a variety of purposes, both public and private. Their surface rationalizations are obvious—slicer droids are experts at restoring corrupted files and salvaging data that might have been accidentally deleted. But most businesses have ulterior motives, such as sneaking a peek at their competitors' upcoming production plans. Even honest companies that don't engage in corporate spying routinely employ slicer droids to test their *own* systems and ensure that their secrets are safely protected.

During the Galactic Civil War, the Rebel Alliance used as many slicer droids as they could lay their hands on, allowing them to monitor Imperial troop movements and sabotage entire logistical networks through the release of crippling computer viruses. Rebel familiarity with the automatons proved to be a great help when the Alliance eventually morphed into the New Republic. After the galactic capital of Coruscant was wrested from the Empire's clutches, New Republic Research and Development started work on a new series of slicer droids.

The NR 1100 was designed for the express purpose of cracking the Imperial Information Center. This cavernous, climate-controlled chamber beneath the Imperial Palace held an astronomical amount of data—from centuries-old weather reports to Emperor Palpatine's nightly dinner menu—but most of the juiciest bits were buried beneath multiple layers of encryption. As soon as each NR 1100 was completed, it was hardwired into place near a mainframe access port and programmed for uninterrupted slicing, sifting, and collating.

The NR 1100 possesses spindly arms, a lumpy carapace, and a generous overbite. Its repulsorlift engine is weak, intended for temporary use only. A scomp-link computer port is centrally located in the lower body and each long finger can be used as a data-probe. Compound scanners ring the elongated cranium, which contains the most advanced slicing hardware available in the New Republic. The mute droid does not have a vocabulator.

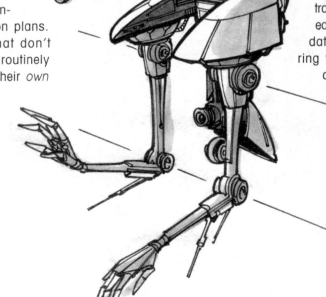

Front View

Side View

Removable Coding Modules ⎯⎯⎯⎯⎯
Datacard Insert Slot
Internal Slicing Hardware Matrix ⎯⎯⎯⎯
Visual/Audio Recorder
Data Scanners (lining groove) ⎯⎯⎯
Holographic Projector

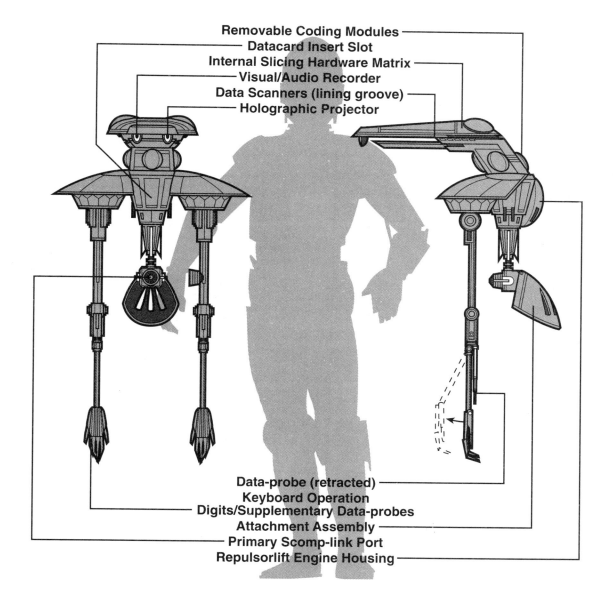

Data-probe (retracted) ⎯⎯⎯⎯
Keyboard Operation
Digits/Supplementary Data-probes
Attachment Assembly ⎯⎯⎯
Primary Scomp-link Port
Repulsorlift Engine Housing ⎯⎯⎯

STAR WARS

ESPIONAGE

POSITRONIC PROCESSOR

Information retrieval is a lucrative business—just look at the corporate proliferation of slicer droids. But while slicer droids can crack codes and restore vast chunks of lost data, they can't manipulate a computer's basic programming. It takes a special machine to whiz past a mainframe's safeties, subvert its core hardware, and make it dance like a scalded ronto. These tiny anarchists are called positronic processors.

MerenData manufactured the first positronic processors as an experimental project for Imperial Intelligence. The silvery titanium B2-X cubes were stuffed with more memory and computing power than units one hundred times their size. Initial performance tests were impressive, but Imperial Intelligence expressed disappointment with the droids' flighty natures. Often, they refused direct orders and aimlessly noodled around in computer networks simply because they were *bored*. MerenData's engineers threw up their hands in resignation—with that much processing power, behavioral quirks were inevitable. Only a few hundred were produced before the experiment was quietly canceled.

Less than six months later the existing B2-Xs found their way into the fringe society of slicers, smugglers, and criminals. The droids' astounding abilities, coupled with their scarcity, made them coveted treasures. One band of outlaw-techs purchased a positronic processor from a bounty hunter, augmented its already remarkable circuitry, and coated it with multiple layers of gleaming blue lacquer.

They named their acquisition Blue Max—"Max"

because of his near-limitless processing capacity, "Blue" for more obvious reasons. In addition to his lapis shell, Blue Max sported a single photoreceptor, a computer interface probe, and a plastron connection socket. For camouflage and mobility, the little cube was nestled into the chest cavity of Bollux, an antique labor droid. Both droids, along with a grumbling freighter captain named Han Solo, stole a top-secret cache of data from the grainworld Orron III in the Corporate Sector.

A second positronic processor, nicknamed Flirt, wound up in the hands of the Wookiee bounty hunter Chenlambec. The droid's previous owner had taken MerenData's basic design and radically modified it by installing unique microcircuitry of his own invention. Flirt's most extraordinary gift was her ability to slice into a computer network from any outlet, even innocuous, and usually unguarded, fueling sockets such as power points and fusion terminals.

Like Blue Max, Flirt had a buoyant and irrepressible personality that belied her small size. Her computer skills proved invaluable to Chenlambec and his partner Tinian when the trio matched wits with the reptilian bounty hunter Bossk following the Battle of Hoth. After successfully subverting Bossk's ship *Hound's Tooth*, Flirt took over the body of a Trandoshan X10-D draft droid so she could move about under her own power.

Bollux with Blue Max

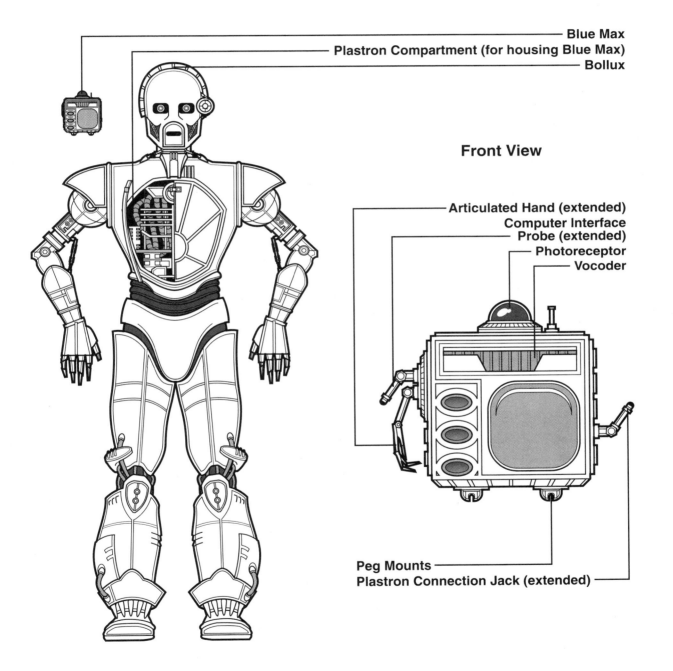

Blue Max
Plastron Compartment (for housing Blue Max)
Bollux

Front View

Articulated Hand (extended)
Computer Interface
Probe (extended)
Photoreceptor
Vocoder

Peg Mounts
Plastron Connection Jack (extended)

HUMAN REPLICA DROID AND SYNTHDROID

There is an unspoken rule in robotics: a limit exists as to how closely machines should resemble their creators. Protocol droids such as the 3PO series were designed to look like humans, but only superficially—two eyes, two arms, two legs. Recent breakthroughs in artificial tissue, however, have ushered in a revolutionary and disturbing new era manifested in the human replica droid and the synthdroid.

Human replica droids, or HRDs, could very well be the most expensive automatons ever assembled. The HRD experiment has its origins in Project Decoy, a Rebel Alliance plan to replace Imperial officials with perfect duplicates. The Rebels, however, lacked sufficient funds to complete their design during the Galactic Civil War and their archenemies beat them to the punch. The Empire hired designers Massad Thrumble and Simonelle the Ingoian to create an Imperial replica droid, and their partnership resulted in a flawless specimen named Guri. Smelling profit, Simonelle established his own HRD workshop in the Minos Cluster, while Thrumble remained with the Empire and developed several lesser HRDs for use in a scheme on Corulag. Guri, meanwhile, was sold to Prince Xizor for a cool nine million credits.

Guri possessed hyper-reflexes and astonishing strength and was modeled in the image of a striking young woman. The masquerade was accomplished through use of a poly-alloy skeleton, skin grown in a clone vat, and internal organs made from bio-fibers. To all but the most advanced medical equipment she appeared completely organic.

Cool, competent, and always professional,

Guri worked as Xizor's bodyguard and private assassin. At the time of her master's death she was the second most powerful figure in the vast Black Sun crime syndicate. This astonishing fact was testament to her cognitive module—a completely redesigned and upgraded AA-1 Verbobrain. Even when the Rebel Alliance completed Project Decoy after the Battle of Endor, they couldn't come close to reproducing Guri's autonomous decision-making skills.

Compared with the sophistication of HRDs, synthdroids seemed like a giant step backward. They were, however, the first organic duplicates made available to the general public, even if their 100,000-credit price tags were still too steep for anyone but the very wealthy.

The Loronar Corporation launched their synthdroid line approximately nine years after Endor. These expensive new novelties were made largely of synthflesh, the artificial skin used by emergency medcenters and burn clinics. A durasteel skeleton with cable and hydraulic joints supported the synthflesh covering and gave the droids inhuman strength. Since synthflesh was malleable, the droids could be sculpted to resemble any famous holo-actor or -actress. This made them quite popular in the pleasure-domes of Carosi and Hesperidium.

The shortcomings of synthdroids included their unsettling lack of scent, their doll-like hair, their vacant expressions, and their minimal brains—each droid's skull contained only a programmable crystal run from a distant control board. When Loronar's only source of these crystals was wiped out in the Battle of Nam Chorios, the company pulled every last synthdroid from the marketplace.

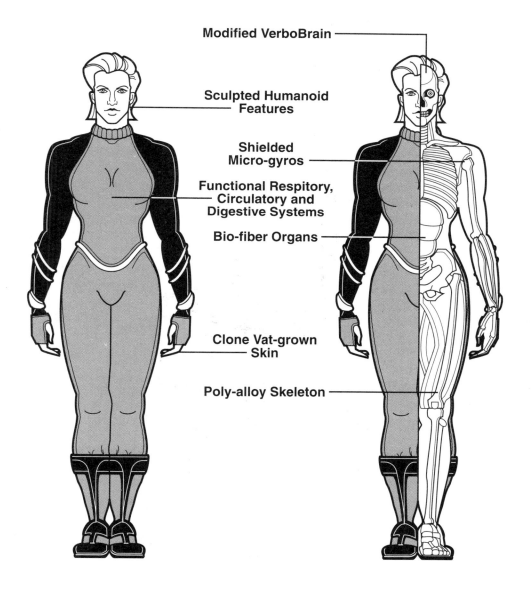

Front View

Front View (cutaway)

Modified VerboBrain

Sculpted Humanoid Features

Shielded Micro-gyros

Functional Respitory, Circulatory and Digestive Systems

Bio-fiber Organs

Clone Vat-grown Skin

Poly-alloy Skeleton

B'OMARR BRAIN WALKER

B'omarr brain walkers aren't true droids. The spiderlike armatures are simply metal machines controlled by preserved organic brains, much like the cloned Emperor's Shadow Droids. But unlike Palpatine's dark destroyers, the B'omarr brain-donation process is voluntary and its subjects are blissfully enthusiastic. For a B'omarr monk, there is no surer path to enlightenment than a disembodied intellect.

Generations ago, an enclave of devout B'omarr ascetics set up shop on Tatooine. Their religion required them to seek spiritual fulfillment at the expense of physical sensation, and the desert planet's sun-scoured wastelands were perfect for focusing the mind. Among the endless dunes the monks constructed a brooding monastery of iron and durasteel and shut themselves off from the local population.

After years of meditation, the most advanced believers had no further use for the distractions of the flesh. In a holy ceremony, the lesser B'omarr acolytes sharpened their scalpels and surgically removed the brains from their masters' skulls. Each lumpy gray mass was reverently dropped into a clear jar of nutrient fluid and arranged on a shelf in the subterranean Great Room of the Enlightened. The unfettered monks were now free to contemplate all the mysteries of creation.

But even a bodiless brain needs to get out once in a while. For this purpose, the B'omarr attendants assembled a series of arachnid armatures. They faithfully maintain

the contrivances to this day, many years after Jabba the Hutt turned their monastery into his personal pleasure palace and forced the religious disciples into the lowest subcorridors.

When a disembodied monk has business to attend to, it telepathically summons a set of spider legs. The metal walker then picks up the brain jar and gingerly affixes it to the unique housing. An on-duty acolyte usually assists with this process.

The brain walkers do not follow a single overriding design pattern. Some have gripper claws, some do not; some have only four legs, some have as many as nine. Almost all, however, have speakers and audio sensors, allowing the monk to communicate, and a row of colored lights at the base of the shatterproof jar. These lights glow blue and green under normal conditions. Bright red indicates that the brain is "screaming" and unable to adjust to its strange new state.

The monks in Jabba's palace were eager to initiate others into their way of life—so eager, in fact, that they forcibly removed a few reluctant brains following the Hutt's death at the Great Pit of Carkoon. Among the victims was Jabba's Twi'lek lieutenant Bib Fortuna, who later managed to shed his brain walker and restore his cerebellum to a new host body.

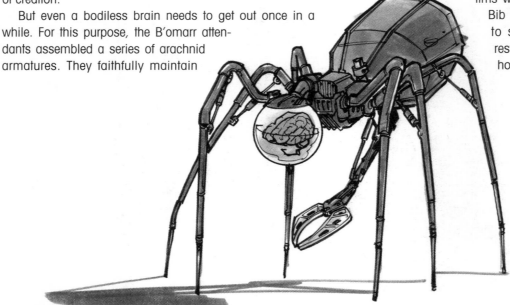

Storage/Transport Model - Side View

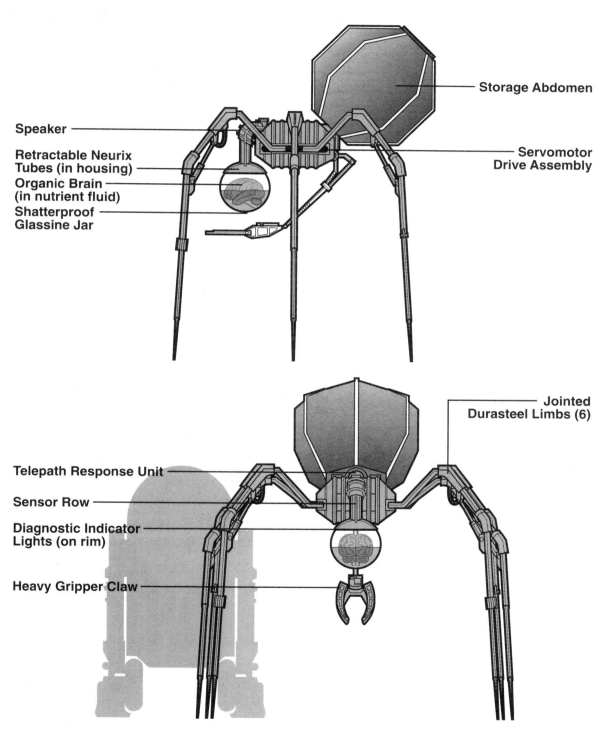

Storage Abdomen

Speaker

Servomotor
Drive Assembly

Retractable Neurix
Tubes (in housing)

Organic Brain
(in nutrient fluid)

Shatterproof
Glassine Jar

Jointed
Durasteel Limbs (6)

Telepath Response Unit

Sensor Row

Diagnostic Indicator
Lights (on rim)

Heavy Gripper Claw

Front View

ONE OF A KIND
VUFFI RAA

Lando Calrissian once called Vuffi Raa the weirdest apparition of the mechanical subspecies he'd ever seen. But at the time, the roguish gambler had no idea that his undersized droid copilot was an exotic alien construct of extraordinary age and astonishing origin.

Eons ago in the Unknown Regions, an advanced alien species was tragically wiped out by a sudden radiation storm. Their droids, however, lived on, becoming fully sentient and modifying their forms into fifty-kilometer spacegoing spheres. But the robotic entities were excessively timid, resulting in a dull and stagnant society. Vuffi Raa was constructed for the purpose of gathering fresh information from the outside galaxy.

Unlike his mechanical "parents," Vuffi was created in the image of the long-extinct starfishlike alien architects. A pentagonal plate of polished chromite made up his body, unadorned save for a single glowing red photoreceptor at top center. The eye was capable of seeing into ultraviolet and infrared wavelengths. Other sensors, and a miniature vocabulator, were hidden out of sight on the droid's underside.

Vuffi Raa possessed five elongated chromite tentacles that served as both arms and legs. These appendages tapered to points, then split into five-tentacled "hands" with one small optic sensor in each palm. What most observers failed to notice was that the tips of these fingers

continued to split into near-microscopic *sub*fingers, able to manipulate the tiniest objects yet still as strong as durasteel cables. Vuffi could shunt heat into his extremities and produce a glowing tentacle tip, quite useful for illuminating a room—or lighting a cigarra.

Remarkably, Vuffi Raa could detach all five limbs from his body and control each one remotely. While a quintet of metal snakes squirming across the face of a damaged console was a startling sight, the peculiar technique allowed Vuffi to do twice the repair work in half the time. The little droid was a gifted mechanic, competent star pilot, determined pacifist, and loyal comrade.

While collecting diverse life experiences for his creators, Vuffi Raa went through dozens of owners in hundreds of systems, including a shameful role in the brutal pacification of Renatasia. Once Lando Calrissian procured Vuffi in the Rafa system, the two became fast friends and partners in crime. The droid helped his new master collar the legendary Mindharp of Sharu, served as a pilot during the Battle of Nar Shaddaa, and saved Lando's skin during the Oseon system's annual Flamewind festival.

But, during a climactic showdown in the ThonBoka nebula, the little droid's people finally arrived to take him back to their home system. Vuffi Raa departed with his kinfolk, and his current fate is unknown.

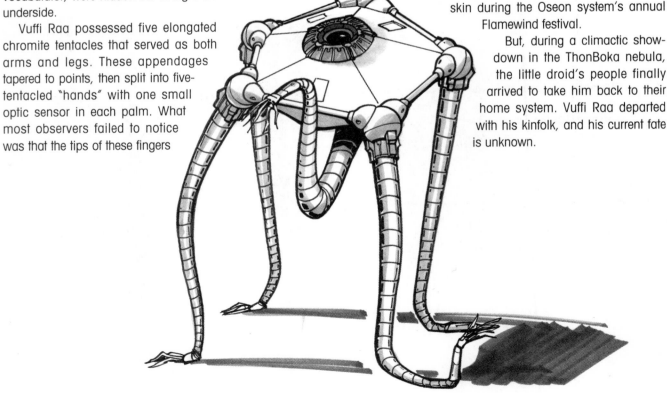

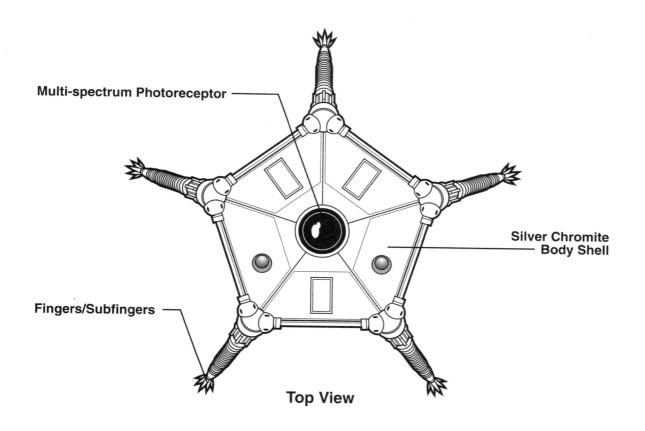

Multi-spectrum Photoreceptor

Silver Chromite
Body Shell

Fingers/Subfingers

Top View

Side View

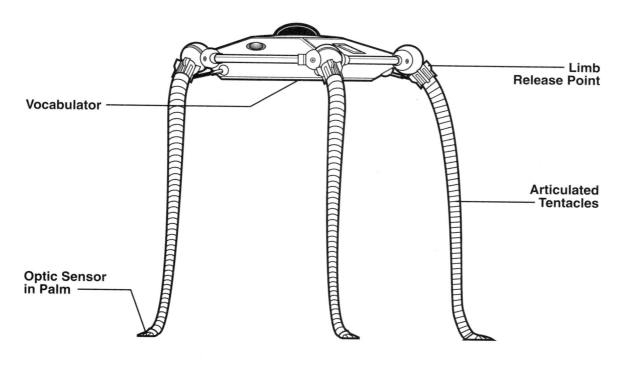

Limb
Release Point

Vocabulator

Articulated
Tentacles

Optic Sensor
in Palm

ONE OF A KIND

Q9-X2

Q9-X2 rolled off the assembly line looking identical to thousands of his fellow astromech units, but not even his own designers would recognize him now. Over the years he has modernized himself into a unique, adaptable—and, some would add, ill-tempered and flighty—jack-of-all-trades.

First, he can talk. Second, he can float. Q9 simply was dissatisfied with his motile and communicative limitations, and upgraded. It's a safe bet that there is no other astromech quite like him in the galaxy.

The reason for this unusual behavior was the highly advanced personality matrix installed in the experimental Q9 series by Industrial Automaton. Based on the R7, the Q9 model was designed for versatility and featured superior analytical and data access skills. But the droids' complexity was their undoing, resulting in systems failures and costly repairs when subjected to periods of extended stress. Most developers consider the Q9 experiment to be an utter disaster.

Q9-X2 would disagree, though he readily admits that traditional astromechs are ill-prepared for life outside a flight hangar. After fitting himself with low-power repulsor pads, Q9 could hover above obstacles; after installing a vocoder, he could speak Basic. But these modifications, while radical, still weren't enough.

Q9 added a sophisticated detection package, including a molecular backtrack

sniffer, a residual heat-trend directionalizer, and retractable sensor wands. He followed this up with a powerful forward-mounted floodlight and two additional lamps that folded into either side of his cylindrical chassis.

On a whim, Q9 fitted a high-tech photography system into his front chest section, reasoning that his holographic projector was a blurry, grainy way to capture images. The new system has a telephoto lens and is capable of surprisingly detailed resolution. Pictures are dispensed through a narrow printout slot.

In addition, Q9 is outfitted with the standard "factory-installed" astromech equipment offered by Industrial Automaton: a retractable grasper arm, an arc welder, a fire extinguisher, and more. The droid does not consider himself fully developed, however, and will likely continue his self-tinkering for some time to come.

Ebrihim the Drall is Q9-X2's current owner. He purchased the bizarre droid for twelve hundred and fifty Drallish crowns at a used-tech market, and so far has not regretted his decision—though Q9 has certainly tested his patience. The droid can be insolent, headstrong, egotistical, temperamental, and oblivious, but his database retrieval skills have proved invaluable in Ebrihim's profession as a tutor.

Q9 is also capable of great heroism, a fact made abundantly clear during the notorious Corellian crisis. Without Q9's timely assistance, Han Solo's children would never have escaped from imprisonment on Drall.

Side View

Front View

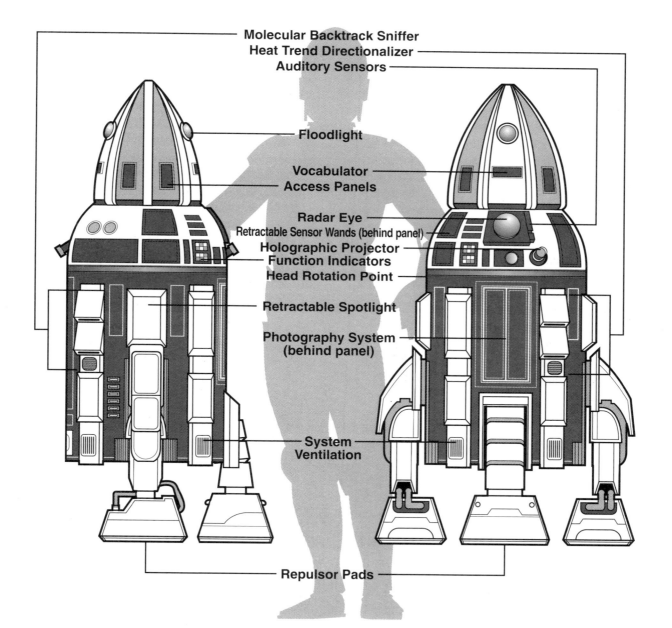

Molecular Backtrack Sniffer
Heat Trend Directionalizer
Auditory Sensors

Floodlight

Vocabulator
Access Panels

Radar Eye
Retractable Sensor Wands (behind panel)
Holographic Projector
Function Indicators
Head Rotation Point

Retractable Spotlight

Photography System
(behind panel)

System
Ventilation

Repulsor Pads

8T88

Owned by no one and contemptuous of everyone, 8t88 is the epitome of a free and self-reliant droid. Since the rise of the Rebellion the autonomous automaton has made quite a name for himself as a top-notch interpreter and data broker. As 8t88 often tells prospective clients, "When someone desires information, they come to me."

8t88 is a variation on the antiquated 88 series, a line of bookkeeping and administrative droids manufactured by a long-forgotten Tiss'sharl company. The line was junked ages ago and no units remain in active use save for 8t88. Through circumstances unknown, the droid's original head/processor assembly was removed and a different cranial unit grafted into its place. When compared to his gangly frame, the new head is disproportionately small, and this fact infuriates 8t88. Though he has only the vaguest memories of his former life as an accountant, he has vowed to find the individual responsible for his "disfigurement" and inflict a suitably gruesome punishment.

The best way to go about this, 8t88 has decided, is to become stinking rich. It helps that the droid considers himself above such petty human concepts as morality and justice. Anyone, from the Rebels to the Empire to the Hutts, can hire his services, and 8t88 won't even think twice about selling out a former associate. His intricate cognitive matrix allows him to easily crack security codes and decipher archaic languages, and he is a genius at uncovering top-secret data. Besides his exorbitant upfront fee, 8t88 has only one condition: don't ask where he gets his information.

8t88's silver skeleton-body is powered by hydraulic tubing, and his squeaky joints are in frequent need of an oil-bath. A number of communications devices are built into his metallic skin. Behind a hinged torso panel is a small storage compartment used as a "pocket," since he doesn't wear clothing.

The droid's head features a central scanner plate and various optical mechanisms rigged on either side, including an infrared sensor, microscopic imager, and holographic projector/recorder. 8t88's audio sensors are extremely perceptive, and his vocabulator is modulated to deliver cultured, intelligent-sounding speech patterns.

8t88 maintains a semipermanent office on Nar Shaddaa, the Smugglers' Moon. It was here that he ran afoul of erstwhile Rebel agent Kyle Katarn following the Battle of Endor. 8t88, secretly in the employ of the Dark Jedi Jerec, double-crossed Katarn and walked away with a data-disc belonging to the human's father. In the subsequent shootout, 8t88 lost his arm.

The droid repaired himself with parts from a scrapped 88-series body shell, but Katarn tracked him down in Baron's Hed on Sulon. This time, the Rebel took the robot's head—which contained the hidden coordinates of the Valley of the Jedi. But decapitation won't kill a droid, and 8t88 is unlikely to stay down for long.

Front View

Rear View

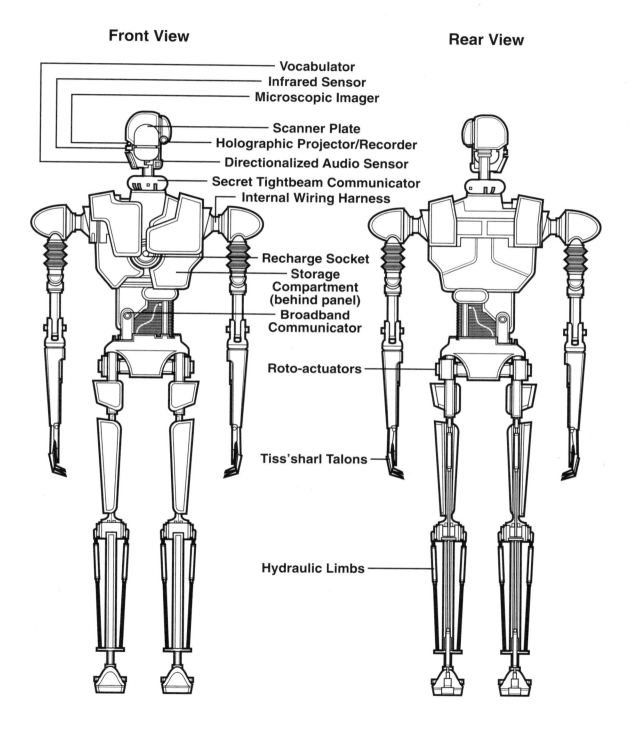

Vocabulator
Infrared Sensor
Microscopic Imager

Scanner Plate
Holographic Projector/Recorder
Directionalized Audio Sensor
Secret Tightbeam Communicator
Internal Wiring Harness

Recharge Socket
Storage
Compartment
(behind panel)
Broadband
Communicator

Roto-actuators

Tiss'sharl Talons

Hydraulic Limbs

ONE OF A KIND
GORM THE DISSOLVER

When one particular bounty hunter strides into a cantina, conversation stills to a hush. Patrons huddle furtively over their lum tankards and trade frightened whispers about the walking jumble of organics and electronics. No one knows if he eats. No one knows if he sleeps. No one even knows if he started life as a human or a droid. But one thing is known by all—if Gorm the Dissolver is on your trail, your life expectancy can be measured in microseconds.

Gorm is a bizarre entity whose origins are swathed in mystery. Very few have heard of the Arkanian Renegades, a group of scientists who attempted to topple the Arkanian Dominion some fifty years before the Battle of Yavin. Their coup was an abysmal failure, but the Renegades' unique handiwork lived on long after their creators' bloody executions.

The ill-fated researchers had tried to create the ultimate mercenary army. Arkanians possess an intimate knowledge of cyborging—just ask any Yaka—and the Renegades were no exception. Through arcane and forbidden practices, they assembled a ruthless fighting force—part droid, part organic, and all attitude. Several of the warriors survived the dustup on Arkania and struck out into the greater galaxy, and Gorm has kept the highest profile as an extravagantly priced manhunter.

Gorm contains parts from six alien species and seven generations of droid electronics. How much of that is original equipment is unclear—the hunter long ago learned how to repair and reassemble himself. In fact, Gorm could theoretically live on for centuries, scrounging body parts from scrapped robots and fallen victims to patch up his lanky frame.

In his current incarnation, Gorm stands an imposing 2.5 meters tall. Twin photoreceptors burn like smoldering coals from beneath a battered Ithullian infantry helmet. His left forearm is barely recognizable as the severed limb of Vultar the Ugly, a Trandoshan who started a brutal underworld power struggle many decades ago.

Gorm earned the sobriquet "the Dissolver" early in his career, when he sported a recycling-droid appendage capable of reducing matter to raw molecular paste. He lost the tool in a savage encounter with the Jedi Knights, and now uses a more conventional arm. Gorm's weapons include a custom-built repeater rifle and an incendiary slugthrower strapped to his chest. For close-quarters finesse, he prefers his concealed molecular garrote.

One of the few beings to ever take down Gorm was the Rodian youngster Greedo, who made a lucky shot in a Nar Shaddaa alleyway. But the only way to truly destroy the Dissolver is to reduce him to constituent atoms. Gorm was soon back in action, accepting a 50,000-credit bounty from Jabba the Hutt to bring fellow hunter Zardra to heel.

Front View

Rear View

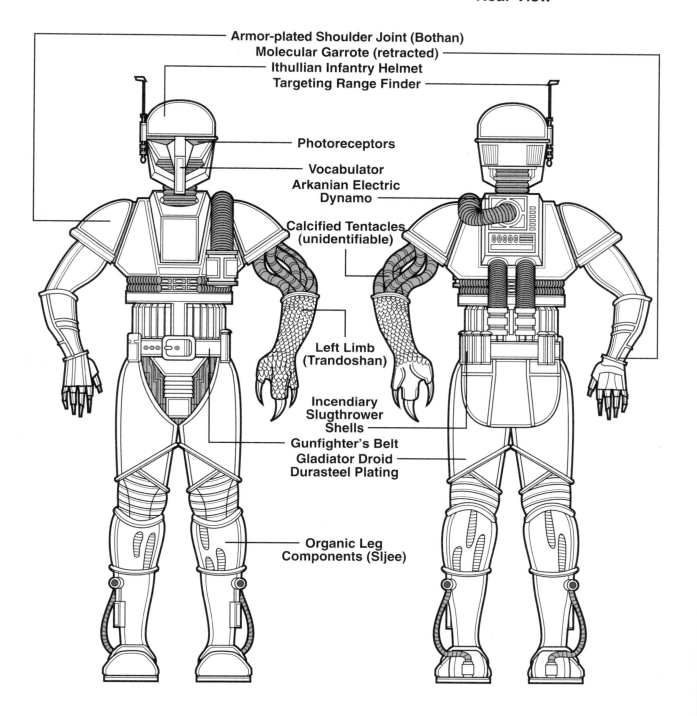

Armor-plated Shoulder Joint (Bothan)
Molecular Garrote (retracted)
Ithullian Infantry Helmet
Targeting Range Finder

Photoreceptors

Vocabulator
Arkanian Electric
Dynamo

Calcified Tentacles
(unidentifiable)

Left Limb
(Trandoshan)

Incendiary
Slugthrower
Shells

Gunfighter's Belt
Gladiator Droid
Durasteel Plating

Organic Leg
Components (Sljee)

ONE OF A KIND
WIDGET

Widget is a walking toolbox. Pieced together from spare parts and junked equipment, he helps his owner Mora repair ships and scrounge up supplies on the remote agrarian world of M'haeli.

Mora, a beautiful young woman raised by a kindhearted H'drachi guardian, has always been a grease-jockey with a knack for keeping the rustiest rattletrap purring like a pittin. At four, she was disassembling her toys; at nine, she was rewiring speeder bikes. By eighteen, she was operating her own fix-it shop in the capital city of N'croth, not far from the H'drachi ghetto. And a dutiful Widget worked right by her side.

The odd little droid came on-line in Mora's early teens, after a half dozen botched attempts to initialize his cognitive processor. Since then, he has faithfully fulfilled his role of making his master a better mechanic, both intentionally and accidentally—his tools are an asset, but it is his frequent system glitches that have given Mora monthly crash courses in droid reconstruction.

Even in a galaxy choked with automatons, Widget's appearance is peculiar. His stumpy legs and wide, heavy base give him a wobbling, splayed gait and a low center of gravity. A flexible waist supports an armored torso with an inset button panel, used to input commands and run

diagnostics when the droid is off-line or inactive.

His scrunched head, nearly invisible beneath a cymbal-shaped metal pan, houses two red photoreceptors and a voice slot. A flawed vocabulator gives Widget a distinctive stutter in times of stress. Twin power cables, which also function as antennae, sprout from the center of the head-pan and connect to a generator on Widget's back. One of Mora's red handkerchiefs occasionally festoons his neck.

The droid's arms are true marvels, each containing dozens of small machinist's tools that can be extended through the digits and palms of both square, blunt-fingered hands. The right forearm holds a magnifier, a spotlight luma, and a full range of wire cutters. The left, covered by ribbed sheathing, holds a laser welder, gripper clamps, and a computer-access link. This is just a fraction of Widget's total accouterment, and he can add or remove items with little effort.

Following the Battle of Yavin, Princess Leia came to M'haeli to support the local insurgency in their fight against Imperial Governor Grigor. Widget proved to be worth his weight in dragite crystals, helping the team rescue prisoners from Grigor's mines and retrieving coded data on the corrupt governor's illegal activities.

Front View

Rear View

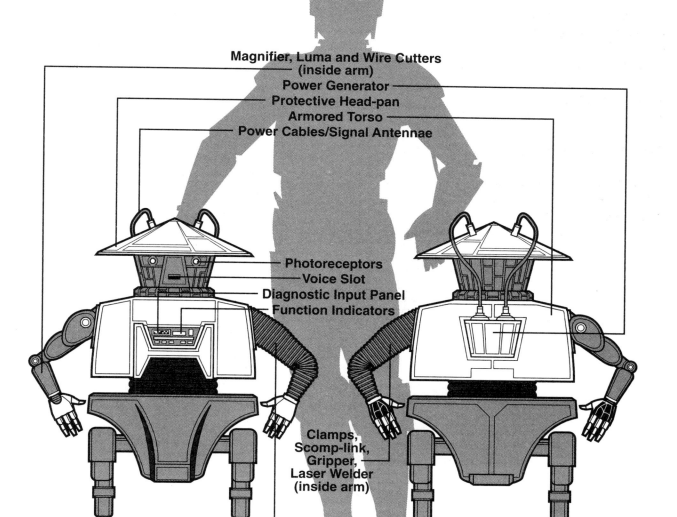

Magnifier, Luma and Wire Cutters
(inside arm)
Power Generator
Protective Head-pan
Armored Torso
Power Cables/Signal Antennae

Photoreceptors
Voice Slot
Diagnostic Input Panel
Function Indicators

Clamps,
Scomp-link,
Gripper,
Laser Welder
(inside arm)

Insulated
Sheathing

About the Author

Daniel Wallace graduated with an advertising degree from Michigan State University and works with new media and promotional communications for one of the world's largest advertising agencies. He is the author or coauthor of several *Star Wars* books, including *Star Wars: The Essential Guide to Planets and Moons*, *Anakin Skywalker: The Story of Darth Vader*, and the forthcoming *Star Wars: The Essential Chronology* (with Kevin Anderson). He lives in the Detroit area with his wife and two enthusiastic sons.

About the Artists

Bill Hughes began designing robots and spaceships at a young age. He self-published his first comic book while still in high school and created special effects–laden television programs while attending the University of Houston. After graduating, Bill worked for several ad agencies and even designed toys for a while. He soon returned to his comic book ambitions with his creations *The SheBuccaneer*™ and *Addam Omega*™. In 1995, he penciled much of the *Star Wars*® *Droids*™ series of comic books for Dark Horse Comics and has been creating children's books and comics for the Star Wars universe ever since.

Bill is currently working and living in Houston, Texas, with his wife, Heidi, and their two children.

Troy Vigil began drawing at age eight and cites the *Star Wars* Trilogy and its wondrous environments as the principal factors in his decision to pursue an art career.

He began his professional career in print production before becoming a freelance computer artist. His work appears in Ballantine/Del Rey's *Star Wars: The Essential Guide to Vehicles and Vessels* and *Star Wars: The Essential Guide to Weapons and Technology*, as well as on trading cards, in portfolio sets, and on posters. He lives in Venice Beach, California, with his partner, Stacey, and eight cats.